C++ FOR C PROGRAMMERS

SECOND EDITION

About the Author

Ira Pohl, Ph.D., is a professor of Computer and Information Sciences at the University of California, Santa Cruz. He has two decades of experience as a software methodologist and is an international authority on C and C++ programming. His teaching and research interests include artificial intelligence and programming languages. Professor Pohl has lectured extensively at U.C. Berkeley, the Courant Institute, Edinburgh University, Stanford, the Vrije University in Amsterdam, and Auckland University in New Zealand. He is the author of the best-selling *Object-Oriented Programming Using C++,* and *C++ for C Programmers,* Second Edition, and coauthor, with Al Kelley, of *A Book on C: Programming in C,* Second Edition; and *C By Dissection,* Second Edition. When not programming, he enjoys riding bicycles in Aptos, California, with his wife Debra and daughter Laura.

C++ FOR C PROGRAMMERS

SECOND EDITION

Ira Pohl

University of California, Santa Cruz

The Benjamin/Cummings Publishing Company, Inc.

Redwood City, California • Menlo Park, California • Reading, Massachusetts
New York • Don Mills, Ontario • Wokingham, U.K. • Amsterdam • Bonn • Sydney
Tokyo • Madrid • San Juan

Sponsoring Editor: J. Carter Shanklin
Production Editor: Gail Carrigan
Editorial Assistant: Melissa Standen
Cover Design: Yvo Riezebos Design
Cover Illustration: Joseph Maas, Paragon[3]
Copy Editor: Barbara Conway
Proofreader: Angela Santos
Composition: G & S Typesetters

© 1994 by The Benjamin/Cummings Publishing Company, Inc.

The programs presented in this book have been included for their instructional value. They have been tested with care but are not guaranteed for any particular purpose. The publisher does not offer any warranties or representations, nor does it accept any liabilities with respect to the programs.

Library of Congress Cataloging-in-Publication Data
Pohl, Ira
    C++ for C Programmers / Ira Pohl
      p.   cm.
    Includes index.
    ISBN 0-8053-3159-X
    1. C++ (Computer program language)   I. Title.
    QA76.73.C153P654   1993
    005.13'3—dc20   93-30685
                                                  CIP

ISBN 0-8053-3159-X
1 2 3 4 5 6 7 8 9 10-DO-97 96 95 94

The Benjamin/Cummings Publishing Company, Inc.
390 Bridge Parkway
Redwood City, CA 94065

PREFACE

This book is intended as an introduction to programming in C++ for the programmer or student already familiar with C. Its approach is to use an evolutionary teaching process with C as a starting point. The programmer can stop and use the language facilities up to that point in the text. We start with C and end with C++. The book is a tutorial on C++ programming.

C++ is a powerful modern successor language to C. C++ was invented at Bell Labs by Bjarne Stroustrup in the mid-1980s. C++ adds to C the concept of *class*, a mechanism for providing user-defined types also called *abstract data types*. It supports *object-oriented* programming by these means and by providing inheritance and run-time type binding. C is the present; C++ is the future.

By carefully developing working C++ programs, using the method of **dissection**, this book presents a simple and thorough introduction to the programming process in C++. Dissection is a technique for explaining new elements in a program that the student is seeing for the first time. It highlights key points in the many examples of working code that are used to teach by example.

This book is intended for use in a first course in programming in C++. It can be used as a supplementary text in an advanced programming course, data structures course, software methodology course, comparative language course, or other courses where the instructor wants C++ to be the language of choice. Each chapter presents a number of carefully explained programs. Many programs and functions are dissected.

All the major pieces of code were tested. A consistent and proper coding style is adopted from the beginning. The style standard used is one chosen by professionals in the C++ community.

For the programmer who has no C experience, this book should be used in conjunction with *A Book on C, Second Edition* by Al Kelley and Ira Pohl (Redwood City, California: Benjamin/Cummings, 1990). As a package, the two books offer an integrated treatment of the C and C++ programming languages and their use that is unavailable elsewhere.

Each chapter has:

Dissections. A program particularly illustrative of the themes of that chapter is analyzed by dissection. Dissection is similar to a structured walk-through of the code. Its intention is to explain to the reader newly encountered programming elements and idioms.

Summary. A succinct list of points covered in the chapter are reiterated as helpful review.

Exercises. The exercises test the student's knowledge of the language. Many exercises are intended to be done interactively while reading the text. This encourages self-paced instruction by the reader. The exercises also frequently extend the reader's knowledge to an advanced area of use.

The book incorporates:

An Evolutionary Approach. The C programmer can immediately benefit from programming in C++. The early chapters show how the language is improved by stronger typing, a new comment style, call-by-reference, and other useful minor additions. The middle chapters show how classes work. Classes are the basis for abstract data types and object-oriented programming. Again the student starts from the C perspective and moves to the C++ view. The later chapters give advanced details of the use of inheritance, templates and exceptions. At any point in the text the programmer can stop and use the new material.

Teaching by Example. The book is a tutorial that stresses examples of working code. Right from the start the student is introduced to full working programs. An interactive environment is assumed. Exercises are integrated with the examples to encourage experimentation. Excessive detail is avoided in explaining the larger elements of writing working code. Each chapter has several important example programs. Major elements of these programs are explained by the method of dissection.

Data Structures in C++. The text emphasizes many of the standard data structures from computer science. Stacks, safe arrays, dynamically allocated multidimensional arrays, lists, trees, and strings are all implemented. Exercises extend the student's understanding of how to implement and use these structures. Implementation is consistent with an abstract data type approach to software.

Object-Oriented Programming. The reader is led gradually to the object-oriented style. Chapter 0 and Chapter 1 discuss how the C programmer can benefit in important ways from a switch to C++ and object-oriented programming. The terminology of object-oriented concepts is defined and the way in which these concepts are supported by C++ is introduced. Chapter 3 introduces classes. This is the basic mechanism for producing modular programs and implementing abstract data types. Class variables are the *objects* being manipulated. Chapter 6 develops inheritance and virtual functions, two key elements in this paradigm. Chapter 9 discusses OOP and a *Platonic* programming philosophy. This book develops and transforms the programmer to an appreciation of this point of view.

ANSI C++ Language and *iostream.h*. C++ continues to change at a rapid pace for an existing widely used language. This book is based on the most recent standard: the ANSI C++ committee language documents. A succinct informal language reference is provided in Appendix C. Chief additions include templates and exception handling. The examples use the *iostream.h* I/O library. This has replaced the older *stream.h* used in the first edition and *stdio.h* used in the C community. The *iostream.h* library and its use is described in Appendix D.

Industry and Course Tested. In its first edition the book won a UNIXWORLD commendation for the professional programmer migrating to C++. It is the basis of many on-site professional training courses given by the author. Its contents have been used to train professionals and students in various forums since 1986. The various changes in the new edition are course tested and reflect considerable teaching and consulting experience by the author.

Acknowledgments

My special thanks go to my wife, Debra Dolsberry, who encouraged me throughout this project. She acted as technical editor and implemented and tested all major pieces of code. Her careful implementations of the code and exercises often led to important improvements. Stephen Clamage of TauMetric Corporation provided wonderfully detailed and insightful comments on language detail. Other reviewers who specifically commented on this second edition were: Douglas Campbell, Brigham Young University, Blayne Mayfield, Oklahoma State University, and Henry Ruston, Polytechnic University. The second edition was developed with assistance from my editor J. Carter Shanklin.

The first edition had help, inspiration and encouragement from: Nan Borreson, Borland International; Skona Brittain; Al Conrad; Steve Demurjian; Samuel Druker, Zortech Limited; Robert Durling; Bruce Eckel; Daniel Edelson; Gene Fisher; Robert Hansen, Lattice, Incorporated; John Hardin, Hewlett-Packard, Incorporated; Al Kelley; Jim Kempf, Sun Microsystems, Incorporated; Ellen Mickanin; Laura Pohl, Cottage Consultants; and Linda Werner. In addition, my editors Alan Apt and Mark McCormick were very supportive. Finally, I thank Bjarne Stroustrup for inventing such a powerful language and encouraging others to help develop and teach it.

Ira Pohl
University of California, Santa Cruz

CONTENTS

To Laura and her mother

CHAPTER 0

OBJECT-ORIENTED PROGRAMMING IN C++

C++ was created by Bjarne Stroustrup in the early 1980s. Stroustrup had two main goals: to make C++ compatible with ordinary C and to extend C using the class construct of Simula 67. The class construct is an extension of the C struct. The language is described in Stroustrup's book, *The C++ Programming Language: Second Edition* [1].

This book teaches C++ to programmers already familiar with C [2]. It does this by building from C to C++. Two aspects of C++ as a successor language to C are stressed. The first is C++'s superiority to C as a general-purpose programming language because of its new features. The second is the success of C++ as an object-oriented programming language. In the next section we define what this new concept means.

A major premise of our approach is that C++ is a superior C, even not taking into consideration the extensions to classes. We expect that C++ will replace C as a general-purpose programming language. With C++ the C programmer can improve on ordinary C code in a number of ways that are illustrated in Chapters 1 and 2.

0.1 OBJECT-ORIENTED PROGRAMMING

We use the terms *abstract data type (ADT)* and *object-oriented programming (OOP)* to refer to a powerful new programming approach. An ADT is a user-defined extension to the existing types available in the language. It consists of a set of values and a collection of operations that can act on those values. For example, C does not have a complex number type, but C++ provides the class construct to add such a type and integrate it with existing types. *Objects* are class variables. Object-oriented programming allows ADTs to be easily created and used. OOP uses the mechanism of *inheritance* to conveniently derive a new type from an existing user-defined type. It allows the programmer to model the objects found in the problem domain by programming their content and behavior with a class.

The new class construct in C++ provides the *encapsulation* mechanism to implement ADTs. Encapsulation packages both the internal implementation details of the type and the externally available operations and functions that can act on objects of that type. The implementation details can be made inaccessible to code that uses the type. Code that uses the ADT is called *client* code for the ADT. For example, stack could be implemented as a fixed-length array, while the publicly available operations would include push and pop. Changing the internal implementation to a linked list should not affect how push and pop are used externally. The implementation of stack is hidden from its clients. The details of how to provide data hiding in classes are introduced in Chapter 1 and developed thoroughly in Chapters 3 and 6.

0.2 WHY C++ IS A BETTER C

Since C++ is based on C, it retains much of that language, including a rich operator set, nearly orthogonal design, terseness, and extensibility. C++ is a highly portable language, and translators for it exist on many different machines and systems. C++ compilers are highly compatible with existing C programs because maintaining such compatibility was a design objective. Unlike other object-oriented languages, such as Smalltalk, C++ is an extension of an existing language widely used on many machines.

If C++ is viewed as an object-oriented language alternative to Smalltalk, it is a relatively inexpensive alternative. Programming in C++

does not require a graphics environment, and C++ programs do not incur run-time expense from type checking or garbage collection.

C++ improves on C in significant ways, especially in supporting strong typing. The function prototype syntax, as now required by Standard C (ANSI C) [2][3][4], is a C++ innovation. In general, C++ has stronger type rules than C, which makes it a safer language.

C++ is a marriage of the low level with the high level. C was designed to be a systems implementation language—a language close to the machine. C++ adds object-oriented features designed to allow a programmer to create or import a library appropriate to the problem domain. The user can write code at the level appropriate to the problem while still maintaining contact with the machine-level implementation details.

Operators can be given new definitions based on the types of their arguments. This operator overloading supports the implementation of new types that may be operated upon transparently. Normal functions, like operators, may be overloaded.

C++ has a reduced reliance on the preprocessor. C programs often use the preprocessor to implement constants and useful macros. However, parameterized #define macros introduce insecurities. In C++, the inline keyword requests the compiler produce inline code for a function having no more overhead than a macro. The inline function has precisely the semantics and syntactic usage of static functions. This preserves type checking while increasing run-time performance as compared with normal functions. Reliance on the preprocessor is further diminished by the const type modifier, which specifies that an object is read-only.

C++ offers a large number of other improvements. A favorite of programmers is the addition of the // symbol for one-line comments. Also, the convenient new I/O library, *iostream.h*, provides a very useful alternative to *stdio.h*. The new and delete operators provide convenient access to free store.

Abstract data types are implemented in C++ through the class mechanism. Classes allow a programmer to control the visibility of the underlying implementation. What is public is accessible and what is private is hidden. Data hiding is one component of object-oriented programming. Classes have member functions, including those that overload operators. Member functions allow the programmer to code the appropriate functionality for the ADT. Classes can be defined through an inheritance mechanism that allows for improved code sharing and library development. Inheritance is another hallmark of object-oriented programming.

C is often criticized as a weakly typed, unsafe language [5]. However, C++ is strongly typed. Conversions between types are allowed, provided they are well defined. In fact, the language allows the programmer to create conversion functions between arbitrary types but not between two non-class types.

Parameter passing in C is unchecked with regard to type or number of actual parameters. This leads to bugs that the compiler cannot catch. In C++, function prototypes allow functions to be fully checked as to count and type. Functions taking variable types or numbers of arguments are also supported. The addition of function prototypes is an aid to the programmer, bringing into the compiler checking that was previously obtainable only through *lint*.

The C array model is pointer-based and one-dimensional without bounds checking. This lack of multidimensional arrays means the programmer must spend more time and effort implementing them using the one-dimensional storage mapping function that is C's paradigm. Development and use of dynamic arrays also require significant work and are not supported in the language. C++ retains the array handling of C; however, classes provide a satisfactory means of transparently implementing general arrays. Multidimensional, dynamic, and bounds-checked arrays can be implemented in libraries.

By and large, the semantics of C++ are much more stringently defined than those of C. For example, type conversion and typing are more carefully implemented. The C need for preprocessor extensibility is curtailed: Function overloading and `inline` can be used to replace macros with arguments, and the `const` type modifier is sufficient for most named constants. The preprocessor's primary remaining uses are file inclusion and conditional compilation.

0.3 WHY SWITCH TO C++?

C++ supports the object-oriented programming style. A chief cost is the increased complexity of the language. Given C++'s objectives, this is hardly surprising. Although the benefits gained by living within the C family and adding improved interface schemes outweigh this cost, the complexity that C++ adds to the C language is one of its biggest drawbacks. This increase reflects the large number of needed new ideas but makes mastery more difficult. To overcome this problem, this book approaches the learning process by gradually transforming the C programmer into a practiced C++ programmer. Each chapter extends from the previous chapter the range of ideas the programmer may use. The reader can stop at any point and still be partly proficient in C++. In effect, the reader evolves from a C programmer to an object-oriented C++ programmer.

C++ is a better C. The use of C++ leads to increased convenience in writing code and increased security in the code. Features such as // for single-line comments, const and inline, new and delete for storage management, and call-by-reference parameters simplify the coding process over C. Stronger typing in general, and function prototypes in particular, enhance security and facilitate software methodology.

0.4 REFERENCES

B. Stroustrup. *The C++ Programming Language: Second Edition*. Reading, Mass.: Addison-Wesley, 1991.
  The de facto language reference manual. This book is very difficult reading.
A. Kelley and I. Pohl. *A Book on C: Second Edition*. Redwood City, Calif.: Benjamin/Cummings, 1990.
  A comprehensive text on the Standard C programming language. It is written in the style of this book.
A. Kelley and I. Pohl. *C by Dissection: Second Edition*. Redwood City, Calif.: Benjamin/Cummings, 1992.
  A popular CS1 text in the C programming language.
S. P. Harbison and G. L. Steele. *C: A Reference Manual, 3d ed.*, Englewood Cliffs, N.J.: Prentice-Hall, 1991.
  The authoritative reference book on the syntax and semantics of the C programming language.
I. Pohl and D. Edelson. "A-Z: C Language Shortcomings." *Computer Languages*, vol. 13, no. 2, 1988, pp. 51-64.
  A brief paper criticizing 26 defects in the original C language.

CHAPTER 1

AN OVERVIEW OF C++ AND OBJECT-ORIENTED PROGRAMMING

This chapter gives an overview of the C++ programming language. It also provides an introduction to using C++ as an object-oriented programming language. Like the rest of the book, it assumes a knowledge of the C programming language. In the chapter a series of programs is presented, and the elements of each program are carefully explained. The programs become increasingly complex as the chapter progresses, and the examples in the later sections illustrate some of the concepts of object-oriented programming. This approach should give the student a sense of how the language works.

Each feature of C++ is explained briefly. The examples in this chapter give simple, immediate, hands-on experience with key features of the C++ language. The chapter introduces the reader to stream I/O, operator and function overloading, reference parameters, classes, constructors, destructors, and inheritance. A programmer can get some of the flavor of writing C++ from this chapter, but mastery of the individual topics requires a thorough reading of the later chapters.

Object-oriented programming is implemented by the class construct. The class construct in C++ is an extension of struct in C. The later examples in this chapter illustrate how C++ implements OOP (object-oriented programming) concepts, such as data hiding, ADTs, inheritance, and type hierarchies.

1.1 OUTPUT

Programs must communicate to be useful. Our first example is a program that prints on the screen the phrase "C++ is an improved C." The complete program is

```
//A first C++ program illustrating output.
//   Title:  improved
//   Author: Richmond Q. Programmer

#include <iostream.h>

int       //The return type for main
main()
{
    cout << "C++ is an improved C.\n";
    return (0);    //signals successful termination
}
```

The program prints on the screen

```
C++ is an improved C.
```

■ DISSECTION OF THE *improved* PROGRAM

```
//A first C++ program illustrating output.
```

- The double slash // is a new comment symbol. The comment runs to the end of the line. The old C bracketing comment symbols /* */ are still available for multiline comments.

```
#include <iostream.h>
```

- The *iostream.h* header introduces I/O facilities for C++.

```
cout << "C++ is an improved C.\n";
```

- This statement prints to the screen. The identifier cout is the name of the standard output stream. The operator << passes the string "C++ is an improved C.\n" to standard output. Used in this way the *output operator* << is referred to as the *put to* or *insertion* operator.

```
return (0);    //signals successful termination
```

- A value of zero is returned to the system, indicating the successful completion of the program. Most systems allow you to ignore this requirement or give you a warning if you fail to return a value from main().

We can rewrite our first program as follows:

```
//A first C++ program illustrating output.

#include <iostream.h>

main()
{
    cout << "C++ is an improved C." << endl;
    return (0);
}
```

Although it is different from the first version, it produces the same output. This version drops the explicit declaration of main() as returning an int and uses the fact that this return type is implicit. Here we use the *put to* operator << twice. Each time we use << with cout, printing continues from the position where it previously left off. In this case the identifier endl forces a new line followed by a *flush*. The endl is a *manipulator* (see Appendix D).

1.2 INPUT

We will write a program to convert to kilometers the distance in miles from Earth to the moon. On average, this distance is 238,857 miles. This number is an integer. To convert miles to kilometers, we multiply by the conversion factor 1.609, a real number.

Our conversion program uses variables capable of storing integer values and real values. In C++ all variables must be declared before they can be used, but unlike in C, they need not be at the head of a block. Declarations may be mixed in with executable statements. Their scope is from the point of the declaration to the end of the block within which they are declared. Identifiers should be chosen to reflect their use in the program. In this way they serve as documentation, making the program more readable.

These programs assume a four-byte int, but on some machines these variables should be declared long. You can check the constant INT_MAX in *limits.h*.

```
//The distance to the moon converted to kilometers.
//    Title: moon

#include <iostream.h>

main()
{
    const int moon = 238857;
    cout << "The moon´s distance from Earth is " << moon;
    cout << " miles." << endl;

    int moon_kilo;
    moon_kilo = moon * 1.609;
    cout << "In kilometers this is " << moon_kilo;
    cout << " km." << endl;
}
```

The output of the program is

```
The moon's distance from Earth is 238857 miles.
In kilometers this is 384320 km.
```

■ DISSECTION OF THE *moon* PROGRAM

```
const int moon = 238857;
```

- The keyword const is new in C++. It replaces some uses of the preprocessor command define to create named literals. Using this type modifier informs the compiler that the initialized value of moon cannot be changed. Thus it makes moon a symbolic constant.

```
cout << "The moon's distance from Earth is " << moon;
```

- The stream I/O in C++ can discriminate among a variety of simple values without needing additional formatting information. Here the value of moon will be printed as an integer.

```
int moon_kilo;
moon_kilo = moon * 1.609;
```

- Declarations can occur after executable statements. This allows declarations of variables to be nearer to their use.

Let us write a program that converts a series of values from miles to kilometers. The program is interactive. The user types in a value in miles, and the program converts this value to kilometers and prints it out.

```
//Miles are converted to kilometers.
//   Title: mi_km

#include <iostream.h>
const double m_to_k = 1.609;
inline int convert(int mi) { return (mi * m_to_k); }

main()
{
   int miles;

   do {
      cout << "Input distance in miles: ";
      cin >> miles;
      cout << "\nDistance is " << convert(miles) << " km." << endl;
   } while (miles > 0);
   return (0);
}
```

This program uses the input stream variable cin, which is normally standard input. The *input operator* >>, called the *get from* or *extraction* operator, assigns values from the input stream to a variable. This program illustrates both input and output.

■ DISSECTION OF THE *mi_km* PROGRAM

```
const double m_to_k = 1.609;
```

- C++ reduces C's traditional reliance on the preprocessor. For example, instead of having to use define, special constants, such as the conversion factor 1.609, are simply assigned to variables specified as constants.

```
inline int convert(int mi) { return (mi * m_to_k); }
```

- The new keyword inline specifies that a function is to be compiled, if possible as inline code. This avoids function call overhead and is better practice than C's use of define macros. As a rule, inline should be done sparingly and only on short functions. Also note how the parameter mi is declared within the function parentheses. Both const and inline can affect linkage rules (see Appendix C). C++ uses *function prototypes* to define and declare functions. This is explained in the next section.

```
do {
    cout << "Input distance in miles: ";
    cin >> miles;
    cout << "\nDistance is " << convert(miles) << " km." << endl;
} while (miles > 0);
```

- The program repeatedly prompts the user for a distance in miles. The program is terminated by a zero or negative value. The value placed in the standard input stream is automatically converted to an integer value assigned to miles.

1.3 FUNCTION PROTOTYPES

The syntax of functions in C++ inspired the new function prototype syntax found in Standard C compilers. Basically, the types of parameters are listed inside the header parentheses. By explicitly listing the type and number of arguments, strong type checking and assignment-compatible conversions are possible in C++. The following example illustrates these points:

```
//A program illustrating function prototypes.
//    Title: add3

#include <iostream.h>

int    add3(int, int, int);
double average(int);

main()
{
    int    score_1, score_2, score_3, sum;

    cout << "\nEnter 3 scores: ";
    cin >> score_1 >> score_2 >> score_3;
    sum = add3(score_1, score_2, score_3);
    cout << "\nTheir sum is " << sum << endl;
    cout << "\nTheir average is " << average(sum) << endl;
    sum = add3(1.5 * score_1, score_2, score_3);
    cout << "\nThe weighted sum is " << sum << "." << endl;
    cout << "\nTheir weighted average is " << average(sum) << "." << endl;
    return (0);
}
```

```
int add3(int a, int b, int c)
{
    return (a + b + c);
}

double average(int s)
{
    return (s / 3.0);
}
```

■ DISSECTION OF THE *add3* PROGRAM

```
int    add3(int, int, int);
double average(int);
```

- These declarations are function prototypes. They inform the compiler of the type and number of arguments to expect for each externally specified function. The list of arguments can optionally include variable names. So,

```
    int add3(int a, int b, int c);
```

is also possible.

```
sum = add3(1.5 * score_1, score_2, score_3);
```

- This would not be correct in traditional C. In traditional C, the first argument 1.5 * score_1 is promoted to double and passed unconverted to a local placeholder expecting an integer. In C++ this expression is converted to an integer value, per the function prototype specification. This single change markedly improves C++ program reliability over traditional C.

```
int add3(int a, int b, int c)
{
    return (a + b + c);
}
```

- Here is the actual function definition. It could just as well have been imported from another file. It is compatible with the function prototype declaration in main.

1.4 CLASSES AND ABSTRACT DATA TYPES

What is novel about C++ is its aggregate type class. A class is an extension of the idea of struct in traditional C. A class provides the means for implementing a user-defined data type and associated functions and operators. Therefore a class can be used to implement an ADT. Let us write a class string that implements a restricted form of string.

```
//An elementary implementation of type string.

#include <string.h>
#include <iostream.h>

const int max_len = 255;

class string {
public:          //universal access
   void assign(const char* st) { strcpy(s, st); len = strlen(st); }
   int  length() { return (len); }
   void print() { cout << s << "\nLength: " << len << "\n"; }
private:         //restricted access to member functions
   char s[max_len];    //implementation by character array
   int  len;
};
```

Two important additions to the structure concept of traditional C are found in this example: It has members that are functions, such as assign, and it has both public and private members. The keyword public indicates the visibility of the members that follow it. Without this keyword the members are private to the class. Private members are available for use only by other member functions of the class. Public members are available to any function within the scope of the class declaration. Privacy allows part of the implementation of a class type to be "hidden." This restriction prevents unanticipated modifications to the data structure. Restricted access or *data hiding* is a feature of object-oriented programming.

The declaration of member functions allows the ADT to have particular functions act on its private representation. For example, the member function length returns the length of the string defined to be the number of characters up to but excluding the first zero value character. The member function print outputs both the string and its length. The member function assign stores a character string into the hidden variable s and computes and stores its length in the hidden variable len.

We can now use this data type string as if it were a basic type of the language. It obeys the standard block structure scope rules of C. Other code that uses this type is a *client*. The client can use only the public members to act on variables of type string.

```
//Test of the class string.
main()
{
    string  one, two;
    char    three[40] = {"My name is Charles Babbage."};

    one.assign("My name is Alan Turing.");
    two.assign(three);
    cout << three;
    cout << "\nLength: " << strlen(three) << endl;
    //Print shorter of one and two.
    if (one.length() <= two.length())
        one.print();
    else
        two.print();
}
```

The variables one and two are of type string. The variable three is of type pointer to char and is not compatible with string. The member functions are called using the dot operator or *structure member operator*. As seen from their definitions, these member functions act on the hidden private member fields of the named variables. One cannot write inside main the expression one.len expecting to access this member. The output of this example program is.

```
My name is Charles Babbage.
Length: 27
My name is Alan Turing.
Length: 23
```

1.5 OVERLOADING

The term *overloading* refers to the practice of giving several meanings to
an operator or a function. The meaning selected depends on the types of
the arguments used by the operator or function. Let us overload the function print used in the previous example. This is a second definition of the
print function.

```
class string {
public:          //universal access
    . . .
    void print() { cout << s << "\nLength: " << len << "\n"; }
    void print(int n)
    {
        for (int i = 0; i < n; ++i)
            cout << s << endl;
    }
    . . .
}
```

This version of print takes a single argument of type int. It prints the
string n times.

```
three.print(2);  //print string three twice
three.print(-1); //string three is not printed
```

We can overload most of the C operators. For example, let us overload + to mean concatenate two strings. To do this we need two new keywords: friend and operator. The keyword operator precedes the operator
token and replaces what would otherwise be a function name in u function declaration. The keyword friend gives a function access to the private members of a class variable. A friend function is not a member of
the class but has the privileges of a member function in the class in
which it is declared.

```
//Overloading the operator + .

#include <string.h>
#include <iostream.h>

const int max_len = 255;

class string {
public:
    void assign(const char* st) { strcpy(s, st); len = strlen(st); }
    int  length() { return (len); }
    void print() { cout << s << "\nLength: " << len << endl; }
    friend string operator+(const string& a, const string& b);
private:
    char s[max_len];
    int  len;
};

string operator+(const string& a, const string& b)   //overload +
{
    string temp;

    temp.assign(a.s);
    temp.len = a.len + b.len;
    if (temp.len < max_len)
        strcat(temp.s, b.s);
    else
        cerr << "Max length exceeded in concatenation.\n";
    return (temp);
}

void print(const char* c)   //file scope print definition
{
    cout << c << "\nLength: " << strlen(c) << "\n";
}
```

```
main()
{
    string   one, two, both;
    char     three[40] = {"My name is Charles Babbage."};

    one.assign("My name is Alan Turing.");
    two.assign(three);
    print(three);           //file scope print called
    //Print shorter of one and two.
    if (one.length() <= two.length())
        one.print();        //member function print called
    else
        two.print();
    both = one + two;       //plus overloaded to be concatenate
    both.print();
    return (0);
}
```

■ DISSECTION OF THE *operator+* FUNCTION

```
string operator+(const string& a, const string& b)
```

- Plus is overloaded. The two arguments it takes are both strings. The arguments are *call-by-reference*. The declaration, written in the form *type& identifier*, declares the identifier to be a reference variable. Use of const indicates that the arguments cannot be modified. This extension to traditional C allows call-by-reference, as found in languages such as Pascal.

```
string temp;
```

- The function needs to return a value of type string. This local variable is used to store and return the concatenated string value.

```
temp.assign(a.s);
temp.len = a.len + b.len;
if (temp.len < max_len)
    strcat(temp.s, b.s);
```

```
Int Cos                 ASOutofRng              lling the strcpy
D                       D                       g concatenated
E ✓                     E ✓                     d the maximum
Int OutofRng            A SFltLim               le, the standard
D                       D                       ; hidden string
E ✓                     E ✓                     temp.s, a.s, and
IntFltLim                                       friend of class
D                       ASCommFail
E ✓                     D
                        E ✓
Int CommFail                                    ;
D                       ASCoS
E ✓                     D                       int an error mes-
                        E                       ly the first string
AccExp
D
E
```

- The operator was given a return type of string, and temp has been assigned the appropriate concatenated string.

1.6 CONSTRUCTORS AND DESTRUCTORS

A *constructor* is a member function whose job is to *initialize* a variable of its class. In OOP terms such a variable is an *object*. In many cases this involves dynamic storage allocation. Constructors are invoked anytime an object of its associated class is created. A *destructor* is a member function whose job is to deallocate or *finalize* a variable of its class. The destructor is called implicitly when an automatic object goes out of scope.

Let us change our string example by dynamically allocating store for each string variable. We replace the private array variable by a pointer. The remodeled class uses a constructor to allocate an appropriate amount of storage dynamically using the new operator.

```
//An implementation of dynamically allocated strings.

class string {
public:
    string(int n) { s = new char[n + 1]; len = n; }  //constructor
    void assign(const char* st) { strcpy(s, st); len = strlen(st); }
    int  length() { return (len); }
    void print() { cout << s << "\nLength: " << len << "\n"; }
    friend string operator+(const string& a, const string& b);
private:
    char* s;
    int   len;
};
```

A constructor is a member function whose name is the same as the class name. The keyword new is an addition to the C language. It is a unary operator that takes as an argument a data type that can include an array size. It allocates the appropriate amount of memory to store this type from free store and returns the pointer value that addresses this memory. In the preceding example, n + 1 bytes is allocated from free store. Thus the declaration

```
string a(40), b(100);
```

allocates 41 bytes for the variable a, pointed at by a.s, and 101 bytes for the variable b, pointed at by b.s. We add 1 byte for the end-of-string value 0. Storage obtained by new is persistent and is not automatically returned on block exit. When storage return is desired, a destructor function must be included in the class. A destructor is written as an ordinary member function whose name is the same as the class name preceded by the tilde symbol ˜ . Typically, a destructor uses the unary operator delete, another addition to the language, to automatically deallocate storage associated with a pointer expression.

```
//Add as a member function to class string.
˜string() { delete []s; } //destructor
```

It is usual to overload the constructor, writing a variety of such functions to accommodate more than one style of initialization. Consider initializing a string with a pointer to char value. Such a constructor is

```
string(const char* p)
{
    len = strlen(p);
    s = new char[len + 1];
    strcpy(s, p);
}
```

A typical declaration invoking this version of the constructor is

```
char*   str = "I came on foot.";
string  a("I came by bus."), b(str);
```

It also is desirable to have a constructor of no arguments.

```
string() { len = 255; s = new char[255]; }
```

This is invoked by declarations without parenthesized arguments and, by default, allocates 255 bytes of memory. Now all three constructors are invoked in the following declaration:

```
string  a, b(10), c("I came by horse.");
```

The overloaded constructor is selected by the form of each declaration. The variable a has no parameters and so is allocated 255 bytes. The variable b has an integer parameter and so is allocated 11 bytes. The variable c has a pointer parameter to the literal string "I came by horse." and is allocated 17 bytes, with this literal string copied into its private s member.

1.7 OBJECT-ORIENTED PROGRAMMING AND INHERITANCE

The central element of OOP is the encapsulation of an appropriate set of data types and their operations. The class construct with its member functions and data members provides an appropriate coding tool. Class variables are the *objects* to be manipulated.

Classes also provide data hiding. Access privileges can be managed and limited to whatever group of functions needs access to implementation details. This promotes modularity and robustness.

Another important concept in OOP is the promotion of code reuse through the *inheritance* mechanism. This is the mechanism of *deriving* a new class from an existing one called the *base class*. The base class can be added to or altered to create the derived class. In this way a hierarchy of related data types can be created that share code.

Many types are variants of one another, and it is frequently tedious and error prone to develop new code for each. A derived class inherits the description of the base class. Hierarchy is a method for coping with complexity. It imposes classifications on objects. For example, the periodic table of elements has elements that are gases. These have properties that are shared by all elements in that classification. Inert gases are an important special type of gas. The hierarchy here is an inert gas, such as argon, is a gas, which in turn is an element. This provides a convenient way to understand the behavior of inert gases. We know they are composed of protons and electrons because this is a description shared by all elements. We know they are in a gaseous state at room temperature, as this behavior is shared by all gases. We know they do not combine in ordinary chemical reactions with other elements, as this is a shared behavior of all inert gases.

Consider designing a database for a college. The registrar must track different types of students. The base class we need to develop captures a description of student. Two main categories of student are graduate and undergraduate.

The OOP design methodology becomes

1. Decide on an appropriate set of types.
2. Design in their relatedness, and use inheritance to share code.

An example of deriving a class is

```
enum support {ta, ra, fellowship, other};
enum year {fresh, soph, junior, senior, grad};

class student {
public:
   student(char* nm, int id, double g, year x);
   void  print();
private:
   int        student_id;
   double     gpa;
   year       y;
   char       name[30];
};

class grad_student: public student {
public:
   grad_student
       (char* nm, int id, double g, year x, support t, char* d, char* th);
   void print();
private:
   support   s;
   char      dept[10];
   char      thesis[80];
};
```

In this example grad_student is the derived class, and student is the base class. The use of the keyword public following the colon in the derived class header means that the public members of student are to be inherited as public members of grad_student. Private members of the base class cannot be accessed in the derived class. Public inheritance also means that the derived class grad_student is a subtype of student.

An inheritance structure provides a design for the overall system. For example, a database that contains all the people at a college can be derived from the base class person. The student-grad_student relation can be extended to extension students, as a further significant category of objects. Similarly, person can be the base class for a variety of employee categories.

1.8 POLYMORPHISM

A *polymorphic function* has many forms. An example in Standard C is the division operator. If the arguments to the division operator are integral, then integer division is used. However, if one or both arguments are floating point, then floating-point division is used.

In C++ a function name or operator is overloadable. A function is called based on its *signature*, defined as the list of argument types in its parameter list.

```
a / b        //divide behavior determined by native coercions

cout << a    //ad-hoc polymorphism through function overloading
```

In the division expression the result depends on the arguments being automatically coerced to the widest type. So if both arguments are integer, the result is an integer division. But if one or both arguments are floating point, the result is floating-point division. In the output statement the shift operator << invokes a function that is able to output an object of type a.

Polymorphism localizes responsibility for behavior. The client code frequently requires no revision when additional functionality is added to the system through ADT-provided code improvements.

In C the technique for implementing a package of routines to provide an ADT shape relies on a comprehensive structural description of any shape. For example, the declaration

```
struct shape{ enum{CIRCLE, . . . } e_val; double center, radius; . . . };
```

has all the members necessary for any shape currently drawable in our system, and an enumerator value so it can be identified. The area routine can then be written as

```
double area(shape* s)
{
  switch(s -> e_val) {
  case CIRCLE:   return (PI * s -> radius * s -> radius);
  case RECTANGLE: return (s -> height * s -> width);
  . . .
}
```

Question: What is involved in revising this C code to include a new shape? Answer: An additional case in the code body and additional members in the structure. Unfortunately, these would have ripple effects throughout our entire code body. Each routine so structured would need an additional case, even if that case were just adding a label to a pre-existing case. Thus what is conceptually a local improvement would require global changes.

OOP coding techniques in C++ for the same problem uses a shape hierarchy. The hierarchy is the obvious one where circle and rectangle are derived from shape. A virtual function allows run-time selection from a group of functions overridden within a type hierarchy. The revision process is one in which code improvements are provided in a new derived class, so additional description is localized. The programmer overrides the meaning of any changed routines—in this case the new area calculation. Client code that does not use the new type is unaffected. Typically, client code that is improved by the new type is minimally changed.

C++ code following this design uses shape as an *abstract base class*, which is a class containing one or more pure virtual functions.

```
//shape is an abstract base class
class shape {
public:
   virtual double area() = 0; //pure virtual function
};

class rectangle: public shape {
public:
   rectangle(double h, double w): height(h), width(w) {}
   double area() { return (height * width); } //overridden function
private:
   double height, width;
};

class circle: public shape {
public:
   circle(double r): radius(r) {}
   double area() { return ( 3.14159 * radius * radius); }
private:
   double radius;
};
```

Client code for computing an arbitrary area is polymorphic. The appropriate area() function is selected at run-time.

```
shape*  ptr_shape;

    . . .
   cout << " area = " << ptr_shape -> area();
    . . .
```

Now imagine improving our hierarchy of types by developing a square class.

```
class square: public rectangle {
public:
    square(double h): rectangle(h,h) {}
    double area() { return (rectangle::area()); }
};
```

The client code remains unchanged. This was not the case with the non-OOP code.

1.9 TEMPLATES

C++ uses the keyword template to provide *parametric polymorphism*. Parametric polymorphism allows the same code to be used with respect to different types, where the type is a parameter of the code body. The code is written generically to act on class T. The template is used to generate different actual classes when class T is substituted for with an actual type.

An especially important use for this technique is in writing generic *container classes*. A container class is used to contain data of a particular type. Stacks, vectors, trees, and lists are all examples of standard container classes. We can develop a stack container class as a parameterized type.

```
//template stack implementation
template <class TYPE>
class stack {
public:
    stack(int size = 1000) :max_len(size)
        { s = new TYPE[size]; top - EMPTY; }
    ~stack() { delete []s; }
    void reset() { top = EMPTY; }
    void push(TYPE c) { s[++top] = c; }
    TYPE pop() { return (s[top--]); }
    TYPE top_of() { return (s[top]); }
    boolean empty() { return boolean(top == EMPTY); }
    boolean full() { return boolean(top == max_len - 1); }
private:
    enum  {EMPTY = -1};
    TYPE* s;
    int    max_len;
    int    top;
};
```

The syntax of the class declaration is prefaced by

```
template <class identifier >
```

This identifier is a template argument that essentially stands for an arbitrary type. Throughout the class definition the template argument can be used as a type name. This argument is instantiated in the actual declarations. An example of a stack declaration using this is

```
stack<char> stk_ch;            // 1000 element char stack
stack<char*>  stk_str(200);    // 200 element char* stack
stack<complex> stk_cmplx(100); // 100 element complex stack
```

This mechanism saves us rewriting class declarations where the only variations would be type declarations.

When processing such a type, the code must always use the angle brackets as part of the declaration. Here are two functions using the stack template:

```
//Reversing a series of char* represented strings
void reverse(char* str[], int n)
{
    stack<char*> stk(n);  //this stack holds char*

    for (int i = 0; i < n; ++i)
        stk.push(str[i]);
    for (i = 0; i < n; ++i)
        str[i] = stk.pop();
}
```

In function reverse() a stack<char*> is used to insert n strings and then pop them in reverse order.

```
//Initializing a stack of complex numbers from an array
void init(complex c[], stack<complex>& stk, n)
{
    for (int i = 0; i < n; ++i)
        stk.push(c[i]);
}
```

In function init() a stack<complex> variable is passed by reference, and n complex numbers are pushed onto this stack.

1.10 EXCEPTIONS

C++ introduces an exception-handling mechanism that is sensitive to context. The context for raising an exception is a try block. An exception is raised by using the throw expression. The exception is handled by invoking the appropriate *handler* selected from a list of handlers found immediately after the handler's try block. Handlers are declared using the keyword catch. A simple example of all this is

```
//stack constructor with exceptions
stack::stack(int n)
{
   if (n < 1)
      throw (n);        //want a positive value
   p = new char[n];    //create a stack of characters
   if (p == 0)          //new returns 0 when it fails
      throw ("FREE STORE EXHAUSTED");
}

void g()
{
   try {
      stack  a(n), b(n);
      . . .

   }
   catch (int n) { . . . } //an incorrect size
   catch (char* error) { . . . } //free store exhaustion
}
```

The first throw() has an integer argument and matches the catch(int n) signature. This handler is expected to perform an appropriate action when an incorrect array size has been passed as an argument to the constructor. For example, an error message and abort are normal. The second throw() has a pointer to character argument and matches the catch(char* error) signature.

1.11 BENEFITS OF OBJECT-ORIENTED PROGRAMMING

The central element of OOP is the encapsulation of an appropriate set of data types and their operations. The class construct, with its member functions and data members, provides an appropriate coding tool. Class variables are the objects to be manipulated.

Classes also provide data hiding. Access privileges can be managed and limited to whatever group of functions needs access to implementation details. This promotes modularity and robustness.

Another important concept in OOP is the promotion of code reuse through the inheritance mechanism. This is the mechanism of deriving a new class from an existing one called the base class. The base class can be added to or altered to create the derived class. In this way a hierarchy of related data types can be created that share code.

Many useful data structures are variants of one another, and it is frequently tedious to produce the same code for each. A derived class inherits the description of the base class. It can then be altered by adding additional members, overloading existing member functions, and modifying access privileges. Without this reuse mechanism each minor variation would require code replication.

The OOP programming task is frequently more difficult than normal procedural programming as found in C. At least one extra design step is required before the programmer can code algorithms. This step involves the hierarchy of types that is useful for the problem at hand. Frequently, the programmer solves the problem more generally than is strictly necessary.

The belief is that this pays dividends in several ways. The solution is more encapsulated and thus more robust and easier to maintain and change. Also, the solution is more reusable. For example, where the code needs a stack, that stack is easily borrowed from existing code. In an ordinary procedural language, such a data structure is frequently "wired into" the algorithm and cannot be exported.

All these benefits are especially important for large coding projects that require coordination among many programmers. In such cases the ability to have header files specify general interfaces for different classes allows each programmer to work on individual code segments with a high degree of independence and integrity.

OOP is many things to many people. Attempts at defining it are reminiscent of the blind sages attempts at describing the elephant. I offer this equation:

OOP = type extensibility + polymorphism

1.12 SUMMARY

1. The double slash // is a new comment symbol. The comment runs to the end of the line. The old C bracketing comment symbols /* */ are still available for multiline comments.

2. The *iostream.h* header introduces I/O facilities for C++. The identifier cout is the name of the standard output stream. The operator << passes its argument to standard out. Used in this way, the << is referred to as the *put to* operator. The identifier cin is the name of the standard input stream. The operator >> is the input operator, called *get from*, that assigns values from the input stream to a variable.

3. C++ reduces C's traditional reliance on the preprocessor. Instead of using define, C++ assigns special constants to variables specified as const. The new keyword inline specifies that a function is to be compiled inline to avoid function call overhead. As a rule, this should be done sparingly and only on short functions.

4. The syntax of functions in C++ inspired the new function prototype syntax found in Standard C compilers. Basically, the types of parameters are listed inside the header parentheses, for example, int add3 (int, int, int). By explicitly listing the type and number of arguments, strong type checking and assignment-compatible conversions are possible in C++.

5. What is novel about C++ is the aggregate type class. A class is an extension of the idea of struct in traditional C. Its use is a way of implementing a data type and associated functions, and operators. Therefore a class is an implementation of an abstract data type (ADT). There are two important additions to the structure concept: It includes members that are functions, and it employs the access keywords public, private, and protected. These keywords indicate the visibility of the members that follow. Public members are available to any function within the scope of the class declaration. Private members are available for use only by other member functions of the class. Protected members are available for use only by other member functions of the class and by derived classes. Privacy allows part of the implementation of a class type to be "hidden."

6. The term *overloading* refers to the practice of giving several meanings to an operator or a function. The meaning selected depends on the types of the arguments used by the operator or function.

7. A constructor is a member function whose job is to initialize a variable of its class. In many cases this involves dynamic storage allocation. Constructors are invoked anytime an object of its associated class is created. A destructor is a member function whose job is to finalize a variable of its class. The destructor is invoked implicitly when an automatic object goes out of scope.

8. The central element of object-oriented programming (OOP) is the encapsulation of an appropriate set of data types and their operations. These user-defined types are ADTs. The class construct with its member functions and data members provides an appropriate coding tool. Class variables are the *objects* to be manipulated.

9. Another important concept in OOP is the promotion of code reuse through the *inheritance* mechanism. This is the mechanism of *deriving* a new class from an existing one, called the *base class*. The base class can be added to or altered to create the derived class. In this way a hierarchy of related data types can be created that share code. This typing hierarchy can be used dynamically by virtual functions. Virtual member functions in a base class are overloaded in a derived class. These functions allow for dynamic or run-time typing. A pointer to the base class can also point at objects of the derived classes. When such a pointer is used to point at the overloaded virtual function, it dynamically selects which version of the member function to call.

10. A *polymorphic* function has many forms. A virtual function allows run-time selection from a group of functions overridden within a type hierarchy. An example in the text is the area calculation within the shape hierarchy. Client code for computing an arbitrary area is polymorphic. The appropriate area() function is selected at run-time.

11. C++ uses the keyword template to provide *parametric polymorphism*. Parametric polymorphism allows the same code to be used with respect to different types, where the type is a parameter of the code body. The code is written generically to act on class T. The template is used to generate different actual classes when class T is substituted for with an actual type.

12. C++ introduces an exception-handling mechanism that is sensitive to context. The context for raising an exception is a try block. An exception is raised by using the throw expression. The exception will be handled by invoking an appropriate *handler* selected from a list

of handlers found immediately after the handler's try block. Handlers are declared using the keyword catch.

1.13 EXERCISES

1. Using stream I/O, write on the screen the words

   `she sells sea shells by the seashore`

   (a) all on one line, (b) on three lines, (c) inside a box.

2. Write a program that converts distances measured in yards to distances measured in meters. The relationship is 1 meter equals 1.0936 yards. Write the program to use cin to read in distances. The program should be a loop that does this calculation until it receives zero or a negative number for input.

3. Most systems allow *redirection* of input/output. In redirection the symbol < means that input is redirected from the named file, and the symbol > means that output is redirected to the named file. Compile the previous program into an executable *mitok* and execute

   mitok < data > answers

   The file data should contain the numbers

   `1  5  10  26  0`

   Print the contents of file *answers* to check the results.

4. Take a working program, omit each line in turn, and run it through the compiler. Record the error message caused by each deletion. For example, use the following code:

```
#include <iostream.h>

main()
{
    int m, n, k;
    cout << "\nEnter two integers: ";
    cin  >> m >> n;
    k = m + n;
    cout << "\nTheir sum is " << k << ".\n";
}
```

5. Write a program that asks interactively for your *name* and *age* and responds with

```
Hello name, next year you will be next_age.
```

where *next_age* is *age* + 1.

6. Write a program that prints out a table of squares, square roots, and cubes. Use either tabbing or strings of blanks to get a neatly aligned table.

```
i      i * i    square root    i * i * i
-------------------------------------------
1        1      1.00000              1
. . .
```

This topic is covered in detail in Section 7.2.

7. The traditional C swapping function is

```
void swap(i, j)
int*  i;
int*  j;
{
    int  temp;

    temp = *i;
    *i = *j;
    *j = temp;
}
```

Rewrite this using reference parameters and test it.

```
void swap(int& i, int& j)
. . .
```

8. In traditional C the following code causes an error:

```
#include <math.h>
#include <stdio.h>

main()
{
    printf("%f is the square root of 2.\n", sqrt(2));
}
```

Explain the reason for this and why function prototypes in C++ avoid this problem. Rewrite the code using *iostream.h*.

9. Add to the class string a member function reverse. This function reverses the underlying representation of the character sequence stored in the private member s.

10. Add to the class string a member function void print(int pos, int k). This function overloads print() and is meant to print the k characters of the string starting at position pos.

11. Overload the operator * in class string. Its member declaration is

    ```
    string string::operator*(int n);
    ```

    The expression s * k is a string that is k copies of the string s. Check that this does not overrun storage.

12. Write a class person that contains basic information such as name, birthdate, and address. Derive class student from person.

13. Write a class triangle that inherits from shape. It needs to have its own area() member function.

14. The function reverse() can be written generically as follows:

    ```
    //generic reversal
    template <class T>
    void reverse(T v[], int n)
    {
        stack<T> stk(n);

        for (int i = 0; i < n; ++i)
            stk.push(v[i]);
        for (i = 0; i < n; ++i)
            v[i] = stk.pop();
    }
    ```

    Try this on your system, using it to reverse an array of characters and to reverse an array of char*.

15. (S. Clamage) Here are three programs that behave differently. We start with

```
//Function declarations at file scope
int f(int);
double f(double); //overloads f(int)
double add_f()
{
    return(f(1) + f(1.0)); //f(int) + f(double)
}
```

We place one function declaration internally.

```
//Function declaration at local scope
int f(int);
double add_f()
{
    double f(double); //hides f(int)
    return(f(1) + f(1.0)); //f(double) + f(double)
}
```

Now we place the other function declaration internally.

```
double f(double);
double add_f()
{
    int f(int);
    return(f(1) + f(1.0)); //What is called here?
}
```

Write some test programs that clearly show the different behaviors.

CHAPTER 2

C++ AS A BETTER C

C++ extends the C programming language in a number of important ways. Its new features make it more reliable and easier to use than C. Many of these features are independent of the additions connected to the class construct. This chapter describes these improvements. Its theme is that C++ can be used as an improved and better C.

Some of the changes described are minor but nonetheless useful. Among these is the new comment style. Some of the changes are major, such as function prototypes, which have been adopted into Standard C. The type compatibility rules are stronger in C++, and the compiler provides much of the checking that is relegated to *lint* in C.

Several features of C++ affect type declarations, including the use of void, void*, enum, and const. These changes were made to the original C language but were adopted in Standard C. Some changes not in Standard C include the use of the keyword inline for function declarations and the use of & to mean the declaration is a reference declaration. All these changes are explained in this chapter along with examples.

In this chapter, then, we discuss the new comment style, the use of the keywords const and inline, the uses of the void and void* types, the function prototype construct, the use of reference declarations, the overloading of functions, and the use of the free store operators new and delete.

2.1 COMMENT STYLE

Programs must be documented to be useful. C++ introduces a one-line comment symbol //. This one-line comment symbol is an addition to rather than a replacement of the bracket-pair multi-line comment symbols /* */ of C. Everything on a single line after the symbol // is treated as a comment. This is not the case when the symbol is part of a character or a string. The one-line comment symbol is the preferred C++ style. In general, it is less error prone; bracket-pair symbols can cause problems, for example, when one of the pair is omitted. The following example shows C++ comment style:

```
//The computation of circumference and area of circles.
//  Title: circles
//                      by
//                Geometrics Inc.
//                Version 2.2

#include <iostream.h>

const  float pi = 3.14159;     //pi accurate to six places
const  int true = 1;           //mnemonic identifier

inline float circum(float rad) { return (pi * 2 * rad); }
inline float area(float rad) { return (pi * rad * rad); }

main()
{
   float  r;

   while (true) {                   //exit with control-C
      cout << "\nEnter radius: ";   //prompt for input
      cin >> r;
      cout << "\nArea is " << area(r);
      cout << "\nCircumference is " << circum(r) << endl;
   }
   return (0);
}
```

2.2 AVOIDING THE PREPROCESSOR: *inline* AND *const*

In the previous example and in examples in Chapter 1, the new keywords
inline and const were used to avoid the use of the preprocessor define.
Using the preprocessor to define macros has a clear drawback: The preprocessor does not understand C syntax. For example,

```
#define SQ(X)    X * X
```

expands the code

```
SQ(a + b)
```

to

```
a + b * a + b
```

This problem is avoided by fully parenthesizing the original macro. However, the solution does not protect against improper types being used. This latter defect is remedied by using `inline`.

```
inline int SQ(int x) { return (x * x); }
```

The keyword `inline` is a request to the compiler that the function be compiled without function call overhead. The compiler may choose to ignore this suggestion, but either way the semantics of the compiled function are identical. Only very short functions, for which function call overhead is an issue, should use this function specifier.

The `const` keyword is a type specifier. When used alone in a declaration, the base type is implicitly `int`. A variable declared as `const` cannot have its value changed. Such a variable can be used in places that otherwise would require a literal, such as an array size. A `const` variable cannot be used on the left side of an assignment. An ordinary variable can be used on the left side of an assignment, as such it is used as an *lvalue*. An *lvalue* is an expression that can be used as an address to be stored into. A `const` variable is a nonmodifiable *lvalue*. This implies that a `const` variable must be initialized where defined. As in the previous program, it is used to create symbolic constants—an important documentation aid. Some examples are

```
const   false = 0;            //implicit type is int
const   double e = 2.71828;   //natural logarithm base
const   int M_size = 100;     //used in an array declaration
const* p = &M_size;           //a pointer to a constant int
char*   const s = "abcde";    //a constant pointer to char
```

The form

```
const type* identifier
```

declares the identifier as a pointer whose pointed at value is constant. This construct is used when pointer arguments to functions will not have their contents modified. The form

```
type* const identifier
```

declares the identifier as a pointer constant. So

```
const int* const cp = &M_size;
```

declares cp to be a constant pointer whose pointed-at value is constant. Also note the following examples:

```
const double pi = 3.14159;
const double *d_p1 = &pi;  //legal: pi is an lvalue
const double *d_p2 = &3.1; //illegal: 3.1 is not an lvalue
pi = 3.141596;   //illegal because pi is nonmodifiable
```

2.3 DECLARATIONS

This section describes changes to declarations in C++. It discusses the meaning of enum and illustrates the fact that declarations can be inter-mixed with executable statements. It also explains that the struct tag name and enum tag name are types.

Let us write a card-shuffling program to illustrate these points. First we define a card as a struct.

```
enum suit {clubs, diamonds, hearts, spades};

struct card {
    suit  s;
    int   pips;
};

card deck[52];   //a declaration using card as the type
```

In Standard C the declaration of deck would be illegal. It would have to be

```
enum suit {clubs, diamonds, hearts, spades};

struct card {
    enum suit  s;
    int        pips;
};

struct card deck[52];
```

In C++ the tag names are types.

Enumerated types were added to C compilers in the early 1980s. They were implemented as a form of int. C++ treats enumerated types as distinct types promotable to an int in expressions. When listed without

initialized values, the identifiers in the enumerated lists are implicitly initialized consecutively starting with 0. These identifiers are named integer
constants and cannot be changed. So the two declarations

```
enum suit {clubs, diamonds, hearts, spades};
enum suit {clubs = 0, diamonds = 1, hearts = 2, spades = 3};
```

are equivalent, as are

```
enum suit {clubs = 5, diamonds, hearts, spades = 3};
enum suit {clubs = 5, diamonds = 6, hearts = 7, spades = 3};
```

As we saw in Chapter 1, C++ allows declarations to be intermixed
with executable statements. Consider a function that initializes a deck of
cards to the normal 52 card values.

```
void init_deck(card d[])
{
   for (int i = 0; i < 52; ++i) {
      switch (i / 13)  {
         case 0: d[i].s = clubs; break;
         case 1: d[i].s = diamonds; break;
         case 2: d[i].s = hearts; break;
         case 3: d[i].s = spades; break;
      }
      d[i].pips = 1 + i % 13;
   }
}
```

In this function the declaration int i occurs inside the for statement
parentheses. The scope of the declaration is the innermost block within
which it is found, and the identifier is visible starting at the point
at which it is declared. Otherwise the scope rules are the same as in C,
which means that declarations can readily be placed near their use.

The program for deck shuffling follows:

```
//Shuffling a card deck.
//    Title: shuffle

#include  <iostream.h>
#include  <stdlib.h>        //has rand()and srand()
#include  <time.h>          //has time()

enum suit {clubs, diamonds, hearts, spades};

struct card {
   suit  s;
   int   pips;
};

void pr_card(card cd)
{
   switch (cd.pips)  {
      case 1 :  cout << "A"; break;
      case 11:  cout << "J"; break;
      case 12:  cout << "Q"; break;
      case 13:  cout << "K"; break;
      default:  cout << cd.pips;
   }
   switch (cd.s)  {
      case clubs:    cout << "C"; break;
      case diamonds: cout << "D"; break;
      case hearts:   cout << "H"; break;
      case spades:   cout << "S"; break;
      default :      cerr << "suit error\n"; exit(1);
   }
   cout << "  ";
}
void init_deck(card d[])
{
   for (int i = 0; i < 52; ++i) {
      switch (i / 13)  {
         case 0: d[i].s = clubs; break;
         case 1: d[i].s = diamonds; break;
         case 2: d[i].s = hearts; break;
         case 3: d[i].s = spades; break;
      }
      d[i].pips = 1 + i % 13;
   }
}
```

```
void shuffle(card d[])
{
    for (int i = 0; i < 52; ++i) {
        int k = rand() % 52;       //choose a random card
        card t = d[i];             //swap two cards
        d[i] = d[k];
        d[k] = t;
    }
}

void pr_deck(const card d[])
{
    for (int i = 0; i < 52; ++i) {
        if (i % 13 == 0)
            cout << "\n";
        pr_card(d[i]);
    }
    cout << endl;
}

main()
{
    card deck[52];

    srand(time(NULL));             //seed rand() using time()
    init_deck(deck);
    pr_deck(deck);                 //print unshuffled deck
    shuffle(deck);
    pr_deck(deck);                 //print shuffled deck
    return (0);
}
```

■ DISSECTION OF THE *shuffle* PROGRAM

```
void shuffle(card d[])
```

- A function returning no value is of type void. The parameter d is of type pointer to card.

```
for (int i = 0; i < 52; ++i) {
    int k = rand() % 52;       //choose a random card
    card t = d[i];             //swap two cards
    d[i] = d[k];
    d[k] = t;
}
```

- Again executable statements and declarations are mixed. Note how the code is more readable than if the declarations were at the head of the function block. The rand() function is a pseudorandom number generator.

2.4 THE USES OF *void*

The type void was introduced in some C compilers in the early 1980s. It is in Standard C. In the previous section we saw two of the normal uses of the keyword void: as the return type of a function not returning a value and to indicate an empty argument list to a function. Two additional uses are as a cast and as part of the type pointer to void.

As the type within the cast operator, it informs the compiler that the expression's computed value is to be discarded.

```
//Simple use of void.
//    Title: void

#include <iostream.h>

int foo(int i)
{
   cout << "i is " << i;
   return (i);
}

main()
{
   int k = 5;

   (void)foo(k);  //throw away the int return value
   return (0);
}
```

Most interesting, however, is the use of void* as a generic pointer type. An arbitrary pointer value can be converted to a void*. A generic pointer may not be dereferenced. Dereferencing is the operation * acting on a pointer value to obtain what is pointed at. It would not make sense to dereference a pointer to a void value.

```
void* gp;      //generic pointer
int*  ip;      //int pointer
char* cp;      //char pointer

gp = ip;       //legal conversion
ip = (int*)gp; //explicit cast required in C++ but not in C
cp = ip;       //illegal conversion
*ip = 15;      //legal dereferencing of a pointer to int
*ip = *gp;     //illegal dereferencing of a generic pointer
```

A key use for this type is as a formal parameter. For example, the library function memcpy is declared in string.h as

```
void* memcpy(void* s1, const void* s2, size_t n);
```

This function copies n characters from the object based at s2 into the object based at s1. The type size_t is a system-dependent, unsigned integer type defined in *stddef.h*. It works with any two pointer types as actual arguments.

2.5 SCOPE RESOLUTION OPERATOR ::

C is a block-structured language. C++ inherits the same notions of block and scope. In such languages the same identifier can be used to mean different objects. Using a name in an inner block *hides* the outer block or external use of the same name. C++ introduces the operator ::, called the scope resolution operator. When used in the form :: *variable*, it allows access to the externally named variable. As in the following example, it is assumed that this uncovers an otherwise hidden object.

```
//  ::  scope resolution operator
//    Title: scope_operator

#include    <iostream.h>
int i = 1;              //external i

main()
{
   int   i = 2;      //redeclares i locally

   {
      cout << "enter inner block\n";
      int  n = i;    //the outer block i is still visible
      int  i = 3;    //hides both the global i and outer block i

      //print the local i and the external i
      cout << i << " " i <> ::i   " << ::i << "\n";
      cout << "n = " << n << "\n";
   }
   cout << "enter outer block\n";
   cout << i << " " i <> ::i  " << ::i << endl;
   return (0);
}
```

The output of this code is

```
enter inner block
3  i <> ::i  1
n = 2
enter outer block
2  i <> ::i  1
```

The major uses of this notation are important for classes. They are discussed later in the book.

2.6 FUNCTION PROTOTYPES

The single feature in C++ that most accounts for its greater reliability over traditional C is its use of function prototypes. By explicitly listing the type and number of arguments, strong type checking and assignment-compatible conversions are possible in C++. The success of this feature inspired ANSI C to adopt it.

In traditional C a function may be declared before it is defined, with the form

type name();

This declaration announces that the function is defined elsewhere with the given return type. However, the compiler makes no assumptions about type and number of arguments. Therefore, in traditional C when a function is invoked with an actual argument, the explicit value of that argument is passed as is, without being converted to the defined function's corresponding argument type. A most common error occurs when functions such as sqrt are passed int valued expressions.

```
printf("%f is sqrt of 4\n", sqrt(4));
```

This prints 0 on many traditional C systems. The function sqrt expects a double, and the bit configuration for the int constant 4, when interpreted as a double, passes sqrt an argument whose value is 0.

In C++ the prototype form is

type name(*argument-declaration-list*);

Examples are

```
double sqrt(double x);
void   make_str(char*, int);      //definition has names
void   print(const char* s);      //s is not modified
int    printf(char* format, ...); //variable no. of args
```

With the above sqrt prototype definition, the call to

```
sqrt(4)
```

causes a conversion from int value 4 to double value 4 to occur before the function call is executed. The argument-declaration-list can either have named arguments or omit them. These names are intended as possible documentation. It is not necessary but it is good style for names in prototype declarations to match names used in the actual definition. The pro-

totype for the stdio.h function printf uses an ellipsis (...) to specify that
the function argument list has unknown length and type.
    The following example illustrates these points:

```
//Compute the average of a set of int values.
//   Title: prototypes

#include <iostream.h>

int data[10] = {99, 87, 67, 90, 66, 43, 89, 88, 97, 76};
void   print_array(const char*, const int*, int);
void   print_double(const char*, double);
double average(const int a[], int size);

main()
{
   print_array("data", data, 10);
   print_double("average", average(data, 10));
   return (0);
}

void pr_int(const char* name, int k)
{
   cout << name << " = " << k << endl;
}

void print_double(const char* name, double x)
{
   cout << name << " = " << x << endl;
}

void print_array(const char* name, const int a[], int size)
{
   cout << name;
   pr_int(" array, size ", size);
   for (int i = 0; i < size; ++i)
      cout << a[i] << "\t";
   cout << endl;
}

double average(const int a[], int size)   //compute average
{
   int  sum = 0;

   for (int i = 0; i < size; ++i)
      sum += a[i];
   return ((double) sum / size);
}
```

The output from this program is

```
data array, size  = 10
99    87    67    90    66    43    89    88    97    76
average = 80.2
```

2.7 REFERENCE DECLARATIONS AND
CALL-BY-REFERENCE

C++ allows *reference to* declarations. These are typically of the form

type& identifier = object

Such declarations declare the identifier to be an alternative name for an object specified in an initialization of the reference. Some examples are

```
int     n;
int&    nn = n;          //nn is an alternative name for n
double  a[10];
double& last = a[9];     //last is an alias for a[9]
const char& new_line = '\n';
```

In these examples the names n and nn are aliases for each other; that is, they refer to the same object. Modifying nn is equivalent to modifying n, and vice versa. The name last is an alternative to the single array element a[9]. These names, once initialized, cannot be changed. In the examples new_line is initialized to the char constant \n, which is allowed for a const reference declaration.

The chief use of reference declarations is in formal parameter lists. This usage allows C++ to have *call-by-reference* arguments directly. Let us use this mechanism to write a function greater that exchanges two values if the first is greater than the second.

```
int greater(int& a, int& b)
{
   if (a > b) {          //exchange
      int temp = a;
      a = b;
      b = temp;
      return (1);
   }
   else
      return (0);
}
```

If i and j are two int variables, then

```
greater(i, j)
```

uses the reference to i and the reference to j to exchange, if necessary, their two values. In traditional C this operation must be accomplished using pointers and dereferencing.

When function arguments are to remain unmodified, it can be efficient and correct to pass them const call-by-reference. This is the case for types that are structures.

```
struct large_size{
   int mem[N];
   //. . . other stuff
};

void print(const large_size& s)
{
   //since s will not be modified
   //avoid call-by-value copying
   //. . .
}
```

2.8 DEFAULT ARGUMENTS

A formal parameter can be given a default argument. This is usually a constant that occurs frequently when the function is called. Use of a default argument saves writing in this default value at each invocation. The following function illustrates the point:

```
int mult(int n, int k = 2)      //k = 2 is default
{
    if (k == 2)
        return (n * n);
    else
        return (mult(n, k - 1) * n);
}
```

We assume that most of the time the function is used to return the value of n squared.

```
mult(i + 5)                    //computes (i + 5) * (i + 5)
mult(i + 5, 3)                 //computes (i + 5) cubed
```

Only the trailing parameters of a function can have default values. Some examples are

```
void foo(int i, int j = 7);              //legal
void goo(int i = 3, int j);              //illegal
void hoo(int i, int j = 3, int k = 7);   //legal
void moo(int i = 1, int j = 2, int k = 3); //legal
void noo(int i, int j = 2, int k);       //illegal
```

A function can have multiple declarations but is given a default value in only one of the visible declarations. The previous defaults are remembered.

```
void foo(int i, int j = 7);
void foo(int i, int j);        //j = 7 is understood
void foo(int i, int j = 7);    //illegal to repeat default
```

2.9 OVERLOADING FUNCTIONS

The term *overloading* refers to using the same name for multiple meanings of an operator or a function. The meaning selected depends on the types and the number of the arguments used by the operator or function. Here we restrict our discussion to function overloading. We leave operator overloading to later chapters, as it is chiefly used in the context of classes.

The usual reason for picking a function name is to indicate the function's chief purpose. Readable programs generally have a diverse and literate choice of identifiers. Sometimes different functions are used for the same purpose. For example, consider a function that averages the values in an array of double versus one that averages the values in an array of int. Both are conveniently named average, as in a previous example.

```
double average(const double a[], int size);
double average(const int a[], int size);
double average(const int a[], const double b[], int size);

double average(const int a[], int size)
{
    int  sum = 0;

    for (int i = 0; i < size; ++i)
        sum += a[i];         //performs int arithmetic
    return ((double) sum / size);
}

double average(const double a[], int size)
{
    double  sum = 0.0;

    for (int i = 0; i < size; ++i)
        sum += a[i];         //performs double arithmetic
    return (sum / size);
}

double average(const int a[], const double b[], int size)
{
    double  sum = 0.0;

    for (int i = 0; i < size; ++i)
        sum += a[i] + b[i]; //performs double arithmetic
    return (sum / size);
}
```

The following code shows how each function is invoked:

```
main()
{
    int    w[5] = {1, 2, 3, 4, 5};
    double x[5] = {1.1, 2.2, 3.3, 4.4, 5.5};

    cout << average(w, 5) << "  int array average\n";
    cout << average(x, 5) << "  double array average\n";
    cout << average(w, x, 5) << "  both arrays averaged\n";
    return (0);
}
```

The compiler chooses the function with matching types and arguments.

2.10 FREE STORE OPERATORS *new* AND *delete*

The unary operators new and delete are available to manipulate *free store*. They are more convenient than and can be used to replace the standard library functions malloc, calloc, and free in many applications. Free store is a system-provided memory pool for objects whose lifetimes are directly managed by the programmer. The programmer creates the object by using new and destroys the object by using delete. This is important for dynamic data structures such as lists and trees.

The operator new is used in the following forms:

> new *type-name*
> new *type-name initializer*
> new (*type-name*)

In each case the operator has minimally two effects. First, an appropriate amount of store is allocated from free store to contain the named type. Second, the base address of the object is returned as the value of the new expression. The new expression is a suitably typed pointer. If the type-name is T or array-of-T, the returned type is T*. The operator new returns the value 0 when memory is unavailable, and this special pointer value should be used to test that allocation has failed (see Section 2.12).

The following examples use new:

```
int* ptr_i, *v;
double (*)[N] q;

//in each case a suitably typed pointer value is returned
//it is the base address of the heap allocated object

ptr_i = new int(5);    //allocate and initialize, so *ptr_i is 5
v = new int[40];       //allocate a vector of 40 integers
                       //v == &v[0]
q = new double[n][N]; //allocate an n by N vector of doubles
                      //q == &q[0][0]
```

In this code the pointer to int variable ptr_i is assigned the address of the store obtained in allocating an object of type int. The location pointed at by ptr_i is initialized to the value 5. This use is not usual for a simple type such as int, because it is far more convenient and natural to automatically allocate an integer variable on the stack or globally.

The operator delete destroys an object created by new, in effect returning its allocated storage to free store for reuse. The operator delete is used in the following forms:

> delete *expression*
> delete [ ] *expression*

The first form is used when single objects are allocated by new. For example, when p = new my_type is executed, delete p is used. The second form must be used when returning store that was allocated as a vector. For example, when p = new my_type[expr] is executed, delete []p is used. The operator delete returns type void. The following example uses these constructs to dynamically allocate an array:

```
//Use of new operator to dynamically allocate an array.
//   Title: dynamic

#include <iostream.h>

main()
{
    int*  data;
    int   size;

    cout << "\nEnter array size: ";
    cin >> size;

    data = new int[size];
    for (int j = 0; j < size; ++j)
        cout << (data[j] = j) << "\t";
    cout << endl;

    delete []data;
    data = new int[size];
    for (j = 0; j < size; ++j)
        cout << data[j] << "\t";
    return (0);
}
```

■ DISSECTION OF THE *dynamic* PROGRAM

```
int* data;
int  size;

cout << "\nEnter array size: ";
cin >> size;

data = new int[size];
```

- The pointer variable data is used as the base address of a dynamically allocated array whose number of elements is the value of size. The user is prompted for the integer-valued size. The new operator is used to allocate storage from free store capable of storing an object of type int[size]. This allocates sizeof(int) * size bytes. At this point data is assigned the base address of this store.

```
for (int j = 0; j < size; ++j)
   cout << (data[j] = j) << "\t";
```

- This statement initializes the values of the data array and prints them.

```
delete []data;
```

- The operator delete returns the storage associated with the pointer variable data to free store. This can be done only with objects allocated by new. The empty brackets indicate that vector allocation was used and therefore vector deallocation should be used.

```
data = new int[size];
for (j = 0; j < size; ++j)
   cout << data[j] << "\t";
```

- We access free store again, but this time we do not initialize the data array. On a typical system, the same memory just returned to free store is used, with the old values reappearing. However, the values that appear in objects allocated from free store are system dependent. Test this on your system. The programmer is responsible for properly initializing such objects.

■

2.11 ODDS AND ENDS

Several other features of C++ that do not appear in traditional C are relatively minor. Among these are the use of signed, the treatment of float, and the use of anonymous unions. We cover these matters briefly.

Standard C introduces the keyword signed, which is analogous to the keyword unsigned. The keywords signed and unsigned are type specifiers for the integral types. The unsigned type does not allow negative values; the signed type does.

The type float in traditional C was always promoted to double when used in expressions. C++, however, reserves the right to do arithmetic in single precision float.

An anonymous union has the following form:

union{*member declarations*};

C++ allows the member names of such unions to be used directly, but they must be distinct from other identifiers defined within the same scope. A global anonymous union must have storage class static. An example is

```
//Anonymous Unions

#include <iostream.h>

static union {
    long int   i;
    char       c[4];
    float      w;
};

main()
{
    i = 65;
    cout << c[0] << "\n";
    c[1] = c[2] = c[3] = 'A';
    cout << w << endl;
    return (0);
}
```

What gets printed is

```
A
12.078431
```

The byte that is used by the integer member i to store the value 65 is accessed by the indexed character member c[0]. The string of four ´A´s stored in the array c[] is interpreted as the floating point value 12.07841. This representation is system dependent. This code is highly machine dependent. In a union the member declarations share the same storage. This technique is used to conserve storage and avoid unnecessary type conversions.

2.12 PRAGMATICS

Standard C community style is used for ordinary code.

```
for (i = 0; i < n; ++i) {   //C style brace on first line
   a[i] = b[i] = c[i];      //typical indent
   cout << a[i] << ", \t" ;
};                          //closing brace matches for
```

The opening brace for a flow-of-control statement is on the first line together with the initial part of the statement. The closing brace matches the first letter of the initial keyword of that statement.

Pascal style is an acceptable alternative.

```
for (i = 0; i < n; ++i)
{                           //Pascal style brace on a separate line
   a[i] = b[i] = c[i];      //typical indent
   cout << a[i] << ", \t" ;
};                          //closing brace matches open brace
```

The pointer value returned by new should be tested to see if it is 0. This value represents a failure to allocate memory and should be used to terminate the program. One method of testing for this value is to use *assert.h.*

```
#include <assert.h>

   . . .
   p = new double[500000000];  //probably fails
   assert(p != 0);             //p == 0 aborts
   . . .
```

The assertion macro aborts the program with relevant diagnostic information when it fails. We believe assertions and exceptions will be used to increase the robustness of C++ code. Assertions can be turned off using the preprocessor command

```
#define NDEBUG
```

For an extended discussion of these ideas, see Chapter 8.

2.13 SUMMARY

1. Programs must be documented to be useful. C++ introduces a one-line comment symbol //. This symbol is an addition to rather than a replacement of the bracket-pair comment symbols /* */ of traditional C. Everything on a single line after the symbol // is treated as a comment.

2. The keyword inline is a request to the compiler that the function be compiled without function call overhead. The const keyword is a type specifier. When used alone in a declaration, the base type is implicitly int. A variable declared as const becomes a symbolic constant. It can be used in places that otherwise would require a literal, such as an array size.

3. Enumerated types were added to C compilers in the early 1980s. They were implemented as a form of int. C++ treats enumerated types as distinct types promotable to an int in expressions. When listed without initialized values, the identifiers in the enumerated lists are implicitly initialized consecutively starting with 0. These identifiers are named integer constants and cannot be changed.

4. The tag names of both enumerated and structure types can be used as type names. Declarations may be intermixed with executable statements.

5. The type void was introduced in some C compilers in the early 1980s. It improves both documentation and type checking over traditional C. The keyword void is used as the return type of a function not returning a value. Three further uses are as a cast, as part of the type pointer to void, or optionally as an empty argument list.

6. C++ introduces the operator ::, called the scope resolution operator. When used in the form :: *variable*, it allows access to the externally named variable.

7. The single feature in C++ that most accounts for its greater reliability over traditional C is its use of function prototypes. By explicitly listing the type and number of arguments, strong type checking and assignment-compatible conversions are possible in C++. In C++ the prototype form is

   type name(argument-declaration-list);

   Examples are

   ```
   double sqrt(double x);
   void   make_str(char*, int);     //definition has names
   void   print(const char* s);     //s is not modified
   int    printf(char* format, ...); //variable no. of args.
   ```

8. C++ allows *reference to* declarations. These are typically of the form

   type & identifier = object

   These declare the identifier to be an alternative name for an object specified in an initialization of the reference. The chief use of reference declarations is in formal parameter lists. This allows C++ to have *call-by-reference* arguments.

9. A formal parameter can be given a default argument. This is usually a constant that occurs frequently when the function is called. Use of the default argument saves writing in this default value at each invocation.

10. The term *overloading* refers to using the same name for various meanings of an operator or a function. The meaning selected depends on the types and number of the arguments used by the operator or function.

11. The unary operators new and delete are available to manipulate *free store*. Free store is a system-provided memory pool for objects whose lifetime is directly managed by the programmer. The programmer creates the object by using new and destroys the object by using delete. The operator new is used in the following forms:

> new *type-name*
> new *type-name initializer*
> new (*type-name*)

The new expression is a suitably typed pointer.

12. The operator delete is used in the following forms:

> delete *expression*
> delete [ ] *expression*

The first form is used when single objects are allocated by new. For example, when p = new my_type is executed, delete p is used. The second form must be used when returning store that was allocated as an vector. For example, when p = new my_type[expr] is executed, delete []p is used. The operator delete returns type void.

2.14 EXERCISES

1. C++ style follows C style in layout. Generally a tab stop of three to five blank spaces is used to indent sections of code to reflect flow of control. Proper commenting and choice of identifier names are important to readable code. Try to understand the following code and rewrite it in good style:

```
#include <iostream.h>
const float f = 3.14159;
inline float v(float b) {return 4*f*b*b*b/3.0; }
main() {float b; while (1) { cout << "enter b"; cin >> b;
cout << "\nVolume is " << v(b) << endl; }}
```

2. Can you have the following as comments in C and C++?

```
//one liner
/*one liner
/*    old style */
/*    is nesting /* allowed */ on your system? */
//what happens if we repeat // on this line
a /*p; where p is a pointer
"/* within a string */"
"// within a string"
//  /* within a one liner */
/*  //okay I give up  */
```

3. Recode the following #define preprocessor lines using const and inline declarations:

```
#define TRUE         1
#define c            299792.4562  //light speed in km/sec
#define EOF          (-1)
#define LARGER(X,Y)  ((X > Y) ? (X) : (Y))
#define CUBE(X)      (X) * (X) * (X)
```

4. Using the declaration of card deck[52] as found in this chapter, write code that deals out and prints 6 five-card hands. A hand should be stored in a two-dimensional array.

```
const int players = 6;
const int nc       = 5;
card  hand[players][nc];
```

5. Continuing with Exercise 4, write code that checks if a hand is a flush. A flush is a hand that contains five or more cards of the same suit. It can be tested by summing for each suit the number of cards of that suit that occur. Write the function

```
int is_flush(card h[]);  //returns 1 if a flush else 0
```

Generate 1000 deals at random, and print out the probability of getting a flush.

6. On some early C compilers the following program runs:

```
char strg[5] = "ABCD";

main()
{
    int  i = 7, *p = &i;
    char* c;

    c = *p;
    c = strg + 1;
    *c = 'X';
    return (0);
}
```

On C++ compilers the program gives a syntax error. Discuss these differences. Which is preferred?

7. The following program uses pointer types and modifies a string:

```
#include <iostream.h>

main()
{
    char*  c;
    char   strg[] = "ABCD";

    cout << "\nstrg is " << strg;
    c = strg + 1;
    *c = 'X';
    cout << "\n strg is " <<  strg;
    return (0);
}
```

What is wrong with changing the strg declaration to

```
const char*  const strg = "ABCD";
```

8. Given the declarations,

```
int    i = 5;
int*   pi = &i;
char   c = 'C';
char*  pc = &c;
void*  pv;
char   s[100];
```

what do the following expressions mean? Are any illegal under C++ typing?

```
*pi = i + c;
*pc = s + 10;
pc  = s + 10;
pv  = pi;
pv  = s + 1;
pv  = ++s;
pc  = pv;
*pc = *pv;
*pc = (char)*pv;
```

9. Use the library function memcpy to copy a string into another character array. Also copy an integer array into another integer array. Finally, copy a character array into an integer array. On most systems the header string.h has memcpy.

10. Implement your own version of memcpy to conform to the function prototype found in Section 2.4.

11. What gets printed by the following code?

```
// :: scope resolution operator

double x = 1.23;

#include  <iostream.h>

main()
{
    double  x = 2.34;

    {
        double y = x;
        double x = 3.45;
        cout << x  << "  x <> ::x  " << ::x << "\n";
        cout << "y = " << y << "\n";
    }
    cout << x  << "  x <> ::x  " << ::x << endl;
    return (0);
}
```

12. The following traditional C function uses pointer variables and dereferencing to implement a circular shift:

```
void shift(pc1, pc2, pc3, pc4)
char* pc1;
char* pc2;
char* pc3;
char* pc4;
{
    char  temp;

    temp = *pc1;
    *pc1 = *pc2;
    *pc2 = *pc3;
    *pc3 = *pc4;
    *pc4 = temp;
}
```

Convert it to a function in C++ using call-by-reference.

```
void shift(char& c1, char& c2, char& c3, char& c4)
. . .
```

Write a test program that prints the before and after values using shift.

13. The following function computes the minimum and maximum values found in an array:

```
//Find both the minimum and maximum values of an array.

void minmax(const int data[], int size, int* min, int* max)
{
    *min = *max = data[0];
    for (int i = 1; i < size; ++i)
        if (*min > data[i])
    *min = data[i];
        else if (*max < data[i])
    *max = data[i];
}
```

Convert it to a function that uses call-by-reference. Write a program to test it.

14. A more efficient method for finding minimum and maximum is as follows: Compare a pair of elements, and use the smaller element for finding the minimum and the larger element for finding the maximum. With this method rewrite the function used in Exercise 13.

How many comparisons are saved over the previous method? A description of this method is found in "A Sorting Method and Its Complexity," *Communications of the ACM*, vol. 15, no. 6, 1972, by Ira Pohl.

15. Change the solution to Exercise 13 to use a default size parameter. Let the default value be 10. *Reminder*: The argument size must now be at the end of the argument list.

16. Write three overloaded functions that each print an array. One prints an array of int, the second an array of float, and the third an array of char.

```
void print(const int data[], int size = 20);   //int version
void print(const float data[], int size = 20); //float version
void print(const char data[], int size = 20);  //char version
```

Note that each declaration has a default value for size. Use stream I/O when writing each function. It is debatable whether this use of defaults is a good idea. The programmer that uses such a function may inadvertently omit the size parameter and still have a running program in which this omission is hard to spot.

17. First write a function that creates a vector of a user-keyed size and that reads in, using cin, its size and initial values.

```
void create_vec(int* &v, int& size);
//get array size from cin
//use new to create v[size]
//and then use a for loop to assign values from cin
```

Next write a function that adds two vectors. If the vectors are not the same size, add them for the lesser of the two sizes.

```
void add_vec(const int* v1, const int* v2, int* sum, int size);
//add_vec  returns vector sum   sum[i] = v1[i] + v2[i]
```

Finally, print out the resulting array.

```
void print_vec (const int* v, int size);
```

18. The following code uses new to allocate a two-dimensional array:

```
//Dynamically allocated two-dimensional arrays
//   Title: two_d_array

#include <iostream.h>

main()
{
   int**  data;
   int    sz1, sz2, i, j;

   cout << "\nEnter two sizes: ";
   cin >> sz1 >> sz2;
   data = new int* [sz1];            //an array of pointers
   for (i = 0; i < sz1; ++i)
      data[i] = new int[sz2];        //each row is allocated
   cout << "\nEnter " << sz1 << " by " << sz2 << " ints\n";
   for (i = 0; i < sz1; ++i)
      for (j = 0; j < sz2; ++j)
         cin >> data[i][j];
   for (i = 0; i < sz1; ++i)
      for (j = 0; j < sz2; ++j)
         cout << data[i][j] << "\t";
   cout << endl;
   return (0);
}
```

Notice that you must do the allocation in two stages because C has a simple linear interpretation of an array. Use the ideas found in this code to write two-dimensional routines, create_matrix and add_matrix. These are analogous to the functions written in Exercise 17.

19. Anonymous unions must be used carefully because they are machine dependent. Let us use them to check on conversion between the types long int and float. Fill in the Prints column in the following table.

Declarations and Assignments

```
//external to main
union {
 long int j;
 float    y;
};
//in main
long int  i = 1024;
float     x = 1.0;
```

Expression	Output Expression	Value
j = i	cout << j	1024
j = i	cout << y	
y = x	cout << j	
y = 2 * x	cout << y	

CHAPTER 3

CLASSES

This chapter introduces the reader to struct and class. The original name given by Stroustrup to his language was "C with Classes." The class concept is an extension of the idea of struct found in traditional C. It is a way of implementing a data type and associated functions and operators. User-defined data types, such as stacks, complex numbers, and card decks, are examples of ADT implementations. Each of these types is coded in C++ and used in a major example in this chapter.

We explain here the new concept of class by first reviewing how traditional C structures work. C++ structures may have member functions, and they also can have parts of their descriptions private. Both of these extensions are described here. These extensions lead naturally to the class concept that, in effect, is a struct with a default access of private.

Allowing private and public access for members gives the programmer control over what parts of the data structure are modifiable. The private parts are hidden from client code, and the public parts are available. It is possible to change the hidden representation but not to change the public access or functionality. If done properly, client code need not change when the hidden representation is modified. A large part of the OOP design process involves thinking up the appropriate ADTs for a problem. Good ADTs not only model key features of the problem but also are frequently reusable in other code.

3.1 THE AGGREGATE TYPE *struct*

The structure type allows the programmer to aggregate components into a single named variable. A structure has components, called *members*, that are individually named. Since the members of a structure can be of various types, the programmer can create aggregates that are suitable for describing complicated data.

As a simple example, let us define a structure that describes a playing card. The spots on a card that represent its numeric value are called *pips*. A playing card, such as the three of spades, has a pip value, 3, and a suit value, spades. As in Chapter 2, we can declare the structure type:

```
enum suit {clubs, diamonds, hearts, spades};

struct card {
   suit  s;
   int   pips;
};
```

In C the declaration of card would be illegal. It would have to be

```
struct card {
   enum suit  s;
   int        pips;
};
```

As we described in Chapter 2, in C++ the tag names are types. Our examples use this C++ innovation. In this declaration struct is a keyword, card is the structure tag name, and the variables pips and s are members of the structure. The variable pips takes values from 1 to 13, representing ace to king.

This declaration creates the derived data type struct card or, in C++, the type card. The declaration can be thought of as a template; it creates the type, but no storage is allocated. The declaration

```
card    c1, c2;
```

allocates storage for the identifiers c1 and c2, which are of type card. We use the structure member operator . to access the members of c1 and c2. Suppose we want to assign to c1 the values representing the five of diamonds and to c2 the values representing the queen of spades. To do this, we can write

```
c1.pips = 5;
c1.s = diamonds;
c2.pips = 12;
c2.s = spades;
```

A construct of the form

structure_variable . member_name

is used as a variable in the same way a simple variable or an element of an array is used. The member name must be unique within the specified structure. Since the member must always be prefaced or accessed through a unique structure variable identifier, there is no confusion between two members having the same name in different structures. An example is

```
struct fruit {
    char    name[15];
    int     calories;
};

struct vegetable {
    char    name[15];
    int     calories;
};
```

```
fruit       a;      //struct fruit     a; in C
vegetable   b;      //struct vegetable b; in C
```

Having made these declarations, we can access a.calories and b.calories without ambiguity.

3.2 STRUCTURE POINTER OPERATOR

We have already seen the use of the member operator . in accessing members. In this section we introduce the structure pointer operator -> .

    C provides the structure pointer operator -> to access the members of a structure via a pointer. This operator is typed on the keyboard as a minus sign followed by a greater-than sign. If a pointer variable is assigned the address of a structure, then a member of the structure can be accessed by a construct of the form

pointer_to_structure -> member_name

An equivalent construct is given by

(**pointer_to_structure*).*member_name*

The operators -> and ., along with () and [], have the highest precedence, and they associate left to right. In complicated situations the two accessing modes can be combined. The following table illustrates their use in a straightforward manner:

Declarations and Assignments

```
card cd, *p = &cd;
card deck[52];

cd.pips = 5;
cd.s = spades;
deck[0] = cd;
```

Expression	Equivalent Expression	Value
cd.pips	p -> pips	5
cd.suit	p -> suit	spades
deck[0].pips	deck -> pips	5
(*p).suit	p -> suit	spades

3.3 AN EXAMPLE: STACK

The stack is one of the most useful standard data structures. A stack is a data structure that allows insertion and deletion of data to occur only at a single restricted element, the top of the stack. This is the last-in-first-out discipline (LIFO). Conceptually, it behaves like a pile of trays that pops up or is pushed down when trays are removed or added. Typically, a stack allows as operations *push*, *pop*, *top*, *empty*, and *full*. The push operator places a value on the stack. The pop operator retrieves and deletes a value off the stack. The top operator returns the top value from the stack. The empty operator tests if the stack is empty. The full operator tests if the stack is full. The stack is a typical ADT.

We want to implement a stack as a C++ data type using struct in its traditional form. An implementation choice is to use a fixed-length char array to store the contents of the stack. The top of the stack is an integer-valued member named top. The various stack operations are implemented as functions, each of whose argument list includes a pointer to stack parameter. This avoids copying a potentially large stack to perform a simple operation.

```
//A traditional C implementation of type stack.

#define max_len    1000
#define EMPTY      -1
#define FULL       (max_len - 1)
enum boolean {false, true};

typedef struct stack {
   char s[max_len];
   int  top;
} stack;

void reset(stack* stk)
{
   stk -> top = EMPTY;
}

void push(char c, stack* stk)
{
   stk -> top++;
   stk -> s[stk -> top] = c;
}

char pop(stack* stk)
{
   return (stk -> s[stk -> top--]);
}

char top(stack* stk)
{
   return (stk -> s[stk -> top]);
}

boolean empty(const stack* stk)
{
   return (boolean)(stk -> top == EMPTY);
}

boolean full(const stack* stk)
{
   return (boolean)(stk -> top == FULL);
}
```

■ DISSECTION OF THE *stack* FUNCTIONS

```
enum boolean {false, true};

typedef struct stack {
   char s[max_len];
   int  top;
} stack;
```

- We declare a new type boolean. In C++ the tag name of an
  enum type is a new type. The struct declaration creates the
  new type stack. It has two members, the array member s
  and the int member top.

```
void reset(stack* stk)
{
   stk -> top = EMPTY;
}
```

- This function is used for initialization. The member top is
  assigned the value EMPTY. The stack starts out as empty. The
  particular stack that this works on is an argument passed in
  as an address.

```
void push(char c, stack* stk)
{
   stk -> top++;
   stk -> s[stk -> top] = c;
}
```

```
char pop(stack* stk)
{
   rcturn (stk > s[stk -> top--]);
}
```

- The operation push is implemented as a function of two
  arguments. The member top is incremented. The value of c
  is shoved onto the top of the stack. This function assumes
  that the stack is not full. The operation pop is implemented
  in like fashion. It assumes the stack is not empty. The value
  of the top of the stack is returned, and the member top is
  decremented.

```
boolean empty(const stack* stk)
{
   return (boolean)(stk -> top == EMPTY);
}

boolean full(const stack* stk)
{
   return (boolean)(stk -> top == FULL);
}
```

- These functions return an enumerated type boolean value. Each tests the stack member top for an appropriate condition. In all functions the stack argument is passed in as address, and the structure pointer operator -> is used to access members.

Given that these declarations reside in the file stack.h, we can test these operations with the following program, which enters the characters of a string onto a stack and pops them, printing each character out in reverse order:

```
//Test of stack implementation by reversing a string.

#include <iostream.h>
#include "stack.h"        //stack implementation imported

main()
{
   stack  s;
   char   str[40] = {"My name is Betty Dolsberry!"};
   int    i = 0;

   cout << str << "\n";     //print the string
   reset(&s);
   while (str[i])           //push onto stack
      if (!full(&s))
        push(str[i++], &s);
   while (!empty(&s))       //print the reverse
      cout << pop(&s);
   cout << "\n";
}
```

The output from this test program is

```
My name is Betty Dolsberry!
!yrrebsloD ytteB si eman yM
```

Note that one of the actual arguments to each function is &s, the address of the stack variable declared in main. This argument is given because each function expects an address of a stack variable.

3.4 MEMBER FUNCTIONS

The concept of struct is augmented in C++ to allow functions to be members. The function declaration is included in the structure declaration and is invoked by using access methods for structure members. The idea is that the functionality required by the struct data type should be directly included in the struct declaration. This construct improves the encapsulation of the ADT stack operations by packaging it directly with its data representation.

Let us rewrite our stack example by declaring as member functions the various functions associated with the stack:

```
struct stack {
    //data representation

    char s[max_len];
    int  top;
    enum {EMPTY = -1, FULL = max_len - 1};

    //operations represented as member functions

    void    reset() { top = EMPTY; }
    void    push(char c) { top++; s[top] = c; }
    char    pop() { return (s[top--]); }
    char    top_of() { return (s[top]); }
    boolean empty() { return (boolean)(top == EMPTY); }
    boolean full() { return (boolean)(top == FULL); }
};
```

The member functions are written much as other functions. One difference is that they can use the data member names as they are. Thus the member functions in stack use top and s in an unqualified manner. When

invoked on a particular object of type stack, they act on the specified
member in that object. The mechanism for passing in the specific
instances of top and s to a member function is through the this pointer
(see Section 4.4).

The following example illustrates these ideas. If two stack variables

```
stack data, operands;
```

are declared, then

```
data.reset();
operands.reset();
```

invoke the member function reset, which has the effect of setting both
data.top and operands.top to EMPTY. If a pointer to stack

```
stack* ptr_operands = &operands;
```

is declared, then

```
ptr_operands -> push('A');
```

invokes the member function push, which has the effect of incrementing
operands.top and setting operands.s[top] to 'A'. One last observation: The
member function top_of had its name changed from the previous implementation because of a naming conflict.

Member functions that are defined within the struct are implicitly
inline. As a rule, only short, heavily used member functions should be
defined within the struct, as is the case for the example just given. To
define a member function outside the struct, the scope resolution operator is used. Let us illustrate this by changing the definition of push to its
corresponding function prototype within the struct stack. We write it out
fully using the scope resolution operator. In this case the function is not
implicitly inline.

```
struct stack {
    //data representation

    char s[max_len];
    int  top;
    enum {EMPTY = -1, FULL = max_len - 1};

    //operations represented as member functions

    void reset() { top = EMPTY; } //implicitly inline
    void push(char c);            //function prototype
    . . .
};

    void stack::push(char c)      //definition, not inline
    {
        top++;
        s[top] = c;
    }
```

The scope resolution operator allows member functions from the different struct types to have the same names. In this case the member function that is invoked depends on the type of object it acts upon. Member functions within the same struct can be overloaded. Consider adding to the data type stack a pop operation that has an integer parameter that is the number of times the stack should be popped. It can be added as the following function prototype within the struct:

```
struct stack {
    . . .
    char pop(int n);
};
char stack::pop(int n)
{
    while(n-- > 1)
        top--;
    return (s[top--]);
}
```

The definition that is invoked depends on the actual arguments to pop.

```
data.pop();                   //invokes standard pop
data.pop(5);                  //invokes iterated pop
```

The declaration

```
stack s, t, u;
```

creates three separate stack objects of sizeof(stack) bytes. Each of these variables has its own data members

```
char s[max_len];
int  top;
```

A member function is conceptually part of the type. There is no distinct member function for each of these three stack variables.

3.5 ACCESS: *private* AND *public*

The concept of struct is augmented in C++ to allow functions to have public and private members. Inside a struct the use of the keyword private followed by a colon restricts the *access* of the members that follow this construct. The private members can be used by only a few categories of functions whose privileges include access to these members. These functions include the member functions of the struct. Other categories of functions having access are discussed later.

We modify our example of stack to hide its data representation.

```
struct stack {
public:
   void   reset() { top = EMPTY; }
   void   push(char c) { top++; s[top] = c; }
   char   pop() { return (s[top--]); }
   char   top_of() { return (s[top]); }
   boolean empty() { return (boolean)(top == EMPTY); }
   boolean full() { return (boolean)(top == FULL); }
private:
   char s[max_len];
   int  top;
   enum {EMPTY = -1, FULL = max_len - 1};
};
```

We now rewrite main from Section 3.3 to test the same operations.

```
main()
{
    stack   s;
    char    str[40] = {"My name is Don Knuth!"};
    int     i = 0;

    cout << str << "\n";
    s.reset();                  //s.top = EMPTY; would be illegal
    while (str[i])
        if (!s.full())
          s.push(str[i++]);
    while (!s.empty())          //print the reverse
        cout << s.pop();
    cout << "\n";
}
```

The output from this version of the test program is

```
My name is Don Knuth!
!htunK noD si eman yM
```

As the comment in main states, access to the hidden variable top is controlled. It can be changed by the member function reset but cannot be
accessed directly. Also notice how the variable s is passed to each member function using the structure member operator form.

The struct stack has a private part that contains its data description
and has a public part that contains member functions to implement stack
operations. It is useful to think of the private part as restricted to the
implementor's use, and the public part to be an interface specification
that clients may use. At a later time, the implementor could change the
private part without affecting the correctness of a client's use of the stack
type.

Hiding data is an important component of OOP. It allows for more
easily debugged and maintained code because errors and modifications
are localized. Client programs need only be aware of the type's interface
specification.

3.6 CLASSES

Classes in C++ are introduced by the keyword class. They are a form of struct whose default access specification is private. Thus struct and class can be used interchangeably with the appropriate privacy specification.

Many scientific computations require complex numbers. Let us write an ADT for complex numbers.

```
struct complex {
public:
   void   assign(double r, double i);
   void   print() { cout << real << " + " << imag; }
private:
   double real, imag;
};

inline void complex::assign(double r, double i = 0.0)
{
   real = r;
   imag = i;
}
```

Here is its equivalent class representation:

```
class complex {
public:
   void   assign(double r, double i);
   void   print() { cout << real << " + " << imag << "i "; }
private:
   double real, imag;
};

inline void complex::assign(double r, double i = 0.0)
{
   real = r;
   imag = i;
}
```

Also possible is

```
class complex {
   double real, imag;
public:
   void   assign(double r, double i);
   void   print() { cout << real << " + " << imag << "i "; }
};
```

Here we are using the fact that the default access to class members is private. It will be our style to prefer class to struct unless all members are data members with public access.

3.7 *static* MEMBER

Data members can be declared with the storage class modifier static. A data member that is declared static is shared by all variables of that class and is stored uniquely in one place. Nonstatic data members are created for each instance of the class. Since a static member is independent of any particular instance, it can be accessed in the form

    class name :: *identifier*

provided it has public visibility. This is a further use of the scope resolution operator (see Section 2.5). A static member of a global class must be explicitly declared and defined in file scope. An example is

```
class str {
public:
   static int  how_many;  //declaration
   void        print();
   void        assign(const char*);
   . . .
private:      //implement as a fixed length char array
   char        s[100];
};

boolean str::how_many = 0; //definition and initialization
```

In our example this can be used to track how much memory is being used to store strs.

```
str s1, s2, s3, *p;

str::how_many = 3;
   . . .
str t;
t.how_many++;        //dot operator to access
   . . .
p = new str;
p -> how_many++;   //pointer operator to access
   . . .
delete p;
str::how_many--;
```

3.8 CLASS SCOPE

Classes add a new set of scope rules to those of the kernel language. One point of classes is to provide an encapsulation technique. Conceptually it makes sense that all names declared within a class be treated as within their own name space distinct from either external names, function names, or other class names. This creates a need for the scope resolution operator.

Scope Resolution Operator ::

The scope resolution operator is new to C++ and is the highest-precedence operator in the language. It comes in two forms, as seen in the following:

```
::i        //unary operator - refer to external scope
foo_bar::i //binary operator - refer to class scope
```

Its unary form is used to uncover or access a name that is at external scope and has been hidden by local or class scope.

```
int count = 0;  //external variable

void how_many(double w[], double x, int& count)
{
   for (int i = 0; i < N; ++i)
      count += (w[i] == x);
   ++ ::count;                      //keep track of calls
}
```

Its binary form is used to disambiguate names that are reused within classes. It is vital to use with inheritance (see Chapter 8).

```
class widgets {public: void f();};
class gizmos  {public: void f();};

void f() { /* whatever */ }              //ordinary external f
void widgets::f() { /* whatever */ }     //f scoped to widgets
void gizmos::f() { /* whatever */ }      //f scoped to gizmos
```

One way of thinking about the scope resolution operator is to view it as providing a path to the identifier. No scope modifier means that normal scope rules apply.

We continue with the previous example:

```
widgets  w;
gizmos   g;

g.f();
w.f();
g.gizmos::f();    //legal and redundant
g.widgets::f();   //illegal widgets::f() cannot act on a gizmo
```

Nested Classes

Classes can be nested. Nested classes, like nested blocks, have inner and outer nomenclature. The rules for nesting classes have changed from rules that existed in C. In C nested structs were permitted, but the inside structs names were visible externally.

The following nested classes illustrate current C++ rules:

```
char c;                //external scope  ::c

class X {              //outer class declaration  X::
public:
    class Y {          //inner class declaration  X::Y::
    public:
        void foo(char e) { ::c = X::c = c = e; }
    private:
        char c;        //X::Y::c
    };
private:
    char c;            //X::c
};
```

In class Y the member function foo, when using ::c, references the global variable c; when using X::c, it references the outer class variable X::Y::c; and when using c, it references the inner class variable X::Y::c. The three variables named c are all accessible using the scope resolution operator.

Furthermore, purely locally scoped classes can be created within blocks. Their definitions are unavailable outside of their local block context.

```
void foo()
{
   class local { . . . } x;
   // whatever
}

local y; //illegal local is scoped within foo()
```

Notice that C++ gives you the ability to nest function definitions by using class nesting to nest member functions. This is a restricted form of function nesting. The member functions must be defined inside the local class and cannot be referred to outside this scope. As in C, ordinary nested functions are not possible.

3.9 AN EXAMPLE: FLUSHING

We want to estimate the probability of being dealt a flush. A flush occurs when at least five cards are of the same suit. We simulate shuffling cards by using a random-number generator to shuffle the deck. This is a form of *Monte Carlo* calculation. The program is written using classes to represent the needed data types and functionality.

```
//A poker calculation on flushing

#include  <iostream.h>
#include  <stdlib.h>       //for random-number generation
#include  <time.h>         //for random-number seed

enum suit {clubs, diamonds, hearts, spades};

class pips {
public:
   void assign(int n) { p = n % 13 + 1; }
   int  getpip() { return (p); }
   void print();
private:
   int  p;
};

class card {
public:
   suit s;
   pips p;
   void assign(int n) { cd = n; (suit)(s = n/13); p.assign(n); }
   void pr_card();
private:
   int  cd;                        //a cd is from 0 to 51
};

class deck {
public:
   void init_deck();
   void shuffle();
   void deal(int, int, card*);
   void pr_deck();
private:
   card d[52];
};
```

We used an enumerated type suit to represent card suits. The enumerated constants are mapped into the integers 0, 1, 2, and 3. So clubs is
the integer value 0, and spades is the integer value 3. Each level of declaration hides the complexity of the previous level. Notice also that we can
plan to code the functions later. For example, we do not use the print routines in this example; they can be added as needed.

A most interesting function is the implicitly inline function

```
   void assign(int n) { cd = n; (suit)(s = n/13); p.assign(n); }
```

which uses the function void pips::assign(int n). We could have used the notation p.pips::assign(n) to show that this function is from the class pips, but this is known because p is type pips. The function maps an integer whose value is between 0 and 51 into a unique pair of suit and pips values. The value 0 becomes the ace of clubs, and the value 51 becomes the king of spades.

The other member functions are not inline and are defined at a later point with the use of the scope resolution operator.

```cpp
void  deck::init_deck()
{
   for (int i = 0; i < 52; ++i)
      d[i].assign(i);
}

void  deck::shuffle()
{
   for (int i = 0; i < 52; ++i) {
      int k = rand() % 52;
      card t = d[i]; d[i] = d[k]; d[k] = t; //swap two cards
   }
}

void deck::deal(int n, int pos, card* hand)
{
   for (int i = pos; i < pos + n; ++i)
      hand[i - pos] = d[i];
}
```

The init_deck function calls card::assign to map the integers into card values. The shuffle function uses the library-supplied pseudorandom number generator rand to exchange two cards for every deck position. Tests show that this approximates shuffling. The deal function takes cards in sequence from the deck and arranges them into hands.

It now remains to use these functions to estimate the probability that a flush occurs when poker hands are dealt. The operator can choose to deal between five and nine cards per hand.

```
main()
{
   card one_hand[9];   //max hand is 9 cards
   deck dk;
   int  i, j, k, fcnt = 0, sval[4];
   int  ndeal, nc, nhand;

   do {
      cout << "\nEnter no. of cards in each hand (5-9): ";
      cin  >> nc;
   } while (nc < 5 || nc > 9);
   nhand = 52 / nc;

   cout << "\nEnter no. of hands to deal: ";
   cin  >> ndeal;

   srand(time(NULL)):            //seed rand() from time()
   dk.init_deck();
   for (k = 0; k < ndeal; k += nhand) {
      if ((nhand + k) > ndeal)
       nhand = ndeal - k;
      dk.shuffle();
      for (i = 0; i < nc * nhand; i += nc) {
       for (j = 0; j < 4; ++j)        //init suit counts to 0
          sval[j] = 0;
       dk.deal(nc, i, one_hand);      //deal next hand
         for (j = 0; j < nc; ++j)
          sval[one_hand[j].s] ++ ;    //increment suit count
         for (j = 0; j < 4; ++j)
          if (sval[j] >= 5)           //5 or more is flush
             fcnt++;
      }
   }
   cout << "\n\nIn " << ndeal << " ";
   cout << nc << "-card hands there were ";
   cout << fcnt << " flushes\n    ";
}
```

■ DISSECTION OF THE *flush* PROGRAM

```
card one_hand[9];         //max hand is 9 cards
deck dk;
int  i, j, k, fcnt = 0, sval[4];
int  ndeal, nc, nhand;
```

- These are variables allocated upon block entry when main is executed. The variable one_hand is an array of nine elements, the maximum hand size allowed. It is used to store dealt-out hands from the deck. The variable dk represents our deck and is automatically allocated. All its data members are created, though some are hidden. The number of cards dealt to each hand is stored as the variable nc, and the number of hands to be dealt is kept in the variable ndeal. The variable fcnt counts the number of flushes. The array sval is used to store the number of cards found in the hand of a particular suit value.

```
do {
    cout << "\nEnter no. of cards in each hand (5-9): ";
    cin  >> nc;
} while (nc < 5 || nc > 9);
nhand = 52 / nc;

cout << "\nEnter no. of hands to deal: ";
cin  >> ndeal;
```

- We prompt for the number of cards to deal to each hand. The operator must respond with a number between 5 and 9 in order to proceed. The number of hands that can be dealt with the deck is computed and put into the variable nhand. We prompt for the number of deals.

```
srand(time(NULL));              //seed rand() from time()
dk.init_deck();
for (k = 0; k < ndeal; k += nhand) {
    if ((nhand + k) > ndeal)
        nhand = ndeal - k;
    dk.shuffle();
```

- The rand function is initialized by srand(), which uses the time() clock information made available in *time.h*. The deck variable dk is initialized, and each time through the main loop the deck is reshuffled. The variable dk is implicitly an argument to the called member functions init_deck and shuffle. The test to check whether the value of ndeal has been exceeded ensures that the total number of hands dealt does not exceed the request if the total number of hands is not an even multiple of the number of hands per shuffle.

```
for (i = 0; i < nc * nhand; i += nc) {
    for (j = 0; j < 4; ++j)              //init suit counts to 0
        sval[j] = 0;
    dk.deal(nc, i, one_hand);            //deal next hand
    for (j = 0; j < nc; ++j)
        sval[one_hand[j].s] ++ ;         //increment suit count
    for (j = 0; j < 4; ++j)
        if (sval[j] >= 5)                //5 or more is flush
            fcnt++;
}
```

- The array sval stores the number of cards of each suit and is
  initialized to zero for each hand. The function deck::deal
  deals a card hand into the array one_hand. The expression
  one_hand[j].s is the suit value of a particular card, for example, 0 if the card were a club. This then is the index of
  the array sval that counts suits. The variable fcnt counts the
  number of flushes dealt over all these trials. Since the number of trials equals ndeal, the expectation of a flush is
  fcnt/ndeal.

3.10 PRAGMATICS

The access order for classes traditionally has been private first, as in

```
class stack {
private:
    char s[max_len];
    int  top;
    enum {EMPTY = -1, FULL = max_len - 1};
public:
    void    reset() { top = EMPTY; }
    void    push(char c) { top++; s[top] = c; }
    char    pop() { return (s[top--]); }
    char    top_of() { return (s[top]); }
    boolean empty() { return (boolean)(top == EMPTY); }
    boolean full() { return (boolean)(top == FULL); }
};
```

This tradition arose because in the original form of the language the keywords private and protected did not exist. By default, member access for
class was private, therefore the private members had to come first.

Our style of public first is becoming more the norm. It follows the rule that the widest audience needs to see the public members. More specialized information is placed later in the class declaration.

Data members should in general be private. This is an important coding heuristic. Generally, data is part of an implementation choice. It should be accessed through public member functions. Such member functions are called *accessor functions* when they do not change (mutate) the data. This is not necessarily inefficient, because simple accessor member functions can be inline. In the class stack the member functions top_of(), empty(), and full() are all inline accessor functions. The member function reset() is a *mutator*. It allows a constrained action on the hidden variable top. Notice how much safer such a design is. If top were directly accessible, it would be easy for it to be inappropriately changed.

3.11 SUMMARY

1. The original name given by Stroustrup to his language was C with Classes. A class is an extension of the idea of struct in traditional C. It is a way of implementing a data type and associated functions and operators. It also is the mechanism in C++ for implementing ADTs, such as complex numbers and stacks.

2. The structure type allows the programmer to aggregate components into a single named variable. A structure has components, called *members*, that are individually named. Critical to processing structures is the accessing of their members. This is done with either the member operator . or the structure pointer operator ->. These operators, along with () and [], have the highest precedence.

3. The concept of struct is augmented in C++ to allow functions to be members. The function declaration is included in the structure declaration and is invoked by using access methods for structure members. The idea is that the functionality required by the struct data type should be directly included in the struct declaration.

4. Member functions that are defined within the struct are implicitly inline. As a rule, only short, heavily used member functions should be defined within the struct. To define a member function outside the struct, the scope resolution operator is used.

5. The scope resolution operator allows member functions from the different struct types to have the same names. In this case the member function that is invoked depends on the type of object it acts upon. Member functions within the same struct can be overloaded.

6. The concept of struct is augmented in C++ to allow functions to have public and private members. This provides *data hiding*. Inside a struct the use of the keyword private followed by a colon restricts the access of the members that follow this construct. The private members can be used by only a few categories of functions whose privileges include access to these members. These functions include the member functions of the struct.

7. Classes in C++ are introduced by the keyword class. They are a form of struct whose default privacy specification is private. Thus struct and class can be used interchangeably with the appropriate access specification.

8. Data members can be declared with the storage class modifier static. A data member that is declared static is shared by all variables of that class and is stored uniquely in one place. Because of this it can be accessed in the form

class name :: *identifier*

9. Classes can be nested. The inner class is inside the scope of the outer class. This is not in accord with C semantics.

3.12 EXERCISES

1. Design a traditional C structure to store a dairy product name, portion weight, calories, protein, fat, and carbohydrates. Twenty-five grams of American cheese has 375 calories, 5 grams of protein, 8 grams of fat, and 0 grams of carbohydrates. Show how to assign these values to the member variables of your structure. Write a function that, given a variable of type struct dairy and a given weight in grams (portion size), returns the number of calories for that weight.

2. Use the struct card defined in Section 3.1 and write a hand-sorting routine. In card games most players keep their cards sorted by pip

value. The routine places aces first, kings next, and so forth, down to twos. A hand is five cards.

3. The following declarations do not compile correctly. Explain what is wrong.

```
struct brother {
     char            name[20];
     int             age;
     struct sister   sib;
} a;

struct sister {
     char            name[20];
     int             age;
     struct brother  sib;
} a;
```

4. Using the struct stack defined in Section 3.3, write the function

```
void reverse(char s1[], char s2[]);
```

The strings s1 and s2 must be the same size. String s2 should become a reversed copy of string s1. Internal to reverse, use a stack to perform the reversal.

5. Rewrite the functions push and pop in Section 3.3 to test that push is not acting on a full stack and pop is not acting on an empty stack. If either condition is detected, print an error message using cerr, and use exit(1) (in *stdlib.h*) to abort the program.

6. Write reverse (see Exercise 4) as a member function for type stack in Section 3.4. Test it by printing normally and reverse the string

```
Gottfried Leibniz wrote Toward a Universal Characteristic
```

7. For the stack type in Section 3.4, write as member functions

```
//push n chars from s1[1] onto the stack
void pushm(int n, const char s1[]);

//pop n chars from stack into char string
void popm(int n, char s1[]);
```

Hint: Be sure to put a terminator character into the string before outputting it.

8. What is the difference in meaning between the structure

```
struct a {
    int i, j, k;
};
```

and the class

```
class a {
    int i, j, k;
};
```

Explain why the class declaration is not useful. How can you use the keyword public to change the class declaration into a declaration equivalent to struct a?

9. We want to define the class deque to implement a double-ended queue. A double-ended queue allows push and pop at both ends.

```
class deque {
    char s[max_len];
    int  bottom, top;
public:
    void reset() { top = bottom = max_len / 2; top--; }
        . . .
};
```

Declare and implement push_t, pop_t, push_b, pop_b, out_stack, top_of, bottom_of, empty, and full. The function push_t stands for *push on top*. The function push_b stands for *push on bottom*. The out_stack function should output the stack from its bottom to its top. The pop_t and pop_b functions correspond to *pop from top* and *pop from bottom*. An empty stack is denoted by having the top fall below the bottom. Test each function.

10. Extend the data type deque by adding a member function relocate. If the deque is full, then relocate is called, and the contents of the deque are moved to balance empty storage around the center max_len / 2 of array s. Its function declaration header is

```
//returns true if it succeeds, false if it fails
boolean deque::relocate()
```

11. Write a swap function that swaps the contents of two strings. If you push a string of characters onto a stack and pop them into a second string, they come out reversed. In a swap of two strings, we want the original ordering. Use a deque to swap two strings. The strings are stored in two character arrays of the same length, but the strings themselves can be of differing lengths. The function prototype is

```
void swap(char s1[], char s2[]);
```

12. Write the following member functions:

```
void pips::print();
void card::pr_card();
void deck::pr_deck();
```

and add them to the *flush* program found in Section 3.9. Let pr_deck use pr_card and pr_card use print. Print the deck after it is initialized.

13. Write a function pr_hand that prints out card hands. Add it to the *flush* program, and use it to print out each flush.

14. In Section 3.9, main detects flushes. Write a function

```
boolean isflush(const card hand[], int nc);
```

that returns true if a hand is a flush.

15. Write a function

```
boolean isstraight(const card hand[], nc);
```

that returns true if a hand is a straight. A straight is five cards that have sequential pip values. The lowest straight is ace, two, three, four, five, and the highest straight is ten, jack, queen, king, ace. Run experiments to estimate the probability that dealt-out cards are a straight, and compare the results of five-card hands with results of seven-card hands. *Hint*: You may want to set up an array of 15 integers to correspond to counters for each pip value. Be sure that a pip value of 1 (corresponding to ace) is also counted as the high card corresponding to a pip value of 14.

16. Use previous exercises to determine the probability that a poker hand is a straight flush. This is a hand that is both a straight and a flush. It is the hardest poker hand to get and has the highest value.

Note that, in a hand of more than five cards, it is not sufficient to merely check for the presence of both a straight and a flush to determine that the hand is a straight flush.

17. Change the suit declaration from an enumerated type to a class as follows:

```
enum  suit_val{clubs, diamonds, hearts, spades};

class suit {
   suit_val s;
public:
   void assign(int n) { s = suit_val(n / 13); }
   int  getsuit() { return (s); }
   void print();
};
```

The expression suit_val(n / 13) is equivalent to (suit_val)(n / 13). Both are cast expressions (see Section 5.2). We add the member function getsuit to access the hidden integer value of a suit variable. Now recode all references to suit throughout the program.

CHAPTER 4

CONSTRUCTORS AND DESTRUCTORS

An object requires memory and some initial value. C++ provides this through declarations that are definitions. In most cases, when we discuss declarations we mean declarations that are definitions. For example, in

```
void foo()
{
    int n = 5;
    double z[10] = {0.0};
    struct gizmo { int i, j; } w = {3, 4};
      . . .
}
```

all these objects are created at block entry when foo() is invoked. A typical implementation uses a run-time system stack. Thus the int object n on a system with four-byte integers gets this allocated off the stack and initialized to the value 5. The gizmo object w requires eight bytes to represent its two integer members. The array of double object z requires ten times sizeof(double) to store its elements. In each case the system provides for the construction and initialization of these objects. Upon exit from foo(), deallocation occurs automatically.

When creating complicated aggregates the user expects similar management of a class-defined object. The class needs a mechanism to specify object creation and object destruction behavior, so that a client can use objects in a like manner to native types.

A constructor is a member function whose name is the same as the class name. It constructs values of the class type. This process involves initializing of data members and, frequently, allocating free store using new. A destructor is a member function whose name is the class name preceded by the character ˜ (tilde). Its usual purpose is to destroy values of the class type, typically by using delete.

Constructors are the more complicated of these two specially named member functions. They may be overloaded and can take arguments, neither of which is possible for destructors. A constructor is invoked when its associated type is used in a definition. They are invoked when call-by-value is used to pass a value to a function. They are also invoked when the return value of a function must create a value of associated type. Destructors are invoked implicitly when an object goes out of scope. Typically this is at block exit for automatic objects and program exit for static objects. Constructors and destructors do not have return types and cannot use return (*expression*) statements.

4.1 CLASSES WITH CONSTRUCTORS

The simplest use of a constructor is for initialization. We develop some examples in this and later sections that use constructors to initialize the values of the data members of the class.

Our first example is an implementation of a data type mod_int to store numbers that are computed with a modulus.

```
// Modulo numbers and constructor initialization

#include <iostream.h>

const int modulus = 60;
class mod_int {
public:
   mod_int(int i) { v = i % modulus; }
   void assign(int i) { v = i % modulus; }
   void print() { cout << v << "\t"; }
private:
   int  v;
};
```

The integer v is restricted in value to 0, 1, 2, ... modulus - 1. It is the programmer's responsibility to enforce this restriction by having all member functions guarantee this behavior.

The member function mod_int::mod_int(int) is a constructor. It does not have a return type. It is invoked when objects of type mod_int are declared. It is a function of one argument. When invoked it requires an expression that is assignment compatible with its int parameter to be passed to it. It then creates and initializes the declared variable.

Some examples of declarations using this type are

```
mod_int  a(0);   // a.v = 0;
mod_int  b(61);  // b.v = 1;
```

but not

```
mod_int  a;      // illegal:no parameter list
```

Since this class has only the one constructor of argument list int, a mod_int declaration must have an integral expression passed as an initializing value. Note that by not allowing a mod_int variable to be declared without an initializing expression we prevent run-time errors due to uninitialized variables.

Using this type, we can write code to convert seconds into minutes and seconds as follows:

```
main()
{
    int     seconds = 400;
    mod_int z(seconds);

    cout << seconds << " seconds equals "
        << seconds / 60 << " minutes ";
    z.print();
    cout << " seconds\n";
}
```

The Default Constructor

A constructor requiring no arguments is called the *default* constructor. This can be a constructor with an empty argument list or a constructor in which all arguments have default values. It has the special purpose of initializing arrays of objects of its class.

It is often convenient to overload the constructor with several function declarations. In our example we might want to have the default value of v be 0. By adding the default constructor

```
mod_int() { v = 0; }
```

as a member function of mod_int, it is possible to have the following declarations:

```
mod_int s1, s2;  // both initialize the private member v to 0
mod_int d[5];    // arrays are properly initialized
```

In both of these declarations, the empty parameter list constructor is invoked.

If a class does not have a constructor, the system provides a default constructor. If a class has constructors but does not have a default constructor, array allocation is a syntactic error.

Notice that our mod_int example could have one constructor serve as both a general initializer and a default constructor.

```
inline  mod_int::mod_int(int i = 0) { v = i % modulus; }
```

4.2 CONSTRUCTING A DYNAMICALLY SIZED STACK

A constructor can also be used to allocate space from free store. Let us modify the stack type from Chapter 3 to have its maximum length be initialized by a constructor.

The design of the object stack includes hidden implementation detail. Data members are placed in the private access region of class stack. The public interface provides clients with the expected stack abstraction. These are all public member functions, such as push() and pop(). Some of these functions are accessor functions that do not change the stack object, such as top_of() and empty. It is usual to make these const member functions. Some of these functions are mutator functions that do change the stack object, such as push() and pop(). The constructor member functions have the job of creating and initializing stack objects.

```
//stack implementation with constructor
class stack {
public:
    //the public interface for the ADT stack
    stack(int size) { s = new char[size];
                    max_len = size; top = EMPTY; }
    void reset() { top = EMPTY; }
    void push(char c) { s[++top]= c; }
    char pop() { return (s[top--]); }
    char top_of() const { return (s[top]); }
    boolean empty() const { return (boolean)(top == EMPTY); }
    boolean full() const { return (boolean)(top == max_len - 1); }
private:
    enum  {EMPTY = -1};
    char* s;          //changed from s[max_len]
    int   max_len;
    int   top;
};
```

Now a client using stack can decide on the size requirement. An example of a stack declaration invoking this constructor is

```
stack data(1000);       // allocate 1000 elements
stack more_data(2 * n); // allocate 2 * n elements
```

Two alternative constructors are an empty parameter constructor that allocates a specific length stack and a two-parameter constructor whose second parameter is a string used to initialize the stack. They can be written as follows:

```
stack::stack()    //default constructor for stack
{
   s = new char[100];
   max_len = 100;
   top = EMPTY;
}

stack::stack(int size, const char str[]) //domain transfer
{
   s = new char[size];
   max_len = size;
   for ( int i = 0; i < max_len && str[i] != 0; ++i)
      s[i] = str[i];
   top = --i;
}
```

The corresponding function prototypes are included as members of the class stack. Let us use these constructors in the following:

```
stack data;    //default constructor creating s[100]
stack d[N];    //default constructor creates  N 100 element stacks
stack w(4, "ABCD");  //w.s[0] = 'A' . . . w.s[3] = 'D'
```

The Copy Constructor

We want to examine our stack and count the number of occurrences of a given character. We can repeatedly pop the stack, testing each element in turn, until the stack is empty. But what if we want to preserve the contents of the stack. Call-by-value parameters accomplish this.

```
int cnt_char(char c, stack s)
{
   int count = 0;

   while (!s.empty())
      count += (c == s.pop());
   return (count);
}
```

The semantics of call-by-value require that a local copy of the argument type be created and initialized from the value of the expression passed as the actual argument. This requires a *copy constructor*. The compiler provides a default copy constructor. Its signature is

```
stack::stack(const stack&);
```

The compiler copies by memberwise initialization. This may not work in all circumstances for complicated aggregates with members who are themselves pointers. In many cases the pointer is the address of an object that is deleted when going out of scope. However, the act of duplicating the pointer value but not the object pointed at can lead to anomalous code. This deletion affects other instances that still expect the object to exist. It is appropriate for the class to explicitly define its own copy constructor.

```
//Copy constructor for stack of characters
stack::stack(const stack& str) //copy constructor
{
    s = new char[str.max_len];
    max_len = str.max_len;
    top = str.top;
    memcpy(s, str.s, max_len);
}
```

The general form of a copy constructor is

```
type :: type (const type &)
```

Constructor Initializer

There is a special syntax for initializing subelements of objects with constructors. Initializers for structure and class members can be specified in a comma separated list following the constructor parameter list and preceding the code body. We recode the previous example as follows:

```
//Copy constructor for stack of characters
stack::stack(const stack& str)
        : max_len(str.max_len), top(str.top);
{
    s = new char[str.max_len];
    memcpy(s, str.s, max_len);
}
```

Notice how initialization replaces assignment. The individual members must be initializable as

member name (expression list)

When members are themselves classes with constructors, the expression list is matched to the appropriate constructor signature to invoke the correct overloaded constructor.

It is not always possible to assign values to members in the body of the constructor. An initializer list is required when a nonstatic member is either a const or a reference.

4.3 CLASSES WITH DESTRUCTORS

A destructor is a member function whose name is the same as the class name preceded by a tilde. Destructors are usually called implicitly at block exit of the block in which the object was declared. They are also invoked when a delete operator is called on a pointer to an object having a destructor, or where they are needed to destroy a subobject of an object being deleted.

Let us augment our stack example with a destructor.

```
//stack implementation with constructors and destructor
class stack {
public:
    stack();                        //default constructor
    stack(int size) { s = new char[size];
                    max_len = size; top = EMPTY; }
    stack(const stack& str)    //copy constructor
    stack(int size, const char str[]);
    ~stack() { delete []s; }   //destructor
        . . .
private:
    enum  {EMPTY = -1};
    char* s;
    int    max_len;
    int    top;
};
```

The addition of the destructor allows the class to return unneeded heap-allocated memory during program execution. All the public member functions perform in exactly the same manner as before. The difference is that the destructor is implicitly invoked upon block and function exit to clean up storage that is no longer accessible. This is good programming practice and allows programs to execute with less available memory.

4.4 THE *this* POINTER

The keyword this denotes an implicitly declared self-referential pointer.
It can only be used in a nonstatic member function. A simple illustration
of its use is as follows:

```
// Use of the this pointer

#include <iostream.h>

class c_pair {
public:
    c_pair(char b): c1(b), c2(b + 1) { }
    c_pair increment() { c1++; c2++; return (*this); }
    unsigned where_am_I() { return ((unsigned)this); }
    void print() { cout << c1 << c2 << "\t"; }
private:
    char    c1, c2;
};

main()
{
    c_pair  a('A'), b('B'), c('D');
    a.print();
    cout << " is at " << a.where_am_I() << "\n";
    b.print();
    cout << " is at " << b.where_am_I() << "\n";
    c.increment().print();
    cout << " is at " << c.where_am_I() << "\n";
}
```

The member function increment uses the implicitly provided pointer this
to return the newly incremented values of both c1 and c2. The member
function where_am_I returns the address of the given object. The this keyword provides for a built-in self-referential pointer. It is as if c_pair
implicitly declared the private member c_pair* const this.

Early C++ systems allowed memory management for objects to be
controlled by assignment to the this pointer. Such code is obsolete
because the this pointer is not modifiable.

4.5 *static* AND *const* MEMBER FUNCTIONS

C++ allows static and const member functions. Syntactically, a static member function has the modifier static precede the return type inside the class declaration. A definition outside the class must not have this modifier.

```
class foo {
   . . .
     static int foo_fcn();   //static goes first
   . . .
};
int foo::foo_fcn()        //no static keyword here
{  /* definition */ }
```

Syntactically, a const member function has the modifier const following the argument list inside the class declaration. A definition outside the class must have this modifier.

```
class foo {
   . . .
     int foo_fcn() const;
   . . .
};
int foo::foo_fcn() const  //const keyword needed
{  /* definition */ }
```

Implementation of the const and static member functions can be understood in terms of this pointer access. An ordinary member function invoked as

```
object.mem(i, j, k);
```

has an explicit argument list i, j, k and an implicit argument list that is the members of *object*. The implicit arguments can be thought of as a list of arguments accessible through the this pointer. In contrast, a static member function cannot access any of the members using the this pointer. A const member function cannot modify its implicit arguments. The following example illustrates these differences:

```
//calculate salary using static members.
//   Title: salary

#include <iostream.h>

class salary {
public:
    salary(int b) : b_sal(b) { }
    void calc_bonus(double perc) { your_bonus = b_sal * perc; }
    static void reset_all(int p) { all_bonus = p; }
    int comp_tot() const
        { return (b_sal + your_bonus + all_bonus); }
private:
    int      b_sal;
    int      your_bonus;
    static int all_bonus;  //declaration
};

int salary::all_bonus = 100; //declaration and definition

main()
{
    salary w1(1000), w2(2000);

    w1.calc_bonus(0.2);
    w2.calc_bonus(0.15);
    salary::reset_all(400);
    cout << " w1 " << w1.comp_tot() << "   w2 " << w2.comp_tot() << "\n";
}
```

■ DISSECTION OF THE *salary* PROGRAM

```
class salary {
    . . .
private:
    int      b_sal;
    int      your_bonus;
    static int all_bonus;  //declaration
```

- There are three private data members. The static member all_bonus requires a file scope declaration. It can exist independently of any specific variables of type salary being declared.

```
salary(int b) : b_sal(b) { }
```

- This constructor uses the initializer syntax following the colon. It has the effect of assigning the value of b to the member b_sal. Thus the code body can be empty.

```
static void reset_all(int p) { all_bonus = p; }
```

- The modifier static must come before the function return type.

```
int comp_tot() const
    { return (b_sal + your_bonus + all_bonus); }
```

- The const modifier comes between the end of the argument list and the front of the code body. It indicates that no data member will have its value changed. As such it makes the code more robust. In effect it means that the self-referential pointer is passed as const salary* const this.

```
salary::reset_all(400);
```

- A static member function can be invoked using the scope resolution operator. It can also be invoked as:

```
w1.reset_all(400);
```

  but this is misleading, in that there is nothing special about using the class variable w1.

■ _____

Note that the static keyword is used only in the class definition and must be omitted when the data or function member is defined outside the class.

4.6 AN EXAMPLE: DYNAMICALLY ALLOCATED STRINGS

C++ lacks a native string type. Strings are represented as pointers to char and are manipulated accordingly. In this representation the end-of-string is denoted by \0. An important drawback to this convention is that many basic string manipulations are proportional to string length. When the string length is known, the efficiency of operations on strings can be significantly improved.

In this section we develop a useful string ADT that stores its length privately. We want our type to be dynamically allocated and able to represent arbitrary length strings. A variety of constructors are coded to initialize and allocate strings, and operations on strings are coded as member functions. The implementation uses the string.h library functions to manipulate the underlying pointer representation of strings.

```
//An implementation of dynamically allocated strings.
#include <string.h>
#include <iostream.h>

class string {
public:
   string(): len(0) { s = new char[1]; s[0] = 0; }
   string(const string& str);   //copy constructor
   string(const char* p);       //conversion constructor
   ~string() { delete []s; }
   void assign(const string& str);
   void print() const { cout << s << endl; }
   void concat(const string& a, const string& b);
private:
   char* s;
   int   len;
};

string::string(const char* p)
{
   len = strlen(p);
   s = new char[len + 1];
   strcpy(s, p);
}
string::string(const string& str):len(str.len)
{
   s = new char[len + 1];
   strcpy(s, str.s);
}
```

```
void string::assign(const string& str)
{
   if (this == &str)
      return;
   else
      delete []s;  //retrieve old string
   len = str.len;
   s = new char[len + 1];
   strcpy(s, str.s);
}

void string::concat(const string& a, const string& b)
{
   char temp[a.len + b.len + 1];

   len = a.len + b.len;
   strcpy(t, a.s);
   strcat(t, b.s);
   delete []s;
   s = new char[len + 1];
   strcpy(s, temp);
}
```

This type allows you to declare strings, assign by copying one string to another, print a string, and concatenate two strings. The hidden representation is a pointer to char and has a variable len in which to store the current string length. The constructors all allocate dynamically from free store.

■ DISSECTION OF THE *string* CLASS

```
string(): len(0) { s = new char[1]; s[0] = 0; }
string(const string& str);    //copy constructor
string(const char* p);        //conversion constructor
```

- There are three overloaded constructors. The first is the empty parameter default used to declare an array of strings. The second is the copy constructor. The third constructor has a pointer to char argument that can be used to convert the char* representation of strings to our class type. It uses two library functions: strlen and strcpy. We allocate one additional character to store the end-of-string character \0, although this character is not counted by strlen. The copy constructor is explained below.

```
~string() { delete []s; }
```

- The destructor automatically returns memory allocated to strings back to free store for reuse. The empty bracket-pair form of delete is used because array allocation was used. The operator delete [] knows the amount of memory associated with the pointer s as the base address for an array.

```
string::string(const string& str): len(str.len)
{
    s = new char[len + 1];
    strcpy(s, str.s);
}
```

- This is a copy constructor. This form of constructor is used to perform copying of one string value into another when:
  - A string is initialized by another string.
  - A string is passed as an argument in a function.
  - A string is returned as the value of a function.

  In C++, if this constructor is not present, these operations are member-by-member initializations of value.

```
void string::assign(const string& str)
{
    if (this == &str)
        return;
    else
        delete []s;   //retrieve old string
    len = str.len;
    s = new char[len + 1];
    strcpy(s, str.s);
}
```

- The assignment semantics are based on *deep copy* semantics. In deep copy the entire aggregate must be replicated and the data values copied into its representation. The copying requires a check against copying over the same string. Each time the value of a string is copied, the value is physically recopied using strcpy(). This is in distinction to a later implementation that shows how to use *shallow copy* semantics. In shallow copy the copying can be effected by setting a pointer to an existing value without replicating the aggregate. As we will see, this can be very efficient.

```
void string::concat(const string& a, const string& b)

{
    char temp[a.len + b.len + 1];

    len = a.len + b.len;
    strcpy(t, a.s);
    strcat(t, b.s);
    delete []s;
    s = new char[len + 1];
    strcpy(s, temp);
}
```

- This is a form of string concatenation. The two string arguments are not modified. The implicit argument, whose hidden member variables are s and len, is modified to represent the string a followed by the string b. Note that in this member function the use of len, a.len, and b.len is possible. Member functions have access not only to the private members of the implicit argument but also to the private representation of any of the arguments of type string.

The following code tests this type by concatenating several strings:

```
main()
{
    char*   str = "The wheel that squeaks the loudest\n";
    string  a(str), b, author("Josh Billings\n"), both, quote;

    b.assign("Is the one that gets the grease\n");
    both.concat(a, b);
    quote.concat(both, author);
    quote.print();
}
```

The printout from this program is

```
The wheel that squeaks the loudest
Is the one that gets the grease
Josh Billings
```

We deliberately use a variety of declarations to show how different constructors can be called. The string variables b, both, and quote all use the default constructor. The declaration for author uses the constructor whose argument type is char*, which is the type of a literal string. The concatenation takes place in two steps. First, strings a and b are concatenated into both. Next, strings both and author are concatenated into quote. Finally, the quotation is printed out.

The constructor string::string(const char*) is invoked to create and initialize objects a and author. This constructor is also called implicitly as a conversion operation when invoking string::assign() on the string literal "Is the one that gets the grease\n".

4.7 A CLASS *vect*

The one-dimensional array in C is a very useful, efficient aggregate type. However, the traditional C array is error prone. A common mistake is to access elements that are *out of bounds*. C++ allows us to control this problem by defining an analogous array type in which bounds can be tested.

```
//Implementation of a safe array type vect
#include <iostream.h>
#include <stdlib.h>      //for exit

class vect {
public:
   vect() { size = 10; p = new int[size]; }
   vect(int n);
   ~vect() { delete []p; }
   int& element(int i);                    //access p[i]
   int  ub() const { return (size - 1); } //upper bound
private:
   int* p;
   int  size;
};

vect::vect(int n)
{
   if (n < 1) {
      cerr << "illegal vect size " << n << endl;
      exit(1);
   }
   size = n;
   p = new int[size];
}

int& vect::element(int i)
{
   if (i < 0 || i >= size) {
      cerr << "illegal vect index " << i << endl;
      exit(1);
   }
   return (p[i]);
}
```

The constructor vect::vect(int n) allows the user to build dynamically allocated arrays. Such arrays are much more flexible than those in languages, such as Pascal and C, in which array sizes must be constant expressions. The constructor also initializes the variable size, whose value is the number of elements in the array. Access to individual elements is through the safe indexing member function

```
int& vect::element(int i)
```

An index that is outside the expected array range 0 through ub causes an error message and error exit. This safe indexing member function returns a reference to int that is the address of p[i] and that can be used as the left operand of an assignment or *lvalue*. The technique is much used in C++ and is an efficient mechanism for operating on complicated types.

As an example, the declarations

```
vect a(10), b(5);
```

construct an array of ten integers and an array of five integers, respectively. Individual elements can be accessed by the member function element, which checks whether the index is out of range. The statements

```
a.element(1) = 5;
b.element(1) = a.element(1) + 7;
cout << a.element(1) - 2;
```

are all legal. In effect, we have a safe dynamic array type.

Classes with default constructors use them to initialize a derived array type. For example,

```
vect a[5];
```

is a declaration that uses the default constructor to create an array a of five objects, each of which is a size 10 vect. The ith element's address in the jth array is given by a[j].element(i).

In Chapter 8 we discuss how assertions or exceptions can be used to check on error conditions. These more systematic methodologies are used in place of

```
if (n < 1) {
    cerr << "illegal vect size " << n << endl;
    exit(1);
}
```

Using assertions is replaced by

```
assert(n < 1);
```

Using exceptions is replaced by

```
if (n < 1)
    throw(n);
```

4.8 MEMBERS THAT ARE CLASS TYPES

In this section we use the type vect as part of a new class. We want to store multiple values for each index. For example, we may want to store the age, weight, and height of a group of individuals. We could group three arrays together inside a new class.

```
#include "vect.h"

class multi_v {
public:
    vect a, b, c;
    multi_v(int i): a(i), b(i), c(i), size(i) {}
    int ub() const { return (size - 1); }
private:
    int size;
};
```

The class has three vect members and a constructor, which has an empty body but a list of constructor calls separated by commas. These constructors are executed with the integer argument i, creating the three class objects a, b, and c. The value of i is also used to initialize size. The members of class are initialized in order of declaration.

Let us test this class by writing code to store and print a set of values for age in years, weight in pounds, and height in inches.

```
main()
{
    multi_v a_w_h(5);   //age weight and height

    for (int i = 0; i <= a_w_h.ub(); ++i) {
        a_w_h.element(i) = 21 + i;
        a_w_h.element(i) = 135 + i;
        a_w_h.element(i) = 62 + i;
    }
    for (i = 0; i <= a_w_h.ub(); ++i) {
        cout << a_w_h.element(i) << " years ";
        cout << a_w_h.element(i) << " pounds ";
        cout << a_w_h.element(i) << " inches\n";
    }
}
```

The declaration of a_w_h creates three vect members, each with five elements. When the program is executed, the individual destructors for each vect member are called upon block exit from main. The ordering of destructor calls is the reverse of the call on constructors. When executed, this program prints

```
21 years 135 pounds 62 inches
22 years 136 pounds 63 inches
23 years 137 pounds 64 inches
24 years 138 pounds 65 inches
25 years 139 pounds 66 inches
```

4.9 AN EXAMPLE: A SINGLY LINKED LIST

In this section we develop a singly linked list data type. This is the prototype of many useful dynamic data structures called *self-referential* structures. These data types have pointer members that refer to objects of their own type.

The following class declaration implements such a type:

```
//A singly linked list

struct listelem {
    char        data;
    listelem*   next;
};

class list {
public:
    list(): h(0) { }          //0 denotes an empty list
    ~list() { release(); }
    void prepend(char c);     //adds to front of list
    void del();
    listelem* first() const { return (h); }
    void print() const;
    void release();
private:
    listelem*   h;            //head of list
};
```

The link member next points to the next listelem in the list. The variable data in this example is a simple variable, but it can be replaced by a complicated type capable of storing a range of information. The constructor initializes the head of list pointer h to the value zero, which is called the *null pointer constant.* It can be assigned to any pointer type. In linked lists it typically denotes the empty list or end-of-list value. The member function prepend() is used to build the list structure.

```
void list::prepend(char c)
{
    listelem* temp = new listelem;    //create new element

    temp -> next = h;                 //link to list
    temp -> data = c;
    h = temp;                         //update head of list
}
```

A list element is allocated from free store, and its data member is initialized from the single argument c. Its link member next points at the old head of the list. The head pointer h is then updated to point at this element as the new first element of the list.

The member function del has the inverse role.

```
void del()
{
    listelem* temp = h;

    h = h -> next;   //presumes a nonempty list
    delete temp;
}
```

It returns the first element of the list to free store. It does this by using the delete operator on the head of list pointer h. The new head of list is the value of the next member. In Exercise 18 the reader is asked to modify this function to work on the empty list without aborting.

Much of list processing is repetitively chaining down the list until the null pointer value is found. The following two functions use this technique:

```
void list::print() const  //object is unchanged
{
    listelem*  temp = h;

    while (temp != 0) {              //detect end of list
        cout << temp -> data << " -> ";
        temp = temp -> next;
    }
    cout << "\n###\n";
}
```

```
void list::release()  //elements are returned to free store
{
   while (h != 0)
      del();
}
```

■ DISSECTION OF THE *print* AND *release* FUNCTIONS

```
void list::print() const  //object is unchanged
{
   listelem*  temp = h;
```

- An auxiliary pointer temp is used to chain down the list. It is initialized to the address of the list head h. The pointer h cannot be used because its value would be lost, in effect destroying access to the list.

```
while (temp != 0) {        //detect end of list
   cout << temp -> data << " -> ";
   temp = temp -> next;
}
```

- The value 0 represents the end-of-list value. It is guaranteed to be such because the constructor list::list initialized it and the list::prepend function maintains it as the end-of-list pointer value. Notice that the internals of this loop could be changed to process the entire list in some other manner.

```
void list::release()    //each element is returned to free store
```

- The release function is used to return all list elements to free store. It marches down the list doing so.

```
while (h != 0)
   del();
```

- Each element of the list must be returned to free store in sequence. This is done for a single element by the member function del, which manipulates the hidden pointer h. Since we are destroying the list, it is unnecessary to preserve the original value of pointer h. This function's chief use is as the body of the destructor list::~list. We cannot use a destructor written

```
list::~list()
{
    delete h;
}
```

because it deletes only the first element in the list.

We demonstrate the use of this type in the following code, in which we have modified the destructor to print a message:

```
list:: ~list()
{
    cout << "destructor invoked" << endl;
    release();
}

main()
{
    list*  p;
    {
        list w;

        w.prepend('A');
        w.prepend('B');
        w.print();
        w.del();
        w.print();
        p = &w;
        p -> print();
        cout << "exiting inner block" << endl;
    }
    //p -> print();  gives system dependent behavior
    cout << "exiting outer block" << endl;
    return (0);
}
```

Notice that an inner block in main is included to test that the destructor is invoked upon block exit, returning storage associated with w to free store. The output of this program is

```
B -> A ->
###
A ->
###
A ->
###
exiting inner block
destructor invoked
exiting outer block
```

The first print() call prints the two-element list storing B and A. After a del operation is performed, the list contains one element storing A. The outer block pointer to list p is assigned the address of the list variable w. When the list is accessed through p in the inner block, it prints A. This output shows that the destructor works at block exit on the variable w.

The commented-out invocation of list::print() is system dependent. It is a run-time error to dereference p here, because the address it refers to possibly has been overwritten at block exit by the deletion routine.

4.10 TWO-DIMENSIONAL ARRAYS

Standard C does not have authentic higher-dimensional arrays. Instead, the programmer must be careful to map such an abstract data structure into a pointer to pointer to ... base type. In C++ the programmer can implement flexible, safe, dynamic higher-dimensional arrays. We demonstrate this by implementing a two-dimensional array type matrix. The observant reader will notice the strong parallels with the class vect.

type of aggregate. We use the class str_obj to create actual object values. The type str_obj is a required implementation detail for string. The detail cannot be directly placed in string without destroying the potential many-one relationship between objects of type string and referenced values of type str_obj. The values of string are in the class str_obj, which is an auxiliary class for its use. The publicly used class string handles the str_obj instances, and therefore is sometimes called a *handler* class.

```
//Reference counted strings.
#include <string.h>
#include <iostream.h>

class str_obj {
public:
    int  len, ref_cnt;
    char* s;
    str_obj(): len(0), ref_cnt(1) { s = new char[1]; s[0] = 0; }
    str_obj(const char* p):ref_cnt(1)
        { len = strlen(p); s = new char[len + 1]; strcpy(s, p); }
    ~str_obj() { delete []s; }
};
```

The str_obj are string objects that are used by string. We explain later how these can be made private and accessed using the friend mechanism (see Chapter 5). Notice how this class is basically used for construction and destruction of objects using free store. Upon construction of a str_obj, the ref_cnt variable is initialized to one.

```
class string {
public:
    string() { st = new str_obj; }
    string(const char* p) { st = new str_obj(p); }
    string(const string& str)
        { st = str.st; st -> ref_cnt++; }
    ~string();
    void assign(const string& str);
    void print() const { cout << st -> s; }
private:
    str_obj* st;
};
```

The client uses objects of type string. These objects are implemented as pointers st to values of type str_obj. Notice the copy constructor for this class and how it uses reference semantics to produce a copy.

The semantics of assign() show some of the subtleties of using reference counting.

```
void string::assign(const string& str)
{
    if (str.st != st) {
        if (--st -> ref_cnt == 0)
            delete st;
        st = str.st;
        st -> ref_cnt++;
    }
}
```

The assignment occurs if the string is not being assigned its same value. The assignment causes the assigned variable to lose the previous value it had. This is equivalent to decrementing the reference count of the pointed-at str_obj value. Anytime an object's reference count is decremented, it gets tested for deletion.

The advantage of this technique over normal copying is clear. A very large aggregate is copied by reference with a small, fixed number of operations. There is a small amount of additional storage for the reference counter. Also, each possible change to a pointer adds a reference count operation. The destructor must also test the reference count before actual deletion.

```
string:: ~string()
{
    if (--st -> ref_cnt == 0)
        delete st;
}
```

4.12 NO CONSTRUCTOR, COPY CONSTRUCTOR, AND OTHER MYSTERIES

Object creation for native types is usually the task of the compiler. The writer of a class wants to achieve the same ease of use for the defined ADT. Let us reexamine some issues in simple terms.

Does every class need an explicitly defined constructor? Of course not, as is already clear from Chapter 3. When no constructor is written by the programmer, the compiler provides a default constructor, if needed.

```
struct pers_data {
    int    age;      //in years
    int    weight;   //in kilograms
    int    height;   //in centimeters
    char   name[20]; //last name
};

void print(pers_data d)
{
    cout << s d.name << " is " << d.age << " years old " << endl;
    cout << "weight : " << d.weight << "kg,  height : "
        << d.height << "cm." << endl;
}

main()
{
    pers_data laura = {3, 14, 88, "POHL"};  //construction off the stack

    print(laura);    //call by value -local copy constructed
}
```

What if we use constructors and allow the copy constructor to be default? We frequently get the wrong semantics; namely, shallow copy semantics. In shallow copy semantics a new value is not created, but instead a pointer variable is assigned the address of the existing value. Take the case of reference semantics, in which a copy implies that the reference counter is incremented. This does not happen in the default case. Thus objects copied in this manner are undercounted and prematurely returned to free store. As a rule of thumb, the class provider should explicitly write out the copy constructor, unless it is self-evident that memberwise copy is safe. Always be cautious if the aggregate has any members that are pointer based.

Are there special rules for unions? Yes, unions are frequently a special case. This should not be surprising, because unions are a technique for having different objects share space. Unions cannot have members that have constructors or destructors. Unions cannot have static data members. Anonymous unions can only have public data members. Also global anonymous unions must be declared static.

new, delete Options and Syntax

Constructors usually involve the application of new. The two standard forms are

new *new type name optional initializer list*
new *(type name) optional initializer list*

These operators return a pointer to the base address of the created object. In the case of an array of objects, this is the address of its first element. The initializer list is a parenthesized list of expressions used by the object's constructor, or a single value used for a native type.

```
p = new int(9);  //p is pointer to int initialized to 9
p = new int[9];  //p is pointer to a 9 element array of int
```

The second form of the new expression is used when parenthesizing of the type name is required to properly parse the object's type.

```
q = new (char*)[9];  //q is a char**
```

If new fails to allocate store, it returns with the value zero. Different strategies exist for coping with this failure (see Chapter 8).

Destructors usually involve the application of delete. The two standard forms are

delete *expression*
delete [] *expression*

The expression is typically a pointer variable used in assignment from a new expression. The brackets are necessary when allocation involved a bracketed expression, meaning an array of objects were allocated off of free store. A bracketed deletion ensures that destructors are called on each object stored in the array.

Deletion of a zero-valued pointer is harmless. Multiple deletions of the same object is an error (system-dependent behavior results), as is a deletion of a pointer value not gotten from a new expression.

Destructor Details

A destructor is implicitly invoked when an object goes out of scope. Common cases include block and function exits.

```
string sub_str(char c, string b)    //friend of string
{
    string  substring;
    for (int i = 0; i <= b.len; ++i)
        if (c == s[i])
            break;

    substring.assign(s + i);
    return (substring);
}
```

In sub_str(), b is a call-by-value argument of type string. Therefore, the copy constructor is invoked to create a local copy when the function is invoked. Correspondingly, a destructor is called upon function exit. There is a local string variable substring that is constructed upon block entry to this function and therefore must have its destructor invoked upon block exit. Finally, the return argument must be constructed and passed back into the calling environment. The corresponding destructor is invoked dependent on the scope of the object to which it is assigned.

It is possible to explicitly call a destructor.

```
p = new string("I dont need you long");
                //invokes string::string(const char*);
. . .
p -> ~string();  //also possible are p -> string::~string()
                 //and the more usual delete p
. . .
```

Constructors as Conversions

Constructors of a single parameter automatically are conversion functions. Consider the following class whose purpose is to print nonvisible characters with their ASCII designations; for example, the code 07 (octal) is alarm or bel.

```
//ASCII printable characters
//   Title: characters

#include <iostream.h>

class pr_char {
public:
   pr_char(int i = 0): c(i % 128) {}
   void print() const { cout << rep[c]; }
private:
   int   c;
   static char* rep[128];
};

char* pr_char::rep[128] = {"nul", "soh", "stx",
      //and so on - see Appendix A
      . . .
      "w", "x", "y", "z", "{", "|", "}", "~", "del"};

main()
{
   int     i;
   pr_char c;

   for (i = 0; i < 128; ++i) {
      c = i;  // also c = pr_char(i); or c = (pr_char)i;
      c.print();
      cout << endl;
   }
   return (0);
}
```

The constructor creates an automatic conversion from integers to pr_char. Notice, the statement in the loop

```
c = i;
```

implies this conversion. It is also possible to explicitly use a cast. Inordinate reliance on implicit conversions can lead to obscure type-insecure code.

Conversions are a major part of the discussion in the next chapter. A reason OOP requires such a possibility is that one wants the user-defined types to have the "look and feel" of the native types.

4.13 PRAGMATICS

In constructors, initialization is preferred to assignment.

```
stack::stack(int size)
        { s = new char[size]; max_len = size; top = EMPTY; }
```

is better written as

```
stack::stack(int size): max_len(size), top(EMPTY)
        { s = new char[size];}
```

As mentioned, data members that are declared const or reference must be initialized. Also the compiler in general can be more efficient about initialization.

In classes that use new to construct objects, a copy constructor should be explicitly provided. The default compiler-provided copy constructor is usually the wrong semantics for such an object.

4.14 SUMMARY

1. A constructor is a member function whose name is the same as the class name. It constructs objects of the class type. This process may involve initializing data members and allocating free store using new. A constructor is invoked when its associated type is used in a definition.

    ```
    TYPE_foo y(3);  //invoke TYPE_foo::TYPE_foo(int)
    extern TYPE_foo x;  //declaration but not definition
    ```

    Again, not all declarations are definitions. When they are not, constructors are not invoked.

2. A destructor is a member function whose name is the class name preceded by the character ˜ (tilde). Its usual purpose is to destroy values of the class type, typically by using delete.

3. A constructor requiring no arguments is called the *default* constructor. This can be a constructor with an empty argument list or a con-

structor where all arguments have default values. It has the special purpose of initializing arrays of objects of its class.

4. An example of a class with both a constructor and destructor is

```
class stack {
public:
    stack(int size) { s = new char[size];
                    max_len = size; top = EMPTY; }
    ~stack() { delete [] s; }
    . . .
private:
    enum { EMPTY = -1};
    char* s;
    int    max_len;
    int    top;
};
```

5. A copy constructor of the form

$$type::type(\text{ const } type\&)$$

is used to perform copying of one *type* value into another when

- A *type* variable is initialized by a *type* value.
- A *type* value is passed as an argument in a function.
- A *type* value is returned from a function.

In C++, if this constructor is not present, these operations are member-by-member initializations of value.

6. A class having a member whose type requires a constructor may have it specified after the argument list for its own constructor. The constructor has a comma-separated list of constructor calls following a colon. The constructor is invoked by using the member name followed by an argument list in parentheses. The initialization is in declaration order of the members.

7. A singly linked list is the prototype of many useful dynamic data structures called *self-referential* structures. A linked list is like a clothesline on which the data elements hang sequentially. The head of the line is the only immediate access point, and items can readily be added to or deleted from this point.

8. The value zero is called the *null pointer constant*. It can be assigned to any pointer type. In linked lists it typically denotes the empty list or end-of-list value.

9. An efficient disposal scheme for large aggregates is *reference counting*. Each dynamically allocated object tracks its active references. When an object is created, its reference count is set to one. Every time the object is newly referenced, a reference count is incremented. Every time the object loses a reference the count is decremented. When the reference count becomes zero, the object's memory is disposed of.

10. Constructors of a single parameter automatically are conversion functions. They convert from the parameter type to the class type. So `my_type::my_type(int)` is a conversion from `int` to `my_type`.

4.15 EXERCISES

1. Discuss why constructors are almost always `public` member functions. What goes wrong if they are `private`?

2. Write a member function for the class `mod_int`.

   ```
   void add_to(int i);   //add i to v modulo 60.
   ```

   It should add the number of seconds in `i` to the current value of `v` while retaining the modulo 60 feature of `v`.

3. Run the following program and explain its behavior. Placing debugging information inside constructors and destructors is a very useful step in developing efficient and correct classes.

```
//Constructors and destructors invoked

#include <iostream.h>

class A {
public:
    A(int n) { xx = n;
        cout << "A(int " << n << ") called\n"; }
    A(double y) { xx = y + 0.5;
            cout << "A(fl " << y << ") called\n"; }
    ~A() { cout << "~A() called A::xx = " << xx << endl; }
private:
    int xx;
};

main()
{
    cout << "enter main\n";
    int x = 14;
    float y = 17.3;
    A z(11), zz(11.5), zzz(0);

    cout << "\nOBJECT ALLOCATION LAYOUT\n";
    cout << "\nx is at " << &x;
    cout << "\ny is at " << &y;
    cout << "\nz is at " << &z;
    cout << "\nzz is at " << &zz;
    cout << "\nzzz is at " << &zzz;
    cout << "\n_____\n";
    zzz = A(x);
    zzz = A(y);
    cout << "exit main\n";
}
```

4. Add a default constructor for class A.

```
A() { xx = 0; cout << "A() called\n"; }
```

Now modify the previous program by declaring an array of type A

```
A d[5];     //declares an array of 5 elements of type A
```

Assign the values 0, 1, 2, 3, and 4 to the data member xx of each d[i]. Run the program and explain its behavior.

5. Use the stack type in Section 4.2 in this exercise, and include the default constructor to allocate a stack of 100 elements. Write a

program that swaps the contents of two stacks, using an array of stacks to accomplish the job. The two stacks will be the first two stacks in the array. One method would be to use four stacks: st[0], st[1], st[2], and st[3]. Push the contents of st[1] into st[2]. Push the contents of st[0] into st[3]. Push the contents of st[3] into st[1]. Push the contents of st[2] into st[0]. Verify that the stacks have their contents in the same order by implementing a print function that outputs all elements in the stack. Can this be done with three stacks only?

6. Add a constructor to the type stack with the following prototype:

```
stack::stack(const char* c);   //initialize from string array
```

7. Use the string type in Section 4.6 in this exercise, and code the following member functions:

```
//strcmp is negative if s < s1,
//         is 0 if s == s1,
//         and is positive if s > s1
//         where s is the implicit string argument
int string::strcmp(const string& s1);

//strrev  reverses the implicit string argument
void string::strrev();

//print  is overloaded to print the first n characters
void string::print(int n);
```

8. Write a function that swaps two strings. Use it and string::strcmp from the previous exercise to write a program that sorts an array of strings.

9. Use the vect type in Section 4.7 in this exercise, and code the following member functions:

```
//adds up all the element values and returns their sum
int vect::sumelem();

//prints all the elements
void vect::print();

//adds two vectors into a third   v(implicit) = v1 + v2
void vect::add(const vect& v1, const vect& v2);

//adds two vectors and returns   v(implicit) + v1
vect vect::add(const vect& v1);
```

10. Write a further constructor for vect that accepts an int array and its size and constructs a vect with these initial values:

```
vect::vect(const int* d, int sz);
```

11. Try to benchmark the speed differences between safe arrays as represented by class vect and ordinary integer arrays. Repeatedly run an ordinary element summation routine on int a[10000] and one using the vect a(10000). Time your trials. Useful timing functions can be found in *time.h*.

12. Define the class multi_v as follows:

```
class multi_v {
public:
    multi_v(int i) : a(i), b(i), c(i), size(i) {}
    void assign(int ind, int i, int j, int k);
    void retrieve(int ind, int& i, int& j, int& k) const;
    void print(int ind) const;
    int ub const ( return (size -1); }
private:
    vect a, b, c;
    int  size;
};
```

Write and test code for each member function: assign, retrieve, and print. The function assign should assign i, j, and k to a[ind], b[ind], and c[ind], respectively. The function retrieve does the inverse of assign. The function print should print the three values a[ind], b[ind], and c[ind].

13. Use the list type in Section 4.9 in this exercise, and code the following member functions:

```
//list a constructor whose initializer is a char array
list::list(const char* c);

//length returns the length of the list
int list::length();

//return the number of elements whose data value is c
int list::count_c(char c);
```

14. Write a member function append that adds a list to the rear of the implicit list argument and then clears the appended string by zeroing the head.

    ```
    void list::append(list& e);
    ```

15. Write a member function copy that copies a list.

    ```
    //the implicit argument ends up a copy of e
    void list::copy(const list& e);
    ```

    Be sure you destroy the implicit list before you do the copy. You want a special test to avoid copying to oneself.

16. Use the list type and add the equivalent five member functions that give you stack functions.

    ```
    reset   push   pop  top_of  empty
    ```

17. Construct a three-dimensional safe array type called v_3_d.

    ```
    //Implementation of a three-dimensional safe array
    class v_3_d {
        int*** p;
        int    s1, s2, s3;
    public:
        int    ub1, ub2, ub3;
        v_3_d(int l1, int l2, int l3);
        ~v_3_d();
        int& element(int i, int j, int k) const;
        void print() const;
    };
    ```

    Initialize and print a three-dimensional array.

18. As written list::del() expects a nonempty list. What goes wrong if it is passed an empty list? See the effect on your system. Modify this routine to test for this condition and continue. Note that this can be tested as an assertion but would then abort on the empty list.

19. Add a constructor to listelem and use it to simplify the coding of the member function list::prepend(char c).

20. We want to define a C++ class that resembles sets in Pascal. The underlying representation is a 32-bit machine word.

```
// Implementation of an ADT for type set.
const unsigned long int masks[32] = {
    0x80000000, 0x40000000, 0x20000000, 0x10000000,
    0x8000000, 0x4000000, 0x2000000, 0x1000000,
    0x800000, 0x400000, 0x200000, 0x100000,
    0x80000, 0x40000, 0x20000, 0x10000,
    0x8000, 0x4000, 0x2000, 0x1000, 0x800, 0x400, 0x200, 0x100,
    0x80, 0x40, 0x20, 0x10, 0x8, 0x4, 0x2, 0x1};

class set {
public:
    set(unsigned long int i) { t = i; }
    set() { t = 0x0; }
    void u_add(int i) const { t |= masks[i]; }
    void u_sub(int i) const { t &= ~masks[i]; }
    boolean in(int i) const
        { return boolean( (t & masks[i]) != 0); }
    void pr_mems() const;
    set set_union(const set& v) const { return (set(t | v.t)); }
private:
    unsigned long int t;
};
```

Write the code for pr_mems to print out all the elements of the set.
Write the code for the member function intersection to return the
resulting set intersection.

21. Improve the reference-counted form of class string by asserting in
    appropriate member functions that ref_cnt is nonnegative. Why
    would you want to do this?

22. Modify the matrix class to have a constructor that performs a trans-
    pose. It must have an enumerated type as a second argument that
    indicates what transformation should be made on the array.

```
enum transform {transpose, negative, upper};

matrix::matrix(const matrix& a, transform t)
{
    //transpose  base[i][j] = a.base[j][i]
    //negative   base[i][j] = -a.base[i][j]
    //upper      base[i][j] = a.base[i][j] i <= j else 0
    . . .
}
```

Also, overload << and >> to work with matrix values.

CHAPTER 5

OPERATOR OVERLOADING AND CONVERSIONS

This chapter describes operator overloading and conversions of data types. Overloading an operator gives it new meaning for an ADT. The ADT can then be used in much the same way as a built-in type. For example, the expression a + b has different meanings depending on the types of the variables a and b. The expression can mean string concatenation, complex number addition, or integer addition, depending, respectively, on whether the variables are the ADT string, the ADT complex, or the built-in type int. Mixed-type expressions are also possible by defining conversion functions. This chapter also discusses friend functions and how they are crucial to operator overloading.

5.1 THE TRADITIONAL CONVERSIONS

An arithmetic expression such as x + y has both a value and a type. For example, if x and y are both variables of the same type, say int, then x + y is also an int. However, if x and y are of different types, then x + y is a *mixed expression*. Suppose x is a short and y is an int. Then the value of x is converted to an int, and the expression x + y has type int. Note carefully that the value of x as stored in memory is unchanged. It is only a temporary copy of x that is converted during the computation of the value of the expression. Now suppose that both x and y are of type short. Even though x + y is not a mixed expression, automatic conversions again take place; both x and y are promoted to int, and the expression is of type int.

The general rules are straightforward.

Automatic conversion in an arithmetic expression x op y

First:
   Any char, short, or enum is promoted to int.
   Integral types unrepresentable as int are promoted to unsigned.

Second:
   If, after the first step, the expression is of mixed type, then, according to the hierarchy of types,

   int < unsigned < long < unsigned long < float < double < long double

   the operand of lower type is promoted to that of the higher type, and the value of the expression has that type.
   Note: unsigned is promoted to unsigned long if long cannot contain all the values of unsigned.

To illustrate implicit conversion, we first make the following declarations:

```
char c;      double d;      float   f;     int i;
long lg;     short  s;      unsigned u;
```

Now we can list a variety of mixed expressions along with their corresponding types.

Expression	Type	Expression	Type
c - s / i	int	u * 3 - i	unsigned
u * 3.0 - i	double	f * 3 - i	float
c + 1	int	3 * s * lg	long
c + 1.0	double	d + s	double

In addition to automatic conversions in mixed expressions, an automatic conversion also can occur across an assignment. For example,

```
d = i
```

causes the value of i, which is an int, to be converted to a double and then assigned to d; double is the type of the expression as a whole. A promotion or widening such as d = i is usually well behaved, but a narrowing or demotion such as i = d can lose information. Here the fractional part of d is discarded. Precisely what happens in each case is machine dependent.

In addition to implicit conversions, which can occur across assignments and in mixed expressions, there are explicit conversions called *casts*. If i is an int, then

```
(double) i
```

casts the value of i so that the expression has type double. The variable i itself remains unchanged. Casts can be applied to expressions. Some examples are

```
(char) ('A' + 1.0)
x = (float) ((int) y + 1)
(double) (x = 77)
```

The cast operator (*type*) is a unary operator having the same precedence and right-to-left associativity as other unary operators. Thus the expression

```
(float) i + 3
```

is equivalent to

```
((float) i) + 3
```

because the cast operator (*type*) has higher precedence than +.

In C and C++ we also have implicit pointer conversions. As we mentioned in Chapter 4, any pointer type can be converted to a generic pointer of type void*. Other pointer conversions include the name of an array used as a pointer to its base element; the null pointer value converted to any type; and the type function returning T converted to a pointer to the function returning T.

5.2 ADT CONVERSIONS

Explicit type conversion of an expression is necessary when either the implicit conversions are not desired or the expression is not otherwise legal. Traditional C casts are augmented in C++ by a functional notation as a syntactic alternative. C++ has as one aim the integration of user-defined ADTs and built-in types. To achieve this, C++ has a mechanism for having a member function provide an explicit conversion.

A functional notation of the form

> *type-name (expression)*

is equivalent to a cast. The type must be expressible as an identifier. Thus the two expressions

```
x = float(i);   //C++ functional notation
x = (float) i;
```

are equivalent. The expression

```
p = (int*) q;   //legal cast
```

cannot be directly expressed functionally as

```
p = int*(q);    //illegal
```

However, a typedef can be used to achieve this result:

```
typedef  int*  int_ptr;
p = int_ptr(q);
```

This use of typedef to create a readable synonym for a multitoken type name and the associated use of functional notation is the preferred style.

A constructor of one argument is de facto a type conversion from the argument's type to the constructor's class type. In Section 4.6 the string type had a constructor

```
string::string(const char* p)
{
    len = strlen(p);
    s = new char[len + 1];
    strcpy(s, p);
}
```

This is automatically a type conversion from char* to string. It is available both explicitly and implicitly. Explicitly it is used as a conversion operation in either cast or functional form. Thus

```
string s;
char*  logo = "Geometrics Inc";

s = string(logo);    //performs conversion then assignment
```

and

```
s = logo;            //implicit invocation of conversion
```

both work.

These are conversions from an already-defined type to a user-defined type. However, it is not possible for the user to add a constructor to a built-in type such as int or double. This can be done by defining a special conversion function inside the class. The general form of such a member function is

```
operator type() { . . . }
```

These functions must be nonstatic member functions. They cannot have parameters and do not have a declared return type. They must return an expression of the designated type. These conversions occur implicitly in assignment expressions, in arguments to functions, and in values returned from functions.

In the string example, one may want a conversion from string to char*. This can be done for the string class, as follows:

```
string::operator char*()
{
   char* p = new char[len + 1];
   strcpy(s, p);
   return (p);
}
```

Notice we did not simply return the value of the private member s. To do this would violate the integrity of string objects.

5.3 OVERLOADING AND FUNCTION SELECTION

Overloaded functions are an important addition in C++. The overloaded meaning is selected by matching the argument list of the function call to the argument list of the function declaration. When an overloaded function is invoked, the compiler must have a selection algorithm with which to pick the appropriate function. The algorithm that accomplishes this depends on what type conversions are available. A best match must be unique. It must be best on at least one argument and as good on all other arguments as any other match.

The matching algorithm for each argument is as follows:

Overloaded Function Selection Algorithm

1. Use an exact match, if found.
2. Try standard type promotions.
3. Try standard type conversions.
4. Try user-defined conversions.
5. Use a match to ellipsis, if found.

The complete rule on promotions is a two-part rule that distinguishes promotions from other standard conversions. A promotion involves going from a narrower type to a wider type. Thus going from char to int is a promotion. Promotions are better than other standard conversions. Among promotions, conversion from float to double and conversion from char, short, or enum to int are better than other promotions. Standard conversions also include pointer conversions.

An exact match is clearly best. Casts can be used to force such a match. The compiler will complain about ambiguous situations. Thus it is poor practice to rely on subtle type distinctions and implicit conversions that obscure the overloaded function that is called. When in doubt use explicit conversions to provide an exact match.

Let us write an overloaded function greater and follow our algorithm for various invocations. In this example the user type complex is available.

```
//overloading functions
//   Title:overloading

#include <iostream.h>
#include <math.h>              //for sqrt

class complex {
public:
   complex(double r) { real = r; imag = 0; }
   void assign(double r, double i) { real = r; imag = i; }
   void print() { cout << real << " + " << imag << "i "; }
   operator double() {return(sqrt(real * real + imag * imag));}
private:
   double real, imag;
};

inline int     greater(int i, int j)
               { return ( i > j ? i : j); }
inline double  greater(double x, double y)
               { return ( x > y ? x : y); }
inline complex greater(complex w, complex z)
               { return ( w > z ? w : z); }

main()
{
   int     i = 10, j = 5;
   float   x = 7.0;
   double  y = 14.5;
   complex w(0), z(0), zmax(0);

   w.assign(x, y);
   z.assign(i, j);
   cout << "compare " << i << " and " << j << "  greater is "
        << greater(i, j) << "\n";
   cout << "compare " << x << " and " << y << "  greater is "
        << greater(x, y) << "\n";
   cout << "compare " << y << " and " ;
   z.print();
   cout << "  greater is " << greater(y, double(z)) << "\n";
   zmax = greater(w, z);
   cout << "compare ";
   w.print();
   cout << "  and  ";
   z.print();
   cout << "  greater is  ";
   zmax.print();
   cout << "\n\n";
}
```

The output from this program is

```
compare 10 and  5  greater is 10
compare 7 and 14.5  greater is 14.5
compare 14.5 and 10 + 5i  greater is 14.5
compare 7 + 14.5i   and   10 + 5i   greater is  7 + 14.5i
```

A variety of conversion rules, both implicit and explicit, are being applied in this program. We explain these in the following dissection.

■ DISSECTION OF THE *overloading* PROGRAM

```
complex(double r) { real = r; imag = 0; }
```

- This constructor provides a conversion from double to complex.

```
operator double() {return(sqrt(real * real + imag * imag));}
```

- This member function provides a conversion from complex to double.

```
inline int     greater(int i, int j)
               { return ( i > j ? i : j); }
inline double  greater(double x, double y)
               { return ( x > y ? x : y); }
inline complex greater(complex w, complex z)
               { return ( w > z ? w : z); }
```

- Three distinct functions are overloaded. The most interesting has complex type for its argument list variables and its return type. The conversion member function operator double is required to evaluate w > z. In a more comprehensive package, the operator> would be overloaded to take two complex arguments. Here the complex variables w and z are converted to double. The explicit equivalent code is

```
return ( double(w) > double(z) ? w : z));
```

Later in this chapter we discuss overloading operators, a construct that allows us to provide new meanings to existing

C++ operators. No conversion is necessary for the return type.

```
w.assign(x, y);
z.assign(i, j);
```

- The first invocation of the member function assign requires the float argument x to be converted to double. The double argument y needs no conversion. The second invocation has both arguments as int, requiring conversion. Integer arguments are assignment-compatible with double.

```
cout << "compare " << i << " and " << j << "  greater is "
    << greater(i, j) << "\n";
cout << "compare " << x << " and " << y << "  greater is "
    << greater(x, y) << "\n";
```

- The first statement selects the first definition of greater because of the exact-match rule. The second statement selects the second definition of greater because of the use of a standard widening conversion float to double. The value of variable x is widened to double.

```
cout << "  greater is " << greater(y, double(z)) << "\n";
```

- The second definition of greater is selected because of the exact-match rule. The explicit conversion double(z) is necessary to avoid ambiguity. The function call

```
greater(y, z);
```

would have two available conversions to achieve a match. The user-defined conversion of double to complex for the argument y matches the third definition. The user-defined conversion from complex to double for the argument z matches the second definition. This violates the uniqueness provision for matching when user-specified conversions are involved.

```
zmax = greater(w, z);
```

- This is an exact match for definition three.

5.4 FRIEND FUNCTIONS

The keyword friend is a function specifier. It gives a nonmember function access to the hidden members of the class. Its use is a method of escaping the data-hiding restrictions of C++. However, we must have a good reason for escaping these restrictions because they are both important to reliable programming.

One reason for using friend functions is that some functions need privileged access to more than one class. A second reason is that friend functions pass all their arguments through the argument list, and each argument value is subject to assignment-compatible conversions. Conversions apply to a class variable passed explicitly and are especially useful in cases of operator overloading, as seen in the next section.

A friend function must be declared inside the class declaration to which it is a friend. The function is prefaced by the keyword friend and can appear in either the public or private part of the class without affecting its meaning. Our preferred style is to place the friend declaration in the public part of the class. The access keyword has no effect on friend declarations, so they are conceptually public. Member functions of one class can be friend functions of another class. In this case they are written in the friend's class using the scope resolution operator to qualify its function name. If all member functions of one class are friend functions of a second class, this can be specified by writing friend class *class name*.

The following declarations illustrate the syntax:

```
class tweedledee {
   . . .
   friend void alice();        //friend function
   int         cheshire();     //member function
   . . .
};

class tweedledum {
   . . .
   friend int tweedledee::cheshire();
   . . .
};

class tweedledumber {
   . . .
   friend class tweedledee;    //all member functions
                               //of tweedledee have access
   . . .
};
```

Consider the class matrix and the class vect in Chapter 4. A function multiplying a vector by a matrix as represented by these two classes could be written efficiently if it had access to the private members of both classes. It would be a friend function of both classes. In our discussion in Chapter 4, safe access was provided to the elements of vect and matrix with their respective member function, element. We could write a function using this access that would multiply without requiring friend status. However, the price in functional call overhead and array bounds checking would make such a matrix multiply unnecessarily inefficiently.

```
class matrix;                    //forward reference

class vect {
public:
    friend vect mpy(const vect& v, const matrix& m);
    . . .
private:
    int*        p;
    int         size;
};

class matrix {
public:
    friend vect mpy(const vect& v, const matrix& m);
    . . .
private:
    int**       p;
    int         s1, s2;
};

vect mpy(const vect& v, const matrix& m)
{
    if (v.size != m.s1) {      //incorrect sizes
        cerr << "multiply failed - sizes incorrect "
            << v.size << " and " << m.s1 << "\n";
        exit(1);
    }
    //use privileged access to p in both classes
    vect ans(m.s2);
    int  i, j;
    for (i = 0; i <= m.ub2; ++i) {
        ans.p[i] = 0;
        for (j = 0; j <= m.ub1; ++j)
            ans.p[i] += v.p[j] * m.p[j][i];
    }
    return (ans);
}
```

A minor point is the necessity of an empty declaration of the class matrix. This is a forward declaration. It is necessary whenever both classes have to know about each other. Here it is necessary because the function mpy must appear in both classes, and it uses each class as an argument type.

The OOP paradigm requires that objects (class variables in C++) be accessed through their public members. Only member functions can have access to the hidden implementation of the ADT. This is a neat, orderly design principle. The friend function, however, straddles this boundary. It is neither fish nor fowl. It has access to private members but is not itself a member function. It can be used to provide quick fixes to code that needs access to the implementation details of a class. But the mechanism is easily abused.

5.5 OVERLOADING OPERATORS

The keyword operator is used to define a type conversion member function. It is also used to overload the built-in C++ operators. Just as a function name, such as print, can be given a variety of meanings that depend on its arguments, so can an operator, such as +, be given additional meanings. Overloading operators allows infix expressions of both ADTs and built-in types to be written. It is an important notational convenience and in many instances leads to shorter and more readable programs.

Unary and binary operators can be overloaded as nonstatic member functions. Implicitly, they are acting on a class value. Unary operators can be overloaded as ordinary functions, in which they take a single argument of class or reference-to-class type. Binary operators can be overloaded as ordinary functions, in which they take one or both arguments of class or reference-to-class type.

```
class foo {
public:
   foo operator-();     //overload unary minus
   foo operator-(int); //overload binary minus for foo - int
   foo operator-(foo); //overload binary minus for foo - foo
};

foo operator-(int, foo); //overload binary minus for int - foo
foo operator-(int, foo*);//illegal: needed foo or foo& argument
```

The previous section's mpy function can be written as

```
vect operator*(const vect& v, const matrix& m)
   . . .
```

If this is done, and if r and s are vect and t is a matrix, then the natural-looking expression

```
r = s * t;
```

invokes the multiply function. This replaces the functional notation

```
r = mpy(s, t);
```

Although meanings can be added to operators, their associativity and precedence remain the same. For example, the multiplication operator remains of higher precedence than the add operator. The operator precedence table for C++ is included in Appendix B. Almost all operators can be overloaded. The exceptions are the member operator ., the member object selector operator .* (see Appendix C, Section 9.9), the ternary conditional expression operator ? :, the sizeof operator, and the scope resolution operator ::.

Available operators include all the arithmetic, logical, comparison, equality, assignment, and bit operators. Furthermore, the autoincrement and autodecrement operators, ++ and --, can have distinct prefix and postfix meanings (see Exercise 16). The subscript operator [] and the function call () can also be overloaded. The class pointer operator -> and the member pointer selector operator ->* can be overloaded (see Exercise 17 and Appendix C, Section 9.9). It is also possible to overload new and delete.

The assignment, function call, subscripting, and class pointer operators can be overloaded only by nonstatic member functions.

5.6 UNARY OPERATOR OVERLOADING

We continue our discussion of operator overloading by demonstrating how to overload unary operators, such as !, ++, ~, and []. For this purpose we develop the class clock, which can be used to store time as days, hours, minutes, and seconds. We develop familiar operations on this clock.

```
class clock {
public:
   clock(unsigned long i); //constructor and conversion
   void print() const;        //formatted printout
   void tick();               //add one second
   clock operator++() { this -> tick(); return(*this); }
private:
   unsigned long  tot_secs, secs, mins, hours, days;
};
```

This class overloads the prefix autoincrement operator. The overloaded operator is a member function and can be invoked on its implicit single argument. The member function tick adds one second to the implicit argument of the overloaded ++ operator.

```
inline clock::clock(unsigned long i)
{
    tot_secs = i;
    secs = tot_secs % 60;
    mins = (tot_secs / 60) % 60;
    hours = (tot_secs / 3600) % 24;
    days = tot_secs / 86400;
}

void clock::tick()
{
    clock  temp = clock(++tot_secs);

    secs = temp.secs;
    mins = temp.mins;
    hours = temp.hours;
    days = temp.days;
}
```

The constructor performs the usual conversions from tot_secs to days, hours, minutes, and seconds. For example, there are 86,400 seconds in a day, and therefore integer division by this constant gives the whole number of days. The member function tick constructs clock temp, which adds one second to the total time. The constructor acts as a conversion function that properly updates the time.

The overloaded operator++() also updates the implicit clock variable and returns the updated value as well. It could have been coded in the same way as tick(), except that the statement

```
return(temp);
```

would be added.

Adding the following code, we can test our functions:

```
void clock::print() const
{
    cout << days << " d :" << hours << " h :"
         << mins << " m :" << secs << " s\n";
}
```

```
main()
{
    clock t1(59), t2(172799); //172799 = 2 days - 1 sec

    cout << "initial times are\n";
    t1.print();
    t2.print();
    ++t1;  ++t2;
    cout << "after one second times are\n";
    t1.print();
    t2.print();
    return (0);
}
```

The output is

```
initial times are
0 d :0 h :0 m :59 s
1 d :23 h :59 m :59 s
after one second times are
0 d :0 h :1 m :0 s
2 d :0 h :0 m :0 s
```

It would have been possible to overload the prefix ++ using an ordinary function as follows:

```
clock operator++(clock& cl)
{
    cl.tick();
    return(cl);
}
```

Note that since the clock variable must advance by one second, we call it by reference.

The decision to choose between a member function representation or a nonmember function typically depends on whether implicit conversion operations are available and desirable. Explicit argument passing allows the argument to be automatically coerced if necessary and possible. When overloaded as a member function,

```
++c
```

is equivalent to

```
c.operator++()
```

When overloaded by a nonmember function,

```
++c
```

is equivalent to

```
operator++(c)
```

5.7 BINARY OPERATOR OVERLOADING

We continue with our clock example and show how to overload binary operators. Basically, the same principles hold. When a binary operator is overloaded using a member function, its first argument is the implicitly passed class variable and its second argument is the lone argument list parameter. Ordinary functions or friend functions have both arguments specified in the parameter list. Of course, ordinary functions cannot access private members.

Let us create an adding operation for type clock that adds two values together.

```
class clock {
   . . .
   friend clock operator+(clock c1, clock c2);
};

clock operator+(clock c1, clock c2)
{
   return (c1.tot_secs + c2.tot_secs);
}
```

The integer expression is implicitly converted to a clock by the conversion constructor clock::clock(unsigned long). Both clock values are passed as function arguments, and both are candidates for assignment conversions. Because plus is a symmetric binary operator, both arguments should be treated identically. Thus it is normal for symmetric binary operators to be overloaded by friend functions.

In contrast, let us overload binary minus with a member function.

```
class clock {
   . . .
   clock operator-(clock c);
};

clock clock::operator-(clock c)
{
   return (tot_secs - c.tot_secs);
}
```

Remember that there is an implicit first argument. This takes some getting used to. It would have been better to use a friend function for binary minus, because of the symmetric treatment of both arguments.

We define a multiplication operation as a binary operation, with one argument an unsigned int and the second argument a clock variable. The operation requires the use of a friend function. A member function must have the first argument from its class.

```
clock operator*(unsigned long m, clock c)
{
   return (m * c.tot_secs);
}
```

This requirement forces the multiplication to have a fixed ordering that is type dependent. To avoid this, it is common practice to write a second overloaded function.

```
clock operator*(clock c, unsigned long m)
{
   return (m * c.tot_secs);
}
```

An alternate implementation defines the second function in terms of the first as follows:

```
clock operator*(clock c, unsigned long m)
{
   return (m * c);
}
```

Defining the second implementation in terms of the first implementation reduces code redundancy and maintains consistency.

5.8 OVERLOADING ASSIGNMENT AND SUBSCRIPTING OPERATORS

C++ has reference declarations. In effect, such type modifiers produce lvalues. On the right side of an assignment expression, an lvalue is automatically dereferenced. On the left side of an assignment expression, it specifies where an appropriate value is to be stored. Subscripting makes use of these properties of lvalues. Passing and returning values from a function can be expensive, especially when the values are large aggregates and require copying. Using reference declarations can avoid this overhead. Multiple assignment expressions ordinarily require the creation of temporaries to perform them. By using reference return types, this can be managed efficiently.

For ADTs, we must define such expressions, unless satisfactory defaults are available. Let us reimplement the class vect from Section 4.4, extending its functionality by applying operator overloading.

The reimplemented class has several improvements to make it both safer and more useful. A constructor that converts an ordinary integer array to a safe array is added. This allows us to develop code using safe arrays and later run the same code efficiently on ordinary arrays. The public data member ub is changed to a member function. This prevents a user from inadvertently introducing a program error by modifying the member. Finally, the subscript operator [] is overloaded and replaces the member function element.

```
//A safe array type vect with [] overloaded
#include <iostream.h>
#include <stdlib.h>                    //for exit

class vect {
public:
   //constructors and destructor
   vect();                            //create a size 10 array
   vect(int n);                       //create a size n array
   vect(const vect& v);               //initialization by vect
   vect(const int a[], int n);        //initialization by array
   ~vect() { delete []p; }
   //other member functions
   int  ub()const { return (size - 1); }  //upper bound
   int& operator[](int i) const;          //range checked element
private:
   int* p;                            //base pointer
   int size;                          //number of elements
};

vect::vect()
{
   size = 10;
   p = new int[size];
}

vect::vect(int n)
{
   if (n <= 0) {
      cerr << "illegal vect size: " << n << "\n";
      exit(1);
   }
   size = n;
   p = new int[size];
}

vect::vect(const int a[], int n)
{
   if (n <= 0) {
      cerr << "illegal vect size: " << n << "\n";
      exit(1);
   }
   size = n;
   p = new int[size];
   for (int i = 0; i < size; ++i)
      p[i] = a[i];
}
```

```
vect::vect(const vect& v)
{
   size = v.size;
   p = new int[size];
   for (int i = 0; i < size; ++i)
      p[i] = v.p[i];
}

int& vect::operator[](int i) const
{
   if (i < 0 || i > ub()) {
      cerr << "illegal vect index: " << i << "\n";
      exit(1);
   }
   return (p[i]);
}
```

An overloaded subscript operator can have any return type and any argument list type. However, it is good style to maintain the consistency between a user-defined meaning and standard usage. Thus a most common function prototype is

class name& operator[](*integral type*);

Such functions return a reference value that can be used on either side of an assignment expression.

It is also convenient to be able to assign one array to another. The user can specify the behavior of assignment by overloading it. It is good style to maintain consistency with standard usage. The following member function overloads assignment for class vect:

```
vect& vect::operator=(const vect& v)
{
   int s = (size < v.size) ? size : v.size;

   if (v.size != size)
      cerr << "copying different size arrays "
           << size << " and " << v.size << "\n";
   for (int i = 0; i < s; ++i)
      p[i] = v.p[i];
   return (*this);
}
```

■ DISSECTION OF THE *vect::operator=(const vect& v)* FUNCTION

```
vect& vect::operator=(const vect& v)
```

- The operator= function returns reference to vect and has one explicit argument of type reference to vect. The first argument of the assignment operator is the implicit argument. The function could have been written to return void, but then it would not have allowed multiple assignment.

```
int s = (size < v.size) ? size : v.size;
```

- The smaller size is used in the element-by-element assignment. This function allows a smaller array to have its contents copied into the beginning of a larger array. When assigning from the larger array, it uses only as many elements as are in the smaller array.

```
if (v.size != size)
    cerr << "copying different size arrays "
        << size << " and " << v.size << "\n";
```

- This is a warning to the user in case this use was inadvertent.

```
for (int i = 0; i < s; ++i)
    p[i] = v.p[i];
return (*this);
```

- The explicit argument v.p[] is the right side of the assignment; the implicit argument, as represented by p[], is the left side of the assignment. The self-referential pointer is dereferenced and passed back as the value of the expression. This allows multiple assignment with right-to-left associativity to be defined.

Expressions of type vect can be evaluated by overloading in appropriate ways the various arithmetic operators. As an example, let us overload binary + to mean element-by-element addition of two vect variables.

```
vect vect::operator+(const vect& v)
{
    int s = (size < v.size) ? size : v.size;
    vect  sum(s);

    if (v.size != size)
        cerr << "adding different size arrays"
            << size << " and " << v.size << "\n";
    for (int i = 0; i < s; ++i)
        sum.p[i] = p[i] + v.p[i];
    return (sum);
}
```

Now with the class vect, as extended, all of the following expressions are meaningful:

```
a = b;                      //a, b are type vect
a = b = c;                  //a, b, c are type vect
a = vect(data, DSIZE);      //convert array data[DSIZE]
a = b + a;                  //assignment and addition
a = b + (c = a) + d;        //complicated expression
```

The class vect is a full-fledged ADT. It behaves and appears in client code much as any built-in type behaves and appears.

Notice that overloading assignment and overloading plus does not imply that operator+= is overloaded. Indeed, it is the class designer's responsibility to make sure the various operators have consistent semantics. When overloading one related set of operators, it is customary to overload them all in a consistent manner.

5.9 SIGNATURE MATCHING

Signature-matching rules are given in simplified form in Section 5.3. A further clarification of these rules and examples are given in this section.

The function argument type list is called its *signature*. The return type is not a part of the signature, but the order of the arguments is crucial.

```
int  sqr(int i);          //signature is int
double  sqr(int i);       //signature is int
void print(int i = 0);    //signature is int
void print(int i, double x); //signature is int, double
void print(double y, int i); //signature is double, int
```

In this example, sqr is illegally redeclared, but print has three distinct signatures. When the print function is invoked, the compiler matches the actual arguments to the different signatures and picks the best match. In general there are three possibilities: a best match, an ambiguous match, and no match. Without a best match, the compiler issues the appropriate syntax error.

```
print(15);                //matches int
print('A');               //converts and matches int
print(9.90);              //converts and matches int
print(str[]);             //no match wrong type
print(15, 9);             //ambiguous
print(15.0, 9);           //matches double, int
print(15, 9.0);           //matches int, double
print(15.0, 9.0);         //ambiguous
print(i, j, k);           //no match too many arguments
print();                  //match  int by default
```

The matching algorithm has two parts. The first part determines a best match for each argument. The second part sees if one function is a unique best match in each argument. The argument list 15.0, 9.0 has a best match in its first argument to print(double, int) and a best match in its second argument to print(int, double). Thus it has no unique best match and is ambiguously overloaded.

For a given argument, a best match is always an exact match. An exact match also includes *trivial conversions*. For type T these are

From	To
//equally good	
T	T&
T&	T
T	const T
T	volatile T
T[]	T*
T(*args*)	(*T) (*args*)
//not as good	
T*	const T*
T*	volatile T*
T&	const T&
T&	volatile T&

The first six trivial conversions cannot be used to disambiguate exact matches. The last four are considered worse than the first six. Thus

```
void print( int i);
void print( const int& i);
```

can be unambiguously overloaded.

The simplified rule in Section 5.3 is replaced by a two part rule that distinguishes promotions from other standard conversions. A promotion involves going from a narrower type to a wider type. The standard promotions are from char, short, or enum to int, and from float to double. Thus going from char to int is a standard promotion. Promotions are better than other standard conversions. Standard conversions also include pointer conversions. These need to be explained in the context of inheritance (see Chapter 6).

It is important to remember that user-defined conversions include constructors of a single argument. Such a constructor can be implicitly called to perform a conversion from the argument type to its class type. This can happen for assignment conversions, as in the argument-matching algorithm. For example,

```
//modify clock from Section 5.6
class clock {
public:
    clock(unsigned long i); //constructor and conversion
    void print() const;         //formatted printout
    void tick();                //add one second
    clock operator++() { this -> tick(); return(*this); }
    void reset(const clock& c);
private:
    unsigned long  tot_secs, secs, mins, hours, days;
};


     . . .


void clock::reset(const clock& c)
{
    tot_secs = c.tot_secs;
    secs = c.secs;
    mins = c.mins;
    hours = c.hours;
    days = c.days;
}

main()
{
    clock c1(900), c2(400);
    . . .
    c1.reset(c2);
    c2.reset(100);
    . . .
}
```

The call to reset(100) involves an argument match between int and clock that is a user-defined conversion invoking the constructor clock(unsigned).

5.10 PRAGMATICS

Explicitly casting arguments can be both an aid to documentation and a useful way to avoid poorly understood conversion sequences. It is not an admission of ignorance to cast or parenthesize arguments or expressions that would be converted or evaluated properly otherwise.

Operator overloading is readily misused. Do not overload operators when such overloading can lead to misinterpretation. The domain of use should have a widely used notation that conforms to your overloading. Also, overload related operators in a manner consistent with C community expectations. For example, the relation operators <, >, <=, and >= should all be meaningful and provide expected inverse behaviors.

Generally speaking, overload symmetric binary operators, such as +, *, ==, !, =, and &&, with friend functions. Both arguments are then passed as ordinary parameters. This subjects both arguments to the same rules of parameter passing. Recall that using a member function to provide overloading for symmetric binary operators causes the first argument to be passed via the this pointer.

Any time a class uses new to constructs objects, it should provide an explicitly overloaded operator=(). This advice is analogous to the rule in Chapter 4 that such a class provide an explicit copy constructor. The compiler-provided default assignment operator semantics in most cases gives spurious behavior. This leads to a suggested normal form for classes with heap-managed memory.

```
//Normal form for heap managed classes illustrated.
class vect{
public:
    vect();                    //default constructor
    vect(const vect&);         //copy constructor
    . . .
    vect& operator=(const vect&);  //assignment returning lvalue
    . . .
};
```

This normal form rule applies as well to reference counted classes, such as the string type in Chapter 4. The reason operator=() returns a reference is to allow assignment to work efficiently. This requires lvalue semantics.

5.11 Summary

1. Overloading operators gives them new meanings for ADTs. The ADT can then be used in much the same way as a built-in type. For example, the expression a + b has different meanings depending on the types of the variables a and b. The expression can mean string concatenation, complex number addition, or integer addition, depending,

respectively, on whether the variables are the ADT `string`, the ADT `complex`, or the built-in type `int`.

2. A functional notation of the form

   type-name (expression)

   is equivalent to a cast. The type must be expressible as an identifier. Thus the two expressions

   ```
   x = float(i);   //C++ functional notation
   x = (float) i;
   ```

   are equivalent.

3. A constructor of one argument is de facto a type conversion from the argument's type to the constructor's class type. A conversion from a user-specified type to a built-in type can be made by defining a special conversion function. The general form of such a member function is

   ```
   operator type() { ... }
   ```

   These conversions occur implicitly in assignment expressions, in arguments to functions, and in values returned from functions.

4. Overloaded functions are an important addition in C++. The overloaded meaning is selected by matching the argument list of the function call to the argument list of the function declaration. The algorithm that accomplishes this depends on what type conversions are available. A best match must be unique. It must be best on at least one argument and as good on all other arguments as any other match. The matching algorithm for each argument is as follows:
   1. Use an exact match, if found.
   2. Try standard type promotions.
   3. Try standard type conversions.
   4. Try user-defined conversions.
   5. Use a match to ellipsis, if found.

5. The keyword `friend` is a function specifier. It allows a nonmember function access to the hidden members of the class of which it is a friend. Its use is a method of escaping the data-hiding restrictions of C++.

6. The keyword operator is also used to overload the built-in C operators. Just as a function name, such as print, can be given a variety of meanings that depend on its arguments, so also can an operator, such as +, be given additional meanings. Overloading operators allows infix expressions of both user types and built-in types to be written. The precedence and associativity remain fixed.

7. Operator overloading typically uses either member functions or friend functions, because they both have privileged access. When a unary operator is overloaded using a member function, it has an empty argument list because the single operator argument is the implicit argument. When a binary operator is overloaded using a member function, it has as its first argument the implicitly passed class variable and as its second argument the lone argument list parameter. Ordinary functions or friend functions have both arguments specified in the parameter list.

8. An overloaded subscript operator can have any return type and any argument list type. However, it is good style to maintain consistency between a user-defined meaning and standard usage. Thus a most common function prototype is

   class name& operator[](*integral type*);

   A reference value is returned in such functions that can be used on either side of an assignment expression.

5.12 Exercises

1. The following table has a variety of mixed-type expressions. Fill in both the type the expression is converted to and its value when well defined.

in
tic

Th

9. Pr
   val
   by
   res
   a f

10. Th

Declarations and initializations		

`int   i = 3, *p = &i;`
`char  c = 'b';`
`float x = 2.14, *q = &x;`		

Expression	Type	Value
`i + c`		
`x + i`		
`p + i`		
`p == & i`		
`*p - *q`		
`(int)x + i`		

2. For the type complex provide a constructor that converts an int to a complex. Explain why this is redundant when a constructor from double has been provided. Write an explicit conversion that converts complex to double with the meaning that its value is its real component.

3. If the following line of code from the greater program

   ```
   cout << "  greater is " << greater(y, double(z)) << "\n";
   ```

   is replaced by

   ```
   cout << "  greater is " << greater(y, z) << "\n";
   ```

   what goes wrong?

It is
in s
fun

11. Exe
    con
    the
    the
    que
    defi

4. Write a function that adds a vect v to a matrix m. The prototype to be added to class matrix and class vect is

   ```
   friend vect add(const vect& v, matrix& m);
   ```

   The vect v is added element-by-element to each row of m.

5. The class complex as defined in this chapter is

This class must be a `friend` of `vect`. Write the code for `iterate`. Then for each declaration of a `vect`, there is a corresponding declaration of its iterator. For example,

```
vect a(5), b(10);
vect_iterator it_a(a), it_b(b);
```

Use this to write a function that finds the maximum element value in a `vect`.

12. Define a new class `matrix_iterator` as the iterator that sequences through all elements of a `matrix` (Section 4.7). Use it to find the maximum element in a `matrix`.

13. Redo the string ADT of Section 4.3 by using operator overloading. Change the member function `assign` to become `operator=`. Change the member function `concat` to become `operator+`. Also, overload `operator[]` to return the ith character in the string. If there is no such character, the value -1 is returned.

14. Redo the list ADT of Section 4.6 by using operator overloading. Change the member function `add` to become `operator+`. Change the member function `del` to become `operator--`. Also, overload `operator[]` to return the ith element in the list.

15. Modify the class set in Chapter 4, Exercise 19, to have overloaded operators `+`, `-`, and `*`.

```
class set {
    . . .
    set operator+(set& v); //define union
    set operator*(set& v); //define intersection
    set operator-(set& v); //define difference
};
```

Test your complete set ADT with the following:

```
main()
{
    set   s(0x5555), t(0x10303021), w, x;
    s.pr_mems(); t.pr_mems(); w.pr_mems(); x.pr_mems();
    w = s + t;          //set union
    x = s * t;          //set intersection
    t = t - s;          //set difference
    s.pr_mems(); t.pr_mems(); w.pr_mems(); x.pr_mems();
}
```

Notice we added a set type that is similar to the built-in Pascal set type.

16. The postfix operators ++ and -- can be overloaded distinct from their prefix meanings. Postfix can be distinguished by defining the postfix overloaded function as having a single unused integer argument, as in

```
class T {
public:
    void operator++(int);  //postfix invoked as t.operator++(0);
    void operator--(int);
};
```

There is no implied semantical relationship between the postfix and prefix forms. Add postfix decrement and increment to class clock. Have them subtract a second and add a second, respectively. Write these operators to use a default integer argument n that is subtracted or added as an additional argument.

```
clock c(60);

    c++; //adds a second
    c--; //subtracts a second
    c.operator++(5); //adds 1 + 5 seconds
    c.operator--(5); //subtracts 6 seconds
```

17. The operator -> is overloadable provided it is a nonstatic member function returning either a pointer to a class object or an object of a class for which operator-> is defined. Such an overloaded structure pointer operator is called a *smart pointer operator*. It usually returns an ordinary pointer after first doing some initial computation. One use for this type of operator is as an iterator function.

```
int* vect::operator ->()const;
//maintain an internal i - increment and return p[i]
```

Code and test this idea.

18. (Difficult) It is a better idea to make a smart pointer class.

```
class vect {
public:
   friend class smart_ptr_vect; //add to vect
     . . .
};

class smart_ptr_vect {
public:
   smart_ptr_vect(const vect& v);
   int* operator->();
private:
   int* ptr;
   int  position;
};

smart_ptr_vect::smart_ptr_vect(const vect& v): position(0), ptr(v.p){}
int* smart_ptr_vect::operator->()
{
   //write this code to access and test that
   //p[position] is not out of range
}
```

Write code that tests this idea.

CHAPTER 6

INHERITANCE

Inheritance is the mechanism of *deriving* a new class from an old one. That is, the existing class can be added to or altered to create the derived class. This is a powerful code reuse mechanism. Through inheritance, a hierarchy of related types can be created that share code and interface.

Many useful types are variants of one another, and it is frequently tedious to produce the same code for each. A derived class inherits the description of the *base class*. It can then be altered by adding members, modifying existing member functions, and modifying access privileges. The usefulness of this concept can be seen by examining how taxonomic classification compactly summarizes large bodies of knowledge. For example, knowing the concept "mammal" and knowing that an elephant and mouse are both mammals allows our descriptions of them to be considerably more succinct than they would be otherwise. The root concept "mammal" contains the information that mammals are warm-blooded animals and higher vertebrates, and that they nourish their young using milk-producing mammary glands. This information is inherited by both the "mouse" and the "elephant," but it is expressed only once: in the root concept. In C++ terms, both the "elephant" and "mouse" classes are derived from the base class "mammal."

C++ supports virtual member functions. These are functions declared in the base class and redefined in a derived class. A class hierarchy that is defined by public inheritance creates a related set of user types, all of whose objects may be pointed at by a base class pointer. By accessing the virtual function through this pointer, C++ selects the appropriate function definition at run-time. The object being pointed at must carry around type information so that this distinction can be made dynamically, a feature typical of OOP code. Each object "knows" how it is to be acted on. This is a form of polymorphism called *pure polymorphism*.

Inheritance should be designed into software to maximize reuse and to allow a natural modeling of the problem domain. With inheritance the key elements of the OOP design methodology becomes

1. Decide on an appropriate set of types.

2. Design in their relatedness, and use inheritance to share code.

3. Use virtual functions to process related objects polymorphically.

6.1 A DERIVED CLASS

A class can be derived from an existing class using the form

```
class class-name: (public|protected|private)optional base-class-name
{

    member declarations
};
```

As usual, the keyword class can be replaced by the keyword struct, with the implication that members are by default public. One aspect of the derived class is the access of its inherited members. The keywords `public`, `protected`, and `private` are used to specify how the base class members are to be accessible to the derived class.

Consider developing a class to represent students at a college or university.

```
enum year {fresh, soph, junior, senior, grad};
class student {
public:
    student(char* nm, int id, double g, year x);
    void  print() const;
protected:
    int       student_id;
    double    gpa;
    year      y;
    char      name[30];
};
```

We can write a program that lets the registrar track such students. While the information stored in `student` variables is adequate for undergraduates, it omits crucial information needed to track graduate students. Such additional information might include their means of support, their department affiliation, and their thesis topic. Inheritance lets us derive a suitable `grad_student` class from the base class `student` as follows:

```
enum support {ta, ra, fellowship, other};
class grad_student: public student {
public:
    grad_student
        (char* nm, int id, double g, year x, support t, char* d, char* th);
    void print() const;
protected:
    support   s;
    char      dept[10];
    char      thesis[80];
};
```

In this example `grad_student` is the derived class and `student` is the base class. The use of the keyword `public` following the colon in the derived class header means that the protected and public members of `student` are to be inherited as protected and public members of `grad_student`, respectively. Private members are inaccessible. Public inheritance also means that the derived class `grad_student` *is a* subtype of `student`. Thus a graduate student is a student, but a student does not have to be a graduate student. This subtyping relationship is called the ISA relationship.

A derived class is a modification of the base class that inherits the public members and protected members of the base class. Only constructors and any member function operator=() cannot be inherited. Thus, in the example of grad_student, the student members student_id, gpa, name, y, and print are inherited. Frequently a derived class adds new members to the existing class members. This is the case with grad_student, which has three new data members and a redefined member function print. The member function print is *overridden*. The definitions of student::print() and grad_student::print() are written out in the next section. The derived class has a different implementation of the member function than the base class. This is different from overloading, which allows the same function name to have different meanings for each unique signature.

The benefits of such a mechanism include the following:

- Code is reused. The grad_student type uses existing tested code from student.

- The hierarchy reflects a relationship found in the problem domain. When speaking of students the special grouping "graduate student" is an outgrowth of the real world and its treatment of this group.

- Various polymorphic mechanisms allow client code to treat grad_student as a subtype of student, simplifying client code while granting it the benefits of maintaining these distinctions among subtypes.

6.2 TYPING CONVERSIONS AND VISIBILITY

A publicly derived class is a *subtype* of its base class. A variable of the derived class can in many ways be treated as if it were the base class type. A pointer whose type is pointer to base class can point to objects having the derived class type.

Let us examine our example of student and grad_student. First we examine the base and derived class constructors.

```
student::student(char* nm, int id, double g, year x)
            :student_id(id), gpa(g), y(x)
{
    strcpy(name, nm);
}
```

The constructor for the base class docs a series of simple initializations.
It then calls strcpy() to copy over the student's name.

```
grad_student::grad_student(
    char* nm, int id, double g, year x,
    support t, char* d, char* th)
    :student(nm, id, g, x), s(t)
{
    strcpy(dept, d);
    strcpy(thesis, th);
}
```

Notice that the constructor for student is invoked as part of the initializer
list. This is usual, and logically the base class object needs to be constructed first, before the complete object can be completed.

The grad_student is a publicly derived type whose base class is student.
In the class student, the members student_id and gpa are protected. This
makes them accessible to the derived class but otherwise treated as
private.

A reference to the derived class may be implicitly converted to a reference to the public base class. For example,

```
grad_student gs("Morris Pohl", 200, 3.2564, grad, ta, "Pharmacy",
                "Retail Pharmacies");
student& rs = &gs;
```

In this case the variable rs is a reference to student. The base class of
grad_student is student. Therefore this reference conversion is appropriate.

The print member functions are overloaded. Let us implement the
print functions.

```
void student::print() const
{
    cout << "\n" << name << " , " << student_id << " , "
        << y << " , " << gpa << endl;
}
```

```
void grad_student::print() const
{
    student::print();     //base class information is printed
    cout << dept << " , " << s << "\n" << thesis << endl;
}
```

For `grad_student::print` to invoke the `student::print` function, the scope-resolved identifier `student::print` must be used; otherwise there is an infinite loop. To see which versions of these functions get called and to demonstrate some of the conversion relationships between base and publicly derived classes, we write a simple test program.

```
//Test pointer conversion rules.
//   Title: student

#include "student.h"  //include relevant declarations

main()
{
    student       s("Mae Pohl", 100, 3.425, fresh), *ps = &s;
    grad_student  gs("Morris Pohl", 200, 3.2564, grad, ta, "Pharmacy",
                     "Retail Pharmacies"), *pgs;

    ps -> print();     //student::print
    ps = pgs = &gs;
    ps -> print();     //student::print
    pgs -> print();    //grad_student::print
    return (0);
}
```

This function declares both class variables and pointers to them. The conversion rule is that a pointer to a publicly derived class may be converted implicitly to a pointer to its base class. In our example, the pointer variable `ps` can point at objects of both classes, but the pointer variable `pgs` can point only at objects of type `grad_student`.

We want to study how different pointer assignments affect the invocation of a version of `print`. The first instance of the statement

```
ps -> print();
```

invokes `student::print`. It is pointing at the variable `s` of type `student`. The multiple assignment statement

```
ps = pgs = &gs;
```

has both pointers pointing at an object of type grad_student. The assignment to ps involves an implicit conversion. The second instance of the statement

```
ps -> print();
```

again invokes student::print. The fact that this pointer is pointing at a grad_student variable gs is not relevant. The statement

```
pgs -> print();    //grad_student::print
```

invokes grad_student::print. The variable pgs is of type pointer to grad_student and, when invoked with an object of this type, selects a member function from this class.

6.3 CODE REUSE: DYNAMIC ARRAY BOUNDS

In Chapter 5 we developed the vect safe array class. We want to reuse that code and extend this type into a safe array whose upper and lower bounds are dynamic. This style of array declaration is more flexible and allows the indices to correspond directly to a problem domain. For example, Fahrenheit temperatures representing water in its liquid range is 32–212 degrees at sea level. So if we collected data on this range of temperatures, it is appropriate to use a lower bound of 32 and an upper bound of 212.

Recall that the dynamic safe array type vect checked array bounds for being in range and created arrays using free store. The class declaration follows:

```
//Implementation of a safe array type vect
class vect {
public:
    //constructors and destructor
    vect();                          //create a size 10 array
    vect(int l);                     //create a size l array
    vect(const vect& v);             //copy constructor
    vect(int a[], int l);            //initialization by array
    ~vect() { delete [] p; }
    int  ub() const { return(size - 1); }      //upper bound
    int& operator[](int i) const;    //obtain range checked element
    vect& operator=(const vect& v);  //is not inherited
    vect operator+(const vect& v);
private:
    int *p;                          //base pointer
    int size;                        //number of elements
};
```

The derived type has members l_bnd and u_bnd that store privately the lower and upper bounds of the constructed safe array. The derived type reuses the base type's representation and code.

```
//Derived safe array type vect_bnd
class vect_bnd: public vect {
public:
    vect_bnd();
    vect_bnd(int, int);
    int& operator[](int) const;
    vect_bnd& operator=(const vect_bnd& v);
    int ub() const { return (u_bnd); }
    int lb() const { return (l_bnd); }
private:
    int l_bnd, u_bnd;
};
```

The derived class constructors invoke the base class constructors. The syntax for this is the same as initialization syntax of members.

function header: *base-class-name(argument list)*

Here are the derived class constructors:

```
vect_bnd::vect_bnd() :vect(10)
{
    l_bnd = 0;
    u_bnd = 9;
}
```

```
vect_bnd::vect_bnd(int lb, int ub) :vect(ub - lb + 1)
{
    l_bnd = lb;
    u_bnd = ub;
}
```

Notice how the derived class constructors call the base class constructors. The additional code initializes the bound's pair. Alternatively, this
can be done in the initializing list.

```
vect_bnd::vect_bnd(int lb, int ub)
        vect(ub - lb + 1), l_bnd(lb), u_bnd(ub) {}
```

We can also reuse code in overloading the indexing operator [].

```
int& vect_bnd::operator[](int i) const
{
    if (i < l_bnd || u_bnd < i) {
        cerr<<"index out of range\n";
        exit(1);
    };
    return  (vect::operator[](i - l_bnd));
}
```

This would be very inefficient. Why? Because bounds checking is now
done twice. To avoid this we must change the access privilege of the
member vect::p to protected. As a result, the derived class has direct
access to the previously private implementation of vect, and p can be
used in the member function vect_bnd::operator[](). The more efficient
code is

```
int& vect_bnd::operator[](int i) const
{
    if (i < l_bnd || u_bnd < i) {
        cerr<<"index out of range\n";
        exit(1);
    };
    return  (p[i - l_bnd]);
}
```

Notice the tradeoff in code reuse and efficiency. This is often the case.
Also notice that inheritance requires us to think about three access
boundaries: What is to be strictly private and what is to be protected
depends on what is potentially reusable.

6.4 CODE REUSE: A BINARY TREE CLASS

Private inheritance does not have a subtype relationship. It is not an ISA relationship. In private inheritance we *reuse a* base class for its code. We call private derivation a REUSEA relationship. This comes in handy when diagramming the class relationships in a complicated software system. Because private (and also protected) inheritance does not create a type hierarchy, it has more limited utility than public inheritance. In a first pass in understanding these concepts, we can skip nonpublic inheritance.

Interface and code reuse are often all that is wanted from inheritance. We can see how private inheritance is used by designing a generic container class that is a binary tree. The class stores void* data members. The idea is to inherit this class privately, so as to turn the apparently useless container into one storing *useful-type* * data.

```
//generic binary search trees
typedef void*   p_gen;   //generic pointer type

class bnode {
private:
   friend  class gen_tree;
   bnode*  left;
   bnode*  right;
   p_gen   data;
   int     count;
   bnode(p_gen d, bnode* l, bnode* r)
         : data(d), left(l), right(r), count(1) {}
   friend int comp(p_gen a, p_gen b);
   friend void print(bnode* n);
};

class gen_tree {
public:
   gen_tree() { root = 0; }
   void insert(p_gen d);
   p_gen find(p_gen d) const { return (find(root, d)); }
   void print() const { print(root); }
protected:
   bnode* root;
   p_gen find(bnode* r, p_gen d) const;
   void print(bnode* r) const;
};
```

The individual nodes in this binary tree store a generic pointer data and an int count that counts duplicate entries. The pointer data matches a pointer type in the derived class. The tree is a binary search tree that stores nodes of smaller value to the left and larger or equal values to the right. We need a method of comparing values that is appropriate to the specific derived type. We use a friend function comp that is a friend of bnode and is coded appropriately for the derived class.

The insert function places nodes in a tree, and it must find the position in the tree for the new nodes. The function p_gen find(bnode* r, p_gen d) searches the subtree rooted at r for the information represented by d. The function p_gen find(p_gen d) searches the entire tree. The member function void print(bnode* r) walks around the subtree rooted at r, applying the friend function print(bnode* n) to each node in turn. This is done for the entire tree by void print().

```
void gen_tree::insert(p_gen d)
{
    bnode* temp = root;
    bnode* old;

    if (root == 0) {
        root = new bnode(d, 0, 0);
        return;
    }
    while (temp != 0) {
        old = temp;
        if (comp(temp -> data, d) == 0) {
            (temp -> count)++;
            return;
        }
        if (comp(temp -> data, d) > 0)
            temp = temp -> left;
        else
            temp = temp -> right;
    }
    if (comp(old -> data, d) > 0)
        old -> left = new bnode(d, 0, 0);
    else
        old -> right = new bnode(d, 0, 0);
}
```

The insert function creates a one-node tree if the tree is initially empty. If the information as represented by the pointer d matches existing information as determined by comp, then count is incremented. Otherwise comp navigates through the tree to the appropriate leaf position, where the new node is constructed and attached. Note that the function comp can be computationally expensive, and multiple evaluations of it can be eliminated (see Exercise 16).

```
p_gen gen_tree::find(bnode* r, p_gen d) const
{
   if (r == 0)
      return (0);
   else if (comp(r -> data, d) ==  0)
      return (r -> data);
   else if (comp(r -> data, d) > 0)
      return (find( r -> left, d));
   else
      return (find( r -> right, d));
}
```

This is a standard recursion. If the information as pointed at by d is not found, 0 is returned.

The print() function is also a standard recursion. At each node the external function ::print() is applied.

```
void gen_tree::print(bnode* r) const
{
   if (r != 0) {
      print (r -> left);
      ::print(r);
      print (r -> right);
   }
}
```

We next derive a class capable of storing a pointer to char as its data member.

```
#include "gentree.h"
#include <string.h>

class s_tree: private gen_tree {
public:
   s_tree() {}
   void  insert(char* d) { gen_tree::insert(d); }
   char* find(char* d) const
         { return ((char*)gen_tree::find(d)); }
   void  print() const { gen_tree::print(); }
};
```

The base class insertion function gen_tree::insert takes a generic pointer type as its argument. The derived class insertion function s_tree::insert takes a pointer to char as its argument. Therefore, in the derived class s_tree,

```
void  insert(char* d) { gen_tree::insert(d); }
```

uses the implicit conversion char* to void*.

We need a function to perform comparison: the promised friend function to class bnode.

```
int comp(p_gen i, p_gen j)
{
    return (strcmp((char*)i, (char*)j));
}
```

We also need an external print() that can properly print the values stored in a single node to be used recursively by s_tree::print() to output the entire tree.

```
void print(bnode* n)
{
    cout << (char*)n -> data << "\t" ;
    cout << n -> count << "\t";
}
```

The design of s_tree has a good deal more abstraction than would a like structure written in C. The payoff for this abstraction is the ease with which further classes can be derived that utilize the underlying binary tree structure. The exercises at the end of this chapter show how to test these routines.

This tree structure is a container class. It is an ideal candidate for being a template class, as explained in Chapter 7.

6.5 VIRTUAL FUNCTIONS

Overloaded member functions are invoked by a type-matching algorithm that includes having the implicit argument matched to an object of that class type. All of this is known at compile-time and allows the compiler to select the appropriate member directly. As will become apparent, it would be nice to dynamically select at run-time the appropriate member function from among base and derived class functions. The keyword virtual is a function specifier that provides such a mechanism, but it may be used only to modify member function declarations. The combination of virtual functions and public inheritance will be our most general and flexible way to build a piece of software. This is a form of pure polymorphism.

An ordinary virtual function must be executable code. When invoked its semantics are the same as other functions. In a derived class it can be *overridden*, and the function prototype of the derived function must have matching signature and return type. The selection of which function definition to invoke for a virtual function is dynamic. The typical case is when a base class has a virtual function and derived classes have their versions of this function. A pointer to base class can point at either a base class object or a derived class object. The member function selected depends on the class of the object being pointed at, not on the pointer type. In the absence of a derived type member, the base class virtual function is used by default.

Note well the difference in selection of the appropriate overridden virtual function from an overloaded member function. The overloaded member function is selected at compile-time based on signature, and it can have distinct return types. A virtual function is selected at run-time based on the type of the object that is passed to it as its this pointer argument. Also, once declared virtual, this property is carried along to all redefinitions in derived classes. It is unnecessary in the derived class to use the function modifier virtual.

Consider the following example:

```
//virtual function selection.
//   Title: pure_polymorphism

#include <iostream.h>

class B {
public:
   int  i;
   virtual void print_i() { cout << i << " inside B\n"; }
};

class D: public B {
public:
   void print_i() { cout << i << " inside D\n"; } //virtual as well
};

main()
{
   B   b;
   B*  pb = &b;      //points at a B object
   D   f;

   f.i = 1 + (b.i = 1);
   pb -> print_i();  //call B::print_i()
   pb = &f;          //points at a D object
   pb -> print_i();  //call D::print_i()
   return (0);
}
```

The output from this program is

```
1 inside B
2 inside D
```

Compare this behavior to the test program *student* of Section 6.2, in which the selection of print() is based on the pointer type known at compile-time. In the *pure_polymorphism* program, print_i() is selected based on what is being pointed at. In this case a different version of print_i is executed. In OOP terminology, the object is sent the message print_i and selects its own version of the corresponding method. Thus the pointer's base type is not determining method (function) selection. Different class objects are processed by different functions determined at run-time. Facilities that allow the implementation of ADTs, inheritance, and the ability to process objects dynamically are the essentials of OOP. Member function overloading and virtual functions cause mixups and confusion. Consider the following:

```
class B {
public:
   virtual foo(int);
   virtual foo(double);
};

class D: public B {
public:
   foo(int);
};

main()
{
   D  d;
   B  b, *pb = &d;

   b.foo(9);          //selects B::foo(int);
   b.foo(9.5);        //selects B::foo(double);
   d.foo(9);          //selects D::foo(int);
   d.foo(9.5);        //selects D::foo(int);
   pb -> foo(9);      //selects D::foo(int);
   pb -> foo(9.5);    //selects B::foo(double);
   return (0);
}
```

The base class member function B::foo(int) is overridden in the derived class. The base class member function B::foo(double) is hidden in the derived class. In the statement d.foo(9.5), the double value 9.5 is converted to an integer value 9. We could have used d.B::foo(double) to call the hidden member function.

The declaration of an identifier in a scope hides all declarations of that identifier in outer scopes. A base class is an outer scope of any class derived from it. This rule is independent of whether the names are declared virtual. Access restrictions (private, protected) are orthogonal to function selection. If the selected function is inaccessible, that is a compile-time error.

Only nonstatic member functions can be virtual. The virtual characteristic is inherited. Thus the derived class function is automatically virtual, and the presence of the virtual keyword is usually a matter of taste. Constructors cannot be virtual. Destructors can be virtual. As a rule-of-thumb, any class having virtual functions should have a virtual destructor.

Run-time decisions are allowed by virtual functions. Consider a computer-aided design application used to compute the area of the shapes in a design. The different shapes are derived from the shape base class.

```
class shape {
public:
    virtual double area() const { return (0); }  //default behavior
protected:
    double x, y;
};

class rectangle: public shape {
public:
    double area() const { return (height * width); }
private:
    double height, width;
};

class circle: public shape {
public:
    double area() const { return (PI * radius * radius); }
private:
    double radius;
};
```

In such a class hierarchy the derived classes correspond to important, well-understood types of shapes. The system is readily added to by deriving further classes. The area calculation is a local responsibility of a derived class.

Client code that uses the polymorphic area calculation looks like

```
shape* p[N];

. . .
for (i = 0; i < N; ++i)
    tot_area += p[i] -> area();
```

A major advantage here is that the client code does not need to change if new shapes are added to the system. Change is managed locally and propagated automatically by the polymorphic character of the client code.

6.6 ABSTRACT BASE CLASSES

A type hierarchy usually has its root class contain a number of virtual functions, which provide for dynamic typing. Often these virtual functions in the root class are dummy functions. They have an empty body in the root class, but they are given specific meanings in the derived classes. In C++ the *pure virtual function* is introduced for this purpose. A pure virtual function is a virtual member function whose body is normally undefined. Notationally it is declared inside the class as follows:

> virtual *function prototype* = 0;

The pure virtual function is used to defer the implementation decision of the function. In OOP terminology it is called a *deferred method*.

A class that has at least one pure virtual function is an *abstract class*. It is useful to have a root class for a type hierarchy be an abstract class. It would have the basic common properties of its derived classes but cannot itself be used to declare objects. Instead it is used to declare pointers that can access subtype objects derived from the abstract class.

We explain this concept while developing a primitive form of ecological simulation. OOP was developed originally as a simulation methodology using Simula 67. Hence conceptually many of its ideas are understandable as attempts to model reality in a particular way.

In our example our world has different forms of life interacting. The abstract base class is living. Its interface is inherited by various forms of life. We have foxes as an archetypical predator and rabbits as its prey. The rabbits eat grass.

```
//A Predator-Prey simulation using class hierarchy living.
const int N = 40;               //size of square board
enum state { EMPTY , GRASS , RABBIT , FOX, STATES };

class living;                           //forward declaration
typedef living* world[N][N];            //world will be simulation

class living {                          //what lives in the world
public:
   virtual state who() = 0;             //state identification
   virtual living* next(world w) = 0;   //compute next
protected:
   int      row, column;                //location
   void     sums(world w, int sm[]);    //sm[#states] used by next()
};

void living::sums(world w, int sm[])
{
   int i, j;
   sm[EMPTY] = sm[GRASS] = sm[RABBIT] = sm[FOX] = 0;

   for (i = -1; i <= 1; ++i)
      for ( j = -1; j <= 1; ++j)
         sm[w[row + i][column +j] -> who()]++;
}
```

This simulation has two pure virtual functions and one ordinary member function sums(). Virtual functions incur a small added run-time cost over normal member functions. Therefore we use them only when necessary to our implementations. Our simulation has rules for deciding who goes on living in a subsequent cycle based on the populations in the neighborhood of a given square. These populations are computed by sums(). This is akin to Conway's "Game of Life" simulation.

The inheritance hierarchy is one level deep.

```
//currently only predator class
class fox:public living {
public:
    fox(int r, int c, int a = 0): row(r), column(c), age(a) {}
    state who() {return (FOX);}   //deferred method for foxes
    living* next(world w);        //deferred method for foxes
protected:
    int age;                      //used to decide on dying
};

//currently only prey class
class rabbit:public living {
public:
    rabbit(int r, int c, int a = 0): row(r), column(c), age(a) {}
    state who() {return (RABBIT);}
    living* next(world w);
protected:
    int age;
};

//currently only plant life
class grass:public living {
public:
    grass(int r, int c): row(r), column(c) {}
    state who() {return (GRASS);}
    living* next(world w);
};

//nothing lives here
class empty:public living {
public:
    empty(int r, int c): row(r), column(c) {}
    state who() {return (EMPTY);}
    living* next(world w);
};
```

Notice how the design allows other forms of predator, prey, and plant life to be developed using a further level of inheritance. The characteristics of how each life form behave are captured in its version of next().

```
living* grass::next(world w)
{
    int sum[STATES];
    sums(w, sum);

    if (sum[GRASS] > sum[RABBIT]) //eat grass
        return (new grass(row, column));
    else
        return (new empty(row, column));
}
```

Grass can be eaten by rabbits. If there is more grass than rabbits in the neighborhood, the grass remains; otherwise the grass is eaten up. (Please substitute your own rules, as these are highly limited and artificial.)

```
living* rabbit::next(world w)
{
    int sum[STATES];
    sums(w, sum);

    if (sum[FOX] >= sum[RABBIT] )     //eat rabbits
        return (new empty(row, column));
    else if (age > DRAB)              //rabbit is too old
        return (new empty(row, column));
    else
        return (new rabbit(row, column, age + 1));
}
```

Rabbits die of old age if they exceed some defined limit DRAB, or they can be eaten if an appropriate number of foxes are in the neighborhood.

```
living* fox::next(world w)
{
    int sum[STATES];
    sums(w, sum);

    if (sum[FOX] > 5)                 //too many foxes
        return (new empty(row, column));
    else if (age > DFOX)              //fox is too old
        return (new empty(row, column));
    else
        return (new fox(row, column, age + 1));
}
```

Foxes die of overcrowding or of old age.

```
//how to fill an empty square
living* empty::next(world w)
{
    int sum[STATES];
    sums(w, sum);

    if (sum[FOX] > 1)
        return (new fox(row, column));
    else if (sum[RABBIT] > 1)
        return (new rabbit(row, column));
    else if (sum[GRASS])
        return (new grass(row, column));
    else
        return (new empty(row, column));
}
```

Empty squares are competed for by the various life forms. The various rules in the different versions of next determine a possibly complex set of interactions. Of course, we can make the simulation more interesting by simulating other behaviors, such as sexual reproduction where the animals have gender and can mate.

The array type world is a container for the life forms. The container has the responsibility for creating its current pattern. It needs to have ownership of the living objects so as to allocate new ones and delete old ones.

```
//world is all empty
void init(world w)
{
    int i, j;

    for (i = 0; i < N; ++i)
        for (j = 0; j < N; ++j)
            w[i][j] = new empty(i,j);
}

//new world w_new is computed from old world w_old
void update(world w_new, world w_old)
{
    int i, j;

    for (i = 1; i < N - 1; ++i)  //borders are taboo
        for (j = 1; j < N - 1; ++j)
            w_new[i][j] = w_old[i][j] -> next(w_old);
}
```

```
//clean world up
void dele(world w)
{
   int i, j;

   for (i = 1; i < N - 1; ++i)
      for (j = 1; j < N - 1; ++j)
         delete(w[i][j]);
}
```

The simulation has an odd and even world. Each alternates as the basis for the next cycle's calculations.

```
main()
{
   world odd, even;
   int    i, row, column, alive;

   init(odd);  init(even);

   //we initialize inside part of world to non-empty types
   eden(even);              //generate initial world
   pr_state(even);          //print garden of eden state

   for (i = 0; i < CYCLES; ++i) {  //simulation
      if (i % 2) {
         update(even, odd);
         pr_state(even);
         dele(odd);
      }
      else {
         update(odd, even);
         pr_state(odd);
         dele(even);
      }
   }
   return (0);
}
```

We leave you to experiment with the writing of pr_state() and eden().

6.7 MULTIPLE INHERITANCE

The examples in the text thus far require only single inheritance; that is, they require that a class be derived from a single base class. This feature can lead to a chain of derivations in which class B is derived from class A, and class C is derived from class B, ..., and class N is derived from class M. In effect, N ends up being based on A, B, ..., M. This chain must not be circular, however, so a class cannot have itself as an ancestor.

Multiple inheritance (MI) allows a derived class to be derived from more than one base class. The syntax of class headers is extended to allow a list of base classes and their privacy designations. An example is

```
class tools {
   . . .

};

class parts {
   . . .

};

class labor {
   . . .

};

class plans: public tools, public parts, public labor {
   . . .

};
```

In this example the derived class plans publicly inherits the members of all three base classes. This parental relationship is described by the inheritance *directed acyclic graph* (DAG). The DAG is a graph structure whose nodes are classes and whose directed edges point from base to derived class. To be legal it cannot be circular, so no class may, through its inheritance chain, inherit from itself.

In deriving an identically named member from different classes, ambiguities may arise. These derivations are allowed, provided the user does not make an ambiguous reference to such a member. For example,

```
class tools {
public:
    int cost();
    . . .
};

class labor {
public:
    int cost();
    . . .
};

class parts {
public:
    int cost();
    . . .
};

class plans: public tools, public parts, public labor {
public:
    int tot_cost() { return (parts::cost() + labor::cost()); }
    . . .
};

int foo()
{
    int  price;
    plans* ptr;

    price = ptr -> cost();
    . . .
}
```

In the body of foo, the reference to cost is inherently ambiguous. It can be resolved by either properly qualifying cost using the scope resolution operator or adding a member cost to the derived class plans.

With multiple inheritance, two base classes can be derived from a common ancestor. If both base classes are used in the ordinary way by their derived class, that class has two subobjects of the common ancestor. This duplication, if not desirable, can be eliminated by using virtual inheritance. An example is

```
class under_grad: public virtual student {
   . . .

};
class grad: public virtual student {
   . . .

};

class department: public under_grad, public grad {
   . . .

};
```

Without the use of `virtual` in this example, `class department` would have objects of `class::under_grad::student` and `class::grad::student`.

The order of execution for initializing constructors in base and member constructors is

1. Base class are initialized in declaration order.

2. Members are initialized in declaration order.

Virtual base classes are constructed before any of their derived classes. They are constructed before any non-virtual base classes. Their construction order depends on their DAG. It is a depth-first, left-to-right order. Destructors are invoked in reverse order of constructors. These rules, although complicated, should conform to one's intuition.

A parenthesized argument list that implicitly calls the base class constructor is allowed for single inheritance, but it is poor style. Finally, the associated destructors are called in the reverse order from constructor invocation.

Let us illustrate by elaborating on a previous example.

```
class tools {
public:
    tools(char*);
    ~tools();
    . . .
};

class parts {
public:
    parts(char*);
    ~parts();
    . . .
};

class labor {
public:
    labor(int);
    ~labor();
    . . .
};

class plans: public tools, public parts, public labor {
public:
    plans(int m): tools("lathe"), parts("widget"), labor(m), a(m)
        { . . . }
    ~plans();
    . . .
private:
    . . .
    special a;   //member class with constructor
};
```

The constructor-initializing list and the member-initializing list appear in declaration order. This is good style as it avoids confusion and should match declaration order, as a documentation aid. Since its constructor was last, the ~a() destructor is invoked first, followed by ~labor(), ~parts(), ~tools(), and ~plans().

These examples are meant to illustrate syntax and semantics for using MI. MI is a feature that many OOP languages do without, and this was also the case for C++ prior to 1988. It is beyond the scope of this book to discuss the nuances of when MI should be used. Some guidelines are that the derived class has a well-understood ISA relationship with all its base classes. In effect, the derived class abstraction is the non-empty intersection of the base classes' abstractions. So one might derive a warship from a class representing boats and a class representing weapons. A warship is a ship. A warship is a weapon. But even this is not clear cut, as a warship is a ship that has weapons. So possibly it should be a class derived from ship with a member array of weapons.

MI is used to provide different concrete implementations of the same abstraction.

```
class Abstraction {/* virtual functions - an interface */ };

class Concrete_1 {/* implementation scheme */ };
class Concrete_2 {/* implementation scheme */ };

class Abs_1 : public Abstraction, private Concrete_1 {
    /*implementation 1*/
};
```

In this scheme we can *mix in* various interfaces and implementations. This can be convenient for building large reusable software libraries.

For a concrete worked-out example of MI, the implementation of the class iostream on many systems is derived from istream and ostream.

6.8 DETAILED C++ CONSIDERATIONS

Learning C++ can be difficult because of the many extensions and rules pertaining to the use of functions. We have now completed describing most of the extensions and can turn to some of the added rules.

1. A virtual function and its derived instances having the same signature must have the same return type. The virtual function redefinition is called *overriding*. Notice that non-virtual member functions having the same signature can have different return types in derived classes (see Exercise 17). The return type rule is undergoing reconsideration by the ANSI standards committee (see Appendix D).

2. All member functions (except constructors) and overloaded new and delete can be virtual.

3. Constructors, destructors, overloaded operator=, and friends are not inherited.

4. Overloading the operators =, (), [], and -> can be done only with non-static member functions. Conversion functions of the form operator

type( ) also must be done only with nonstatic member functions. Overloading operators `new` and `delete` can be done only with static member functions. Other overloadable operators can be done with either friend, member, or ordinary functions.

5. A `union` may have constructors and destructors but not virtual functions. A `union` cannot serve as a base class, nor can it have a base class. Members of a `union` cannot require constructors or destructors.

6. Access modification is possible, but using it with public inheritance destroys the subtype relationship. Access modification cannot broaden visibility. This can be seen in the following example:

```
//Access modification
class B {
public:
    int k;
protected:
    int j, n;
private:
    int i;
};

class D: public B {
public:
    int m;
    B::n;        //illegal protected access cannot be broadened
private:
    B::j;        //otherwise default is protected
};
```

6.9 PRAGMATICS

Single inheritance (SI) conforms to a hierarchical decomposition of the key objects in the domain of discourse. Multiple inheritance (MI) is more troubling as a modeling or problem-solving concept. In MI we are saying that the new object is composed of several pre-existing objects and is usefully thought of as a form of each. The *mix in* concept is sometimes used to mean a class composed using MI, in which each base class is orthogonal. Much of the time there is an alternative HASA formulation. For example, is a vampire bat a mammal that happens to fly, a flying machine that happens to be an animal, or both a flying machine

6.10 Summary

1. Inheritance is the mechanism of deriving a new class from an old one. That is, the existing class can be added to or altered to create the derived class. Through inheritance, a hierarchy of related ADTs can be created that share code.

2. A class can be derived from an existing class using the form

   class *class-name*: (public|protected|private)*optional base-class-name*
   {
       member declarations
   };

   As usual, the keyword class can be replaced by the keyword struct, with the usual implication that members are by default public.

3. The keywords public, private, and protected are available as visibility modifiers for class members. A public member is visible throughout its scope. A private member is visible to other member functions within its own class. A protected member is visible to other member functions within its class and any class immediately derived from it. These visibility modifiers can be used within a class declaration in any order and with any frequency.

4. The derived class has its own constructors that invoke the base class constructor. A special syntax passes arguments from the derived class constructor back to the base class constructor.

   function header: *base-class-name* (*argument list*)

5. A publicly derived class is a subtype of its base class. A variable of the derived class can in many ways be treated as if it were the base class type. A pointer whose type is pointer to base class can point to objects of the publicly derived class type.

6. A reference to the derived class may be implicitly converted to a reference to the public base class. It is possible to declare a reference to a base class and initialize it to a reference to an object of the publicly derived class.

7. The keyword virtual is a function specifier that provides a mechanism to dynamically select at run-time the appropriate member function

from among base and derived class functions. It may be used only to modify member function declarations. This is called *overriding*. This ability to dynamically select a routine appropriate to an object's type is also called *polymorphism*.

8. Inheritance provides for code reuse. The derived class inherits the base class code. Typically the derived class modifies and extends the base class. Public inheritance also creates a type hierarchy. It allows further generality by providing additional implicit type conversions. It also, at a run-time cost, allows for run-time selection of overridden virtual functions. Facilities that allow the implementation of ADTs, inheritance, and the ability to process objects dynamically are the essentials of OOP.

6.11 Exercises

1. Change the declaration of grad_student found in Section 6.1 to

```
enum {ta, ra, fellowship, other} support;
class grad_student: student {
public:
   grad_student
      (char* nm, int id, double g, year x, support t, char* d, char* th);
   char dept[10];
   char thesis[80];
   void print();
};
```

Explain what goes wrong in the following code:

```
main()
{
   grad_student s;

   strcpy(s.name, "Charles Babbage");
   . . .
}
```

2. The safe array member vect_bnd::operator[] in Section 6.3 is guaranteed to be passed a properly indexed element in the return statement

```
return (vect::operator[](i - l_bnd));
```

This means that the array index is unnecessarily checked twice. Add an unchecked access function as a member function of class vect.

```
int& elem(int i);   //unchecked indexing
```

Use this to modify the return statement so as not to recheck the index.

3. Write a member function print that prints out a variable of type vect_bnd.

4. Write two new constructors for vect_bnd.

```
//initialize by vect_bnd
vect_bnd::vect_bnd(const vect_bnd& v);

//initialize by array
vect_bnd::vect_bnd(const int a[], int l, int u);
```

5. Develop a type matrix_bnd.

```
class matrix_bnd: public matrix {
public:
    matrix_bnd(const matrix_bnd& m); //copy existing matrix
    matrix_bnd();                    //5 x 5 matrix
    matrix_bnd(int l1, int u1, int l2, int u2);
    void print();
       . . .
private:
    int lb1, lb2, ub1, ub2;
    int size1, size2;
};
```

This is a two-dimensional safe array type that has both upper and lower bounds for each index. Write constructors for this type and a print member function. You should write a member function

```
//reference to an individual element
int& element(int i, int j);
```

that accesses individual elements because overloading [] will not work. *Hint*: You can start by modifying the basic matrix class in Chapter 5, Exercise 4, or see the matrix code in Section 5.4. Also see Exercise 20.

6. For student and grad_student as defined in Section 6.2, code respective input member functions read that input data for each data member in their class. Use student::read to implement grad_student::read.

7. Pointer conversions, scope resolution, and explicit casting create a wide selection of possibilities. Using main from the *student* program in Section 6.2, which of the following work, and what is printed?

```
((grad_student *)ps) -> print();
((student *)pgs) -> print();    //grad_student::print
pgs -> student::print();
ps -> grad_student::print();
```

Print out and explain the results.

8. Modify class D from the *pure_polymorphism* program in Section 6.5 to be

```
class D2: private B {
public:
   B::i;   //access modification
   void print_i()
   {
      cout << i << " inside D2 and B::i is "
      << B::i << endl;
   }
};
```

What is changed in the output from that program?

9. The following uses class s_tree:

```
main()
{
   s_tree t;
   char    dat[80], *p;

   cout << "\nEnter strings; exit with an end-of-file\n";
   while ( cin >> dat ) {
      p = new char[strlen(dat) + 1];
      strcpy(p, dat);
      t.insert(p);
   }
   t.print();
   cout << "\n\n\n";
}
```

Use this code with redirection to produce an ordered count of each string occurrence in a file. The function cin >> dat returns true if the operation succeeds.

10. Change the code in Exercise 9 so as to use an arbitrary input file. To accomplish this, read a file name from a command-line argument and use that to open an ifstream. Appendix D shows how to use *fstream.h*.

11. For class gen_tree, write a destructor. Remember, this must traverse and individually delete nodes.

12. For class s_tree, write a destructor.

13. The printing routine for s_tree as written in this chapter is an *inorder* tree traversal.

```
void gen_tree::print(bnode* r);
{
   if (r != 0) {
      print (r -> left);
      ::print(r);    //inorder
      print (r -> right);
   }
}
```

Run the program using both *preorder* and *postorder* traversal. For preorder, the statement ::print(r) goes first, and for postorder it goes last.

14. Develop a class gen_vect that is a safe array of generic pointers. Derive a class s_vect that is a safe array of char*.

15. (Difficult) Using gen_tree derive a class itree that stores a vector of type int pointed at by the data member of each node. You must write an appropriate comp function.

16. Rewrite the code for gen_tree::insert to be more efficient. Do this by assigning the value of comp(temp -> data, d) to a temporary variable. This avoids the recomputation of a potentially expensive function call.

17. For the following program explain when overriding takes place? Also explain when overloading takes place.

```
//Override v. Overload
//    Title: overriding

#include <iostream.h>

class B {
public:
   B(int j = 0): i(j) {}
   virtual void print() const { cout << " i = " << i << endl; }
   void print(char *s) const { cout << s << i << endl; }
private:
   int i;
};

class D: public B {
public:
   D(int j = 0): B(5), i(j) {}
   void print() const { cout << " i = " << i << endl; }
   int print(char *s) const { cout << s << i << endl; return (i); }
private:
   int i;
};

main()
{
   B  b1, b2(10), *pb;
   D  d1, d2(10), *pd = &d2;

   b1.print();
   b2.print();
   d1.print();
   d2.print();
   b1.print("b1.i = ");
   b2.print("b2.i = ");
   d1.print("d1.i = ");
   d2.print("d2.i = ");
   pb = pd;
   pb -> print();
   pb -> print("d2.i = ");
   pd -> print();
   pd -> print("d2.i = ");
   return (0);
}
```

18. Define a base class person that contains information that is universal for all people. Include name, address, birthdate, and gender information. Derive from this class the following classes:

```
class student: virtual public person {
// . . . relevant additional state and behavior
};

class employee: virtual public person {
// . . . relevant additional state and behavior
};

class student_employee: public student, public employee {
// . . .
};
```

Write a program that reads a file of information and creates a list of persons. Process the list to create, in sorted order by last name, a list of all people, a list of people who are students, a list of people who are employees, and a list of people who are student-employees. On your system can you easily produce a list in sorted order of all students that are not employees?

19. **Project**: Design and implement a graphical user interface (GUI) for the predator-prey simulation. It is beyond the scope of this book to describe various available GUI toolkits. The InterViews package is one such that works on top of X and is written in C++. The program should draw each iteration of the simulation on the screen. You should be able to directly input "a garden of Eden" starting position. You should also be able to provide other settings for the simulation, such as the size of the simulation. More generally, can you allow the user to define other life forms and their rules for existing, eating, and reproducing? Make the GUI as easy to use as possible. The user should be able to position it on the screen and resize it. The user should have the ability to select icons for the various available life forms.

20. For the class matrix_bnd in Exercise 5, add the member

```
int& matrix_bnd::operator()(int i, int j)const;
```

It will have exactly the same semantics as the member matrix_bnd::assign(). There are several interesting things about overloading the function call operator. It can only be overloaded as a nonstatic member function and is unary. However, you get to specify the signature it accepts. In essence, its arguments are the this pointer arguments and the arguments conforming to the signature.

```
m(3, 5) = 6
```

is equivalent to

```
m.operator()(3, 5) = 6
```

CHAPTER 7

TEMPLATES

C++ uses the keyword template to provide *parametric polymorphism*. Parametric polymorphism allows the same code to be used with respect to different types where *the type is a parameter of the code body*. Many of our classes have been used to contain data of a particular type. Processing the data has the same form, regardless of type. Template class definitions and template function definitions give us the ability to reuse code in a simple type safe manner that allows the compiler to automate the process of type instantiation.

7.1 TEMPLATE CLASS STACK

Let us modify the stack type from Chapter 4 to have a parameterized type.

```
//template stack implementation
template <class TYPE>
class stack {
public:
    stack() :max_len(1000), top(EMPTY)
        { s = new TYPE[1000]; }
    stack(int size) :max_len(size), top(EMPTY)
        { s = new TYPE[size]; }
    ~stack() { delete []s; }
    void reset() { top = EMPTY; }
    void push(TYPE c) { s[++top] = c; }
    TYPE pop() { return (s[top--]); }
    TYPE top_of() const { return (s[top]); }
    boolean empty() const { return boolean(top == EMPTY); }
    boolean full() const { return boolean(top == max_len - 1); }
private:
    enum {EMPTY = -1};
    TYPE* s;
    int    max_len;
    int    top;
};
```

The syntax of the class declaration is prefaced by

```
template <class identifier>
```

This identifier is a template argument that essentially stands for an arbitrary type. Throughout the class definition the template argument can be used as a type name. This argument is instantiated in the actual declarations. An example of a stack declaration using this is

```
stack<char> stk_ch;            // 1000 element char stack
stack<char*>  stk_str(200);    // 200 element char* stack
stack<complex> stk_cmplx(100); // 100 element complex stack
```

This mechanism saves our rewriting class declarations when the only variation would be type declarations. It is an alternative scheme to using void* as a universal pointer type.

When processing such a type, the code must always use the angle brackets as part of the declaration.

```
//Reversing a series of char* represented strings
void reverse(char* str[], int n)
{
    stack<char*> stk(n);

    for (int i = 0; i < n; ++i)
        stk.push(str[i]);
    for (i = 0; i < n; ++i)
        str[i] = stk.pop();
}


//Initializing a stack of complex numbers from an array
void init(complex c[], stack<complex> stk, n)
{
    for (int i = 0; i < n; ++i)
        stk.push(c[i]);
}
```

Member functions, when declared and defined inside the class, are as usual inline. When defined externally the full angle bracket declaration must be used. So the function

```
TYPE top_of() const { return (s[top]); }
```

when defined outside the template class, is written as

```
template<class TYPE> TYPE stack<TYPE>::top_of() const { return (s[top]); }
```

Yes, this is ugly and takes some getting used to, but otherwise the compiler does not know that TYPE is a template argument.

7.2 FUNCTION TEMPLATES

Many functions have the same code body, regardless of type—for example, initializing the contents of one array from another of the same type. The essential code is

```
for (i = 0; i < n; ++i)
    a[i] = b[i];
```

Most C programmers automate this with a simple macro.

```
void swap(char* s1, char* s2)
{
   int max_len;

   max_len = (strlen(s1) >= strlen(s2)) ? strlen(s1) : strlen(s2);
   char* temp = new char[max_len + 1];

   strcpy(temp, s1);
   strcpy(s1, s2);
   strcpy(s2, temp);
   delete []temp;
}
```

With this explicit case added, this nontemplate version, when an exact match to the signature of a swap() invocation, takes precedence over the exact match found by a template substitution.

The overloading function selection algorithm is as follows:

1. Exact match on a nontemplate function.

2. Exact match using a function template.

3. Ordinary argument resolution on a nontemplate function.

Note well that this algorithm is not universally in use. ATT C++ Release 3.0 relaxes the exact match condition on function templates, allowing both trivial conversions and base/derived pointer conversions. This is also expected to change in the ANSI C++ Standard.

7.3 CLASS TEMPLATES

In the stack<T> example we have an ordinary case of class parameterization. In this section we discuss various special features of parameterizing classes.

Friends

Template classes can contain friends. A friend function that does not use a template specification is universally a friend of all instantiations of the template class. A friend function that incorporates template arguments is specifically a friend of its instantiated class.

```
template <class T>
class matrix {
public:
   friend void foo_bar();  //universal
   friend vect<T> product(vect<T> v); //instantiated
   . . .
};
```

Static Members

Static members are not universal but are specific to each instantiation.

```
template <class T>
class foo {
public:
   static int count;
   . . .
};
foo<int> a;
foo<double> b;
```

The static variables foo<int>::count and foo<double>::count are distinct.

Class Template Arguments

Both classes and functions can have several class template arguments.
Let us write a function that converts one type of value to a second type,
provided the first type is at least as wide as the second.

```
template <class T1, class T2>
boolean coerce(T1& x, T2 y)
{
   if (sizeof(x) < sizeof(y))
      return false;
   x = (T1)y;
   return true;
}
```

In this template function two possibly distinct types are specified as template arguments.

   Other template arguments include constant expressions, function
names, and character strings.

```
template <int n, class T>
class assign_array {
public:
   T a[n];
};
```

```
assign_array<50, double> x, y;
x = y;  //should work efficiently
```

The benefits of this parameterization include allocation of the stack as opposed to allocation from free store. On many systems this is the more efficient regime. The type is bound to the particular integer constant, so operations involving compatible length arrays are type safe and checked at compile-time.

7.4 PARAMETERIZING THE CLASS *vect*

The class vect is a natural candidate for parameterization. We parameterize it and code an associated iterator class.

```
//Template based safe array type

enum boolean {false, true};

template <class T> class    vect_iterator;
template <class T>
class vect {
public:
   vect();                              //create a size 10 array
   vect(int n);                         //create a size n array
   vect(const vect& v);                 //initialization by vect
   vect(const T a[], int n);            //initialization by array
   ~vect() { delete []p; }              //destroy T's
   int  ub() const { return (size - 1); }  //upper bound
   T& operator[](int i) const;          //range checked element
   vect& operator=(const vect& v);
   void print() const;
   friend class vect_iterator<T>;
private:
   T* p;                                //base pointer
   int size;                            //number of elements
};
```

Basically, everywhere the previous vect class used int as the value to be stored in individual elements, the template definition uses T. So the declaration of the private base pointer p is now of type T.

Note the need for a forward declaration of the associated iterator class vect_iterator. It also follows template syntax.

```
template<class T>
class vect_iterator {
public:
    vect_iterator(vect<T>& v):cur_ind(0),pv(&v) {}
    boolean successor();
    boolean predecessor();
    T& item() const { return (pv -> p[cur_ind] ); }
    void reset(int n = 0){cur_ind = n % pv -> size;}
    int position() const { return (cur_ind); }
private:
    vect<T>* pv;
    int cur_ind;
};
```

Obviously the associated iterator class also requires parameterization. The member function syntax, when defined outside of the class declaration, requires the preface template<class T>.

```
template<class T>
boolean vect_iterator<T>::successor()
{
    if (cur_ind >= pv -> size - 1)
        return (false);
    else {
        ++cur_ind;
        return ( truc );
    }
}

template<class T>
boolean vect_iterator<T>::predecessor()
{
    if (cur_ind <= 0)
        return (false);
    else {
        --cur_ind;
        return ( true );
    }
}
```

A member function's definition in file scope includes the scope-resolved label *class name*<T>. The following constructors for vect<T> use T as the type specification to new.

```
template<class T>
vect<T>::vect()
{
  size = 10;
  p = new T[size];
}

template<class T>
vect<T>::vect(int n)
{
  if (n < 1) {
     cerr << "illegal vect size: " << n << endl;
     exit(1);
  }
  size = n;
  p = new T[size];
}

template<class T>
vect<T>::vect(const T a[], int n)
{
  if (n < 1) {
     cerr << "illegal vect size: " << n << endl;
     exit(1);
  }
  size = n;
  p = new T[size];
  for (int i = 0; i < size; ++i)
     p[i] = a[i];
}

template<class T>
vect<T>::vect(const vect<T>& v)
{
  size = v.size;
  p = new T[size];
  for (int i = 0; i < size; ++i)
     p[i] = v.p[i];
}
```

The return type for the bracket operator is again T, as this is an item value stored in the container cell.

```
template<class T>
T& vect<T>::operator[](int i) const
{
   if (i < 0 || i > ub()) {
      cerr << "illegal vect index: " << i << endl;
      exit(1);
   }
   return (p[i]);
}

template<class T>
vect<T>& vect<T>::operator=(const vect<T>& v)
{
   int s = (size < v.size) ? size : v.size;

   if (v.size != size)
      cerr << "copying different size arrays "
           << size << " and " << v.size << endl;
   for (int i = 0; i < s; ++i)
      p[i] = v.p[i];
   return (*this);
}
```

Client code is almost as simple as with nonparameterized declarations. To use these declarations, one only adds within angle brackets the specific type that instantiates the template. These types can be native types, such as int in the example, or user-defined types. We leave as an exercise writing template<class T> void vect<T>::print().

The following code uses these templates:

```
main()
{
   vect<int> v(8);  vect_iterator<int> a(v);

   for (int i = 0; i < 8; ++i)
      v[i] = i * i;
   do
      cout << a.item() << '\t';
   while (a.successor());
   cout << endl;
   v.print();
}
```

7.5 PARAMETERIZED BINARY SEARCH TREE

Parametric polymorphism is achievable with void * generic pointers. We saw this in Section 6.4. In this section, for comparison purposes, we develop the same code as a parameterized binary search tree type.

We start by parameterizing b_node. The key is to change the p_gen variables into a parameterized type.

```
//Template Version of GenTree.
#include <iostream.h>
template <class T> class gen_tree; //forward decl

template <class T>
class bnode {
private:
   friend  class gen_tree<T>;
   bnode<T>*  left;
   bnode<T>*  right;
   T       data;
   int     count;
   bnode(T d, bnode<T>* l, bnode<T>* r)
        : data(d), left(l), right(r), count(1){}
   void print() const { cout << data << " : " << count << '\t'; }
};
```

Notice that the tree stores type T data. This need not be a pointer type. Notationally the internal self-referential pointers left and right are of type bnode<T>*. The notation is ugly but necessary. The inline bnode<T>::print() function is expected to have operator<<() defined as an output operator. If this is not the case, the instantiation fails at compile-time.

```
template <class T>
class gen_tree {
public:
   gen_tree() { root = 0; }
   void insert(T d);
   T find(T d) const { return (find(root, d)); }
   void print() const { print(root);}
private:
   bnode<T>* root;
   T find(bnode<T>* r, T d) const;
   void print(bnode<T>* r) const;
};
```

The generic tree type gentree<T> is instantiated to store T data using the insertion routine insert() to build the binary sorted tree. Because this class is not designed for inheritance, as was the case with the corresponding class in Section 6.4, auxiliary functions can be given private access.

The friend function comp() is a parameterized external function. We have two forms of it. In its general form it uses existing or user-supplied meanings for == and <. When lexicographic comparison on char* is needed, a specific implementation of this function is required.

```
#include <string.h>
template <class T>  //general case
int comp(T i, T j)
{
    if (i == j)    //assumes == < defined for T
        return 0;
    else
        return (i < j)? -1 : 1;
}

int comp(char* i, char* j) //specific case for char*
{
    return (strcmp(i, j));
}
```

The implementation of specific generic member functions requires little modification from the code in Section 6.4. Notice how the new operator needs to create a bnode<T> object.

```
template <class T>
void gen_tree<T>::insert(T d)
{
   bnode<T>* temp = root;
   bnode<T>* old;

   if (root == 0) {
      root = new bnode<T>(d, 0, 0);
      return;
   }
   while (temp != 0) {
      old = temp;
      if (comp(temp -> data, d) == 0) {
         (temp -> count)++;
         return;
      }
      if (comp(temp -> data, d) > 0)
         temp = temp -> left;
      else
         temp = temp -> right;
   }
   if (comp(old -> data, d) > 0)
      old -> left = new bnode<T>(d, 0, 0);
   else
      old -> right = new bnode<T>(d, 0, 0);
}
```

Other member functions require simple modifications to accommodate parameterization. Almost all changes to the concrete case occur in declarations.

```
template <class T>
T gen_tree<T>::find(bnode<T>* r, T d) const
{
   if (r == 0)
      return (0);
   else if (comp(r -> data, d) ==  0)
      return (r -> data);
   else if (comp(r -> data, d) > 0)
      return (find( r -> left, d));
   else
      return (find( r -> right, d));
}
```

```
template <class T>
void gen_tree<T>:: print(bnode<T> *r)
{
   if (r != 0) {
      print( r -> left);
      r -> bnode<T>::print();
      print ( r -> right);
   }
}
```

Client code needs only instantiation of the particular type to be stored in the binary trees. Here we show two uses: one to sort char* strings and the second to sort integers.

```
main()
{
   char dat[256];
   gen_tree<char*>   t;
   char*   p;

   while (cin>>dat){
      p = new char[strlen(dat) + 1];
      strcpy(p, dat);
      t.insert(p);
   }
   t.print();
   cout << "EOF\n\n";

   gen_tree<int>  i_tree;

   for (int i = 15; i > -5; --i)
      i_tree.insert(i), i_tree.insert(i);
   i_tree.print();
}
```

7.6 INHERITANCE

Parameterized types can be reused through inheritance. Such use parallels the use of inheritance in deriving ordinary classes. Templates and inheritance are both mechanism for code reuse, and both can involve polymorphism. They are distinct features of C++ and as such combine in different forms. A template class can be derived from an ordinary class.

An ordinary class can derive from an instantiated template class. A template class can derive from a template class. Each of these possibilities leads to different relationships.

In some situations templates lead to unacceptable cost in the size of the object module. Each instantiated template class requires its own compiled object module. Consider the gen_tree class in Chapter 6. It provided reuse by providing code that was readily converted through inheritance and casting to specifically useful pointer types. Its drawback was that each pointer type required individual coding of its class definition. This can be remedied by using a template to inherit the base class.

```
//Base class is used to keep code body small.

template <class T>
class pointer_tree : private gen_tree {
public:
   pointer_tree() {}
   void  insert(T* d) { gen_tree::insert(d); }
   T* find(T* d)   const
 { return ((T*)gen_tree::find(d)); }
   void  print() { gen_tree::print(); }
};
```

The object code for gen_tree is relatively large and is needed only once. The interface pointer_tree<*type*> requires only a small object module for each instantiation. This is a major saving vis-a-vis the template solution of Section 7.5. This implementation has the drawback of hand-coding each friend function.

The derivation of a class from an instantiated template class is basically no different than ordinary inheritance. In the following example we reuse stack<char> as a base class for a safe character stack.

```
//safe character stack
#include <assert.h>

class safe_char_stack : public stack<char> {
public:
   // test push and pop
   void push(char c) { assert (!full()); stack<char>::push(c);}
   char pop() { assert (!empty()); return (stack<char>::pop());}
};
```

The instantiated class stack<char> is generated and reused by safe_char_stack.

This last example can be usefully generalized to a template class.

```
//parameterized safe stack
template <class TYPE>
class safe_stack : public stack<TYPE> {
public:
    void push(TYPE c) { assert (!full()); stack<TYPE>::push(c);}
    TYPE pop() { assert (!empty()); return (stack<TYPE>::pop());}
};
```

It is important to notice the linkage between base class and derived class. Both require the same instantiated type. Each pair of base and derived classes is independent of all other pairs.

7.7 PRAGMATICS

Orthogonality is the property of a design that chooses independent features interacting together to form its basis. One benefit of an orthogonal design is a user can expect a feature of a design to work in the same way with other features without special restrictions. Orthogonality is a form of minimalism. It is a useful guideline in assessing a class design or a language design.

Among the nonorthogonal features of C++ is the distinction between what can be a template parameter for functions versus what can be a template parameter for classes. Recall for functions, only class arguments are possible. Furthermore, these class arguments must occur in the template function as part of the type description of at least one of the function parameters. Therefore, this is okay:

```
template <class TYPE>
void maxelement(TYPE a[], TYPE& max, int size);

template <class TYPE>
int find(TYPE* data);
```

But this is illegal:

```
template <class TYPE>
TYPE convert(int i) { TYPE temp(i); return (temp); }
```

This restriction exists because the compiler must use the arguments at function invocation to deduce which actual functions will be created. An argument in favor of this restriction is that a function definition allows for parameters that are not type parameters already. Also we can work around this by creating a class whose sole member is a static function appropriately parameterized.

```
template <class TYPE>  //also other arguments are possible
class conversion {
    static TYPE convert(int i) { TYPE temp(i); return (temp); }
};
```

7.8 Summary

1. C++ uses the keyword `template` to provide *parametric polymorphism*. Parametric polymorphism allows the same code to be used with respect to different types where *the type is a parameter of the code body*.

2. The syntax of the class declaration is prefaced by

```
template <class identifier >
```

This identifier is a template argument that essentially stands for an arbitrary type. Throughout the class definition the template argument can be used as a type name. This argument is instantiated in the actual declarations.

3. Templates provide a further polymorphic language mechanism for parameterizing function definitions. For example,

```
template<class TYPE>
void swap(TYPE& a, TYPE& b)
{
    TYPE temp = a;

    a = b;
    b = temp;
}
```

can be used to generate any simple swapping function for two variables.

4. Both classes and functions can have several class template arguments. In addition to class template arguments, class template definitions can include constant expressions, function names, and character strings as template arguments. A common case is to have an int argument that parameterizes an important size characteristic within the class definition, as in

```
template <int n, class T>
class assign_array {
public:
    T a[n];
};
assign_array<50, double> x, y;
```

5. Parameterized types can be reused through inheritance. Such use parallels the use of inheritance in deriving ordinary classes. Templates and inheritance are both mechanism for code reuse, and both can involve polymorphism. A template class can be derived from an ordinary class. An ordinary class can derive from an instantiated template class. A template class can derive from a template class.

6. The overloading function selection algorithm is as follows:

   1. Exact match on a nontemplate function.
   2. Exact match using a function template.
   3. Ordinary argument resolution on a nontemplate function.

   Note well that this algorithm is not universally in use. ATT C++ Release 3.0 relaxes the exact match condition on function templates, allowing both trivial conversions and base/derived pointer conversions. This is also expected to change in the ANSI C++ Standard.

7. Orthogonality is the property of a design that chooses independent features interacting together to form its basis. One benefit of an orthogonal design is a user can expect a feature of a design to work in the same way with other features without special restrictions. Orthogonality is a form of minimalism. It is a useful guideline in assessing a class design or a language design.

7.9 Exercises

1. Rewrite stack<T> to accept an integer value for the default size of the stack. Now client code can use declarations such as

   ```
   stack<int, 100> s1, s2;
   stack<char, 5000> sc1, sc2, sc3;
   ```

   Discuss the pros and cons of this additional parameterization.

2. Define a template for fixed-length stacks that allocate a compile-time-determined size array to store the stacked values.

3. Write a generic cycle() function with the following definition and test it:

   ```
   template<class TYPE>
   void cycle(TYPE& a, TYPE& b, TYPE& c)
   {
       // replace a's value by b's and b's by c's and c's by a's

   }
   ```

4. Write a generic function that, given an arbitrary array and its size, rotates its values with

   ```
   a[1] = a[0] , a[1] = a[2], ...,
   a[size - 1] = a[size - 2], a[0] = a[size - 1]
   ```

5. Write the member function template<class T> void vect<T>::print().

6. Write a generic function that requires that two arrays of different type be swapped. You can assume that both array types have elements that are assignment-convertible.

7. In the following code using the safe character stack s, will an assertion fail? If it fails, what will the last value of i be before the error exit?

```
main()
{
    safe_char_stack s;
    int i = 0;

    while ( 1 ) {
        cout << ++i << endl;
        s.push('a');
        s.push('a');
        cout << s.pop();
    }
}
```

8. Write a parameterized set type whose parameter is the size of the set. Create a set conversion operator that works between different-sized sets. A larger-sized set should be truncated in a "natural" way in being converted to a smaller set type. Is there any reasons to prefer this design to one that allows a universal set type that can handle arbitrary size sets? In this case the size parameter would be an argument to the set constructor.

9. Using vect<T> and its associated iterator class, code a generic vector sorting routine.

10. **Project:** Create a parametric string type. The basic type is to act as a container class that contains a class T object. In the prototype case the object is a char. The normal *end-of-string* sentinel is 0. The standard behavior models the functions found in *string.h*. The class definition could parameterize the sentinel as well.

11. Sorting functions are natural candidates for parameterization. The following is a generic bubblesort:

CHAPTER 8

EXCEPTIONS

This chapter describes exception handling in C++, which is based on the proposed ANSI standard and as such may not be currently released with your compiler. *Exceptions* generally are unexpected error conditions. Normally these conditions terminate the user program with a system-provided error message. An example is floating-point division by zero. Usually the system aborts the running program. With C++ the programmer can attempt to recover from these conditions and continue program execution.

We discuss *assertions* as a means to cope with error conditions and exceptions. An exception can be considered a breakdown in the contractual guarantee between the code provider, or the *manufacturer*, and the user of the code, or the *client* (see Section 9.3). In this model the client guarantees that the conditions for applying the code exist, and the manufacturer guarantees that, under these provisions, the code will work correctly. Assertions provide the various guarantees.

8.1 USING *assert.h*

Program correctness can be viewed in part as a proof that the computation terminated with correct output dependent on correct input. The invoker of the computation had the responsibility of providing correct input. This was a precondition. The computation, if successful, satisfied a postcondition. The intention of providing a fully formal proof of correctness is an idealization that is not usually done. Nevertheless, such assertions can be monitored at run-time to provide very useful diagnostics. Indeed, the discipline of thinking out appropriate assertions frequently causes the programmer to avoid bugs and pitfalls.

In the C and C++ community, an increasing emphasis is placed on the use of assertions. The standard library *assert.h* provides a macro assert and is invoked as though its function signature is

```
void assert(int expression);
```

If the expression evaluates as false, then execution is aborted with diagnostic output. The assertions are discarded if the macro NDEBUG is defined. Consider allocation to our safe array type vect (Chapter 4):

```
vect::vect(int n)
{
    if (n < 1) {
        cerr << "illegal vect size " << n << endl;
        exit(1);
    }
    size = n;
    p = new int[size];
}
```

We replace this with

```
vect::vect(int n)
{
    assert (n > 0);  //contractual precondition
    size = n;
    p = new int[size];
    assert (p != 0); //contractual postcondition
}
```

The use of assertions replace the ad hoc use of conditional tests with a more uniform methodology. This is conducive to better practice. The down side is that the assertion methodology does not allow a retry or other repair strategy to continue program execution. Also asserions do not allow a customized error message. Though it would be easy to add this capability.

It is possible to make this a slightly more sophisticated scheme by providing different testing levels, as found in the Borland C++ *checks.h* file. Under this package the flag _DEBUG can be set to

```
_DEBUG 0   no testing
_DEBUG 1   PRECONDITION tests only
_DEBUG 2   CHECK tests also
```

The idea is that once the library functions are thought to be correct, the level of checking is reduced to only testing preconditions. Once the client code is debugged, all testing can be suspended.

8.2 C++ EXCEPTIONS

C++ introduces an exception-handling mechanism that is sensitive to context. It is not intended to handle the asynchronous exceptions defined in *signal.h*, such as a floating-point exception indicated by SIGFPE. The context for raising an exception is a try block. Handlers are declared at the end of a try block with the keyword catch.

C++ code can directly raise an exception in a try block by using the throw expression. The exception is handled by invoking an appropriate *handler* selected from the list found immediately after the handler's try block. A simple example is

```
vect::vect(int n)
{
    if (n < 1)
        throw (n);
    p = new int[n];
    if (p == 0)
        throw ("FREE STORE EXHAUSTED");
}

void g()
{
    try {
        vect  a(n), b(n);
        . . .

    }
    catch(int n) { . . . } //catches an incorrect size
    catch(char* error) { . . . } //catches free store exhaustion
}
```

The first throw() has an integer argument and matches the catch(int n) signature. This handler is expected to perform an appropriate action when an incorrect array size has been passed as an argument to the constructor. For example, an error message and abort are normal actions. The second throw() has a pointer to character argument and matches the catch(char* error) signature.

8.3 THROWING EXCEPTIONS

Syntactically, *throw expressions* come in two forms:

```
throw
throw expression
```

The throw expression raises an exception. The innermost try block in which an exception is raised is used to select the catch statement that processes the exception. The throw expression with no argument "rethrows" the current exception. Typically it is used when one wants a second handler called from the first handler to further process the exception.

The expression thrown is a temporary static object that persists until exception handling is exited. The expression is caught by a handler that may use this value.

```
void foo()
{
   int i;
   . . .
   throw i;
}

main()
{
   try {
      foo();
   }
   catch(int n) { . . . }
}
```

The integer value thrown by throw i persists until the handler with the integer signature catch(int n) exits. This value is available for use within the handler as its argument.

When a nested function throws an exception, the process stack is "unwound" until an exception handler is found. This means that block exit from each terminated local process causes automatic objects to be destroyed.

```
void foo()
{
   int i, j;
   . . .
   throw i;
   . . .
}

void call_foo()
{
    int k;
    . . .
    foo();
    . . .
}

main()
{
   try {
      call_foo();  //foo is exited with i and j destroyed
   }
   catch(int n) { . . . }
}
```

An example of rethrowing of an exception is as follows:

```
catch(int n)
{
  . . .
  throw;  //rethrown
}
```

Assuming the thrown expression was of integer type, the rethrown exception is the same persistent integer object that is handled by the nearest handler suitable for that type.

Conceptually, the thrown expression "passes" information into the handlers. Frequently the handlers do not need this information. For example, a handler that prints a message and aborts needs no information from its environment. However, the user might want additional information printed or additional information that can be used to select or help decide the handler's action. In such cases, it is appropriate to package the information as an object.

```
class vect_error {
private:
   enum  error { bounds, heap, other} e_type;
   int  ub, index, size;
public:
   vect_error(error, int, int); //package out of bounds
   vect_error(error, int);      //package out of memory
   . . .
};
```

Now a throw expression using an object of type vect_error can be more informative to a handler than just throwing expressions of simple types.

```
   . . .
throw vect_error(bounds, i, ub);
   . . .
```

8.4 TRY BLOCKS

Syntactically, a *try block* has the form

```
try
compound statement
handler list
```

The try block is the context for deciding which handlers are invoked on a raised exception. The order in which handlers are defined determines the order in which a handler for a raised exception of matching type will be tried.

```
try {
    . . .
    throw ("SOS");
    . . .
    io_condition eof(argv[i]);
    throw (eof);
    . . .
}
catch(const char*) {  . . . }
catch(io_condition& x) {  . . . }
```

A throw expression matches the catch argument, if it is one of the following:

- An exact match.

- A public base class of a derived type that is what is thrown.

- A thrown object type that is a pointer type convertible to a pointer type that is the catch argument.

It is an error to list handlers in an order that prevents them from being called. An example is

```
catch(void*)  //any char* would match
catch(char*)
catch(BaseTypeError&)  //would always be called for DerivedTypeError
catch(DerivedTypeError&)
```

Try blocks can be nested. If no matching handler is available in the immediate try block, a handler is selected from its immediately surrounding try block. If no handler can be found that matches, then a default behavior is used.

8.5 HANDLERS

Syntactically, a *handler* has the form

```
catch ( formal argument )
compound statement
```

The catch looks like a function declaration of one argument without a
return type.

```
catch(char* message)
{
   cerr << message << endl;
   exit(1);
}

catch( ... )  //default action to be taken
{
   cerr << "THAT'S ALL FOLKS." << endl;
   abort();
}
```

An ellipsis signature matching any argument type is allowed. Also, the
formal argument can be an abstract declaration, meaning it can have type
information without a variable name.

The handler is invoked by an appropriate throw expression. At that
point the try block in effect is exited. The system calls cleanup functions
that include destructors for any objects that were local to the try block. A
partially constructed object will have destructors invoked on any parts of
them that are constructed subobjects.

8.6 EXCEPTION SPECIFICATION

Syntactically, an exception specification is part of a function declaration
and has the form

function header throw (*type list*)

The type list is the list of types that a throw expression within the function
can have. If the list is empty, the compiler may assume that no throw will
be executed by the function, either directly or indirectly.

```
void foo() throw(int, over_flow);
void noex(int i) throw();
```

If an exception specification is left off, then the assumption is that an
arbitrary exception can be thrown by such a function. Violations of these
specifications are run-time errors.

8.7 *terminate()* AND *unexpected()*

The system-provided handler `terminate()` is called when no other handler has been provided to deal with an exception. By default, the `abort()` function is called. Otherwise a `set_terminate()` can be used to provide a handler.

The system-provided handler `unexpected()` is called when a function throws an exception that was not in its exception specification list. By default, the `abort()` function is called. Otherwise a `set_unexpected()` can be used to provide a handler.

8.8 EXAMPLE EXCEPTION CODE

In this section we discuss some examples of exception code and their effects. Let us return to catching a size error in our *vect* constructor.

```
vect::vect(int n)
{
   if (n < 1)
      throw (n);
   p = new int[n];
   if (p == 0)
      throw ("FREE STORE EXHAUSTED");
}

void g(int m)
{
   try {
      vect a(m);
         . . .

   }
   catch(int n)
   {
      cerr << "SIZE ERROR " << n << endl;
      g(10);  //retry g with legal size
   }
   catch(const char* error)
   {
      cerr << error << endl;
      abort();
   }
}
```

The handler replaces an illegal value with a default legal value. This may be reasonable in the debugging phase for a system, where many routines are being integrated and tested. The system attempts to continue providing further diagnostics. It is analogous to a compiler attempting to continue to parse an incorrect program after a syntax error. Frequently the compiler provides additional error messages that prove useful.

The above constructor checks that only one variable has a legal value. It looks artificial because it replaces code that could directly replace the illegal value with a default by throwing an exception and allowing the handler to repair the value. However, in this form the separation of what is an "error" and how it is "handled" is clear. It is a clear methodology for developing fault-tolerant code.

More generally, one could have an object's constructor look like

```
Object::Object(arguments)
{
   if (illegal argument1 )
     throw expression1;
   if (illegal argument2 )
     throw expression2;
   . . .
   //attempt to construct
   . . .
}
```

The Object constructor now provides a set of thrown expressions for an illegal state. The try block can now use the information to repair or abort incorrect code.

```
try {

   . . . //fault tolerant code

}
catch(declaration1) { /* fixup this case */ }
catch(declaration2) { /* fixup this case */ }
   . . .
catch(declarationK) { /* fixup this case */ }
//correct or repaired - state values are now legal
```

When many distinct error conditions are useful for a given object's state, a class hierarchy can be used to create a selection of related types to be used as throw expressions.

```
class Object_Error {
public:
    Object_Error(arguments); //capture useful information
    members that contain thrown expression state
    virtual void repair()
        { cerr << "Repair failed in Object " << endl; abort(): }
};

class Object_Error_S1 : public Object_Error {
public:
    Object_Error_S1 (arguments);
    added members that contain thrown expression state
    void repair(); //override to provide suitable repair
};

   . . . //other derived error classes as needed
```

These hierarchies allow an appropriately ordered set of catches to handle exceptions in a logical sequence. Recall that a base class type should come after a derived class type in the list of catch declarations.

8.9 PRAGMATICS

Error recovery is chiefly and paradoxically concerned with writing correct programs. Exception handling is primarily a mechanism for error recovery and secondarily for transfer of control. In the client/manufacturer model, the manufacturer has a responsibility to provide software that produces correct output when used in an acceptable input state. The question for the manufacturer is how much error detection, and conceivably correction, should be built-in. The client is often better served by fault-detecting libraries and can decide whether to attempt to continue the computation.

Error recovery is based on transfer of control. Undisciplined transfer of control leads to chaos. In error recovery one assumes an exceptional condition has corrupted the computation. It becomes "dangerous" to continue the computation. It is analogous to driving a car after an indication that the steering is damaged. The disciplined recovery when "damage" happens is what useful exception handling entails.

In most cases programming that raises exceptions should print a diagnostic message and gracefully terminate. Special forms of processing, such as real-time processing, and fault-tolerant computing require that the system not go down. In these cases heroic attempts at repair are legitimate.

What can be agreed upon is that classes can usefully be provided with error conditions. The most common condition is the object has member values in illegal states—values they are not allowed to have. The system raises an exception for these cases, with the default action being program termination. This is analogous to the native types raising system-defined exceptions, such as `SIGFPE`.

Controversy arises regarding what kind of intervention is reasonable to keep the program running and to where the flow of control should return. C++ uses a termination model forcing the current try block to terminate. Under this regime one will either retry the code or ignore or substitute a default result and continue. Retrying the code seems the most likely to give a correct result.

Experience shows that code is usually too thinly commented. It is hard to imagine a program that would be too rich in assertions. Assertions and simple throws and catches that terminate the computation are parallel techniques. A well-conceived set of error conditions detectable by the user of an ADT is an important part of a good design. An over-reliance on exception handling in normal programming, beyond error detection and termination, is a sign that a program was ill-conceived with too many holes in its original form.

8.10 Summary

1. Exceptions are generally unexpected error conditions. Normally these conditions terminate the user program with a system-provided error message. An example is floating-point division by zero.

2. The standard library *assert.h* provides the macro

   ```
   void assert(int expression);
   ```

   If the `expression` evaluates as false, then execution is aborted with diagnostic output. The assertions are discarded if the macro `NDEBUG` is defined.

3. C++ code can directly raise an exception in a `try` block by using the `throw` expression. The exception is handled by invoking an appropriate

handler selected from a list found immediately after the handler's try block.

4. Syntactically, throw expressions come in two forms:

```
throw
throw expression
```

The throw expression raises an exception in a try block. The throw expression with no argument "rethrows" the current exception.

5. Syntactically, a try block has the form

```
try
compound statement
handler list
```

The try block is the context for deciding which handlers are invoked on a raised exception. The order in which handlers are defined determines the order in which a handler for a raised exception of matching type is tried.

6. Syntactically, a handler has the form

```
catch ( formal argument )
compound statement
```

The catch looks like a function declaration of one argument without a return type.

7. Syntactically, an exception specification is part of a function declaration and has the form

```
function header throw ( type list )
```

The type list is the list of types that a throw expression within the function can have. If the list is empty, the compiler may assume that no throw will be executed by the function, either directly or indirectly.

8. The system-provided handler terminate() is called when no other handler has been provided to deal with an exception. The system-provided handler unexpected() is called when a function throws an exception that was not in its exception specification list. By default, each of these call the abort() function.

8.11 Exercises

1. The following bubblesort does not work correctly:

```
//Incorrect bubblesort.
#include <iostream.h>

void swap(int a, int b)
{
    int temp = a;
    a = b;
    b = temp;
}

void bubble(int a[], int size)
{
    int i, j;

    for (i = 0; i != size; ++i)
        for (j = i ; j != size; ++j)
            if (a[j] < a [j + 1])
                swap (a[j], a[j + 1]);
};

main()
{
    int t[10] = { 9, 4, 6, 4, 5, 9, -3, 1, 0, 12};

    bubble(t, 10);
    for (int i = 0; i < 10; ++i)
        cout << t[i] << '\t';
    cout << "\nsorted? " << endl;
}
```

Place assertions in this code that test whether the code is working properly. Use this technique to write a correct program.

2. Use templates to write a generic version of the correct bubblesort, complete with assertions. Use a random-number generator to generate test data. On what types can this be made to work generically?

3. Code the member function vect::operator[](int) to throw an out-of-range exception if an incorrect index is used. Also code a reasonable catch that prints out the incorrect value and terminates. Execute a try block in which the exception occurs to test the code. Write a catch that

allows user intervention at the keyboard to produce a correct index and continue or retry the computation. Can this be done in a reasonable manner?

4. Recode the stack class of Chapter 6 to throw exceptions for as many conditions as you think are reasonable. Use an enumerated type to list the conditions.

```
enum stack_error {overflow, underflow, . . . };
```

Write a catch that uses a switch statement to select an appropriate message and terminate the computation.

5. Write a stack_error class that replaces the enumerated type of the previous exercise. Have this be a base class for a series of derived classes that encapsulates each specific exception condition. The catches should be able to use overridden virtual functions to process the various thrown exceptions.

CHAPTER 9

OOP USING C++

C++ is a hybrid language. The kernel language developed from C is classically used as a systems implementation language. Thus it is suitable for writing very efficient code that uses machine resources efficiently. The class-based additions to the language support the full range of OOP requirements; therefore it can be used to write reusable libraries, and it supports a polymorphic coding style.

Object-oriented programming (OOP) and C++ have been embraced by industry within a very short time frame. C++ is a hybrid OOP language. As such it allows a multiparadigmatic approach to coding. What surfaces as new is the use of polymorphism and inheritance. The traditional advantages of the C language as an efficient, powerful programming language are not lost. The new key ingredient is polymorphism—the ability to assume many forms.

9.1 OOP LANGUAGE REQUIREMENTS

An OOP language has

- *Encapsulation with data hiding:* the ability to distinguish an object's internal state and behavior from its external state and behavior.

- *Type extensibility:* the ability to add user-defined types to augment the native types.

- *Inheritance:* the ability to create new types by importing or reusing the description of existing types.

- *Polymorphism with dynamic binding:* the ability of objects to be responsible for interpreting function invocation.

These features cannot substitute for programmer discipline and community-observed convention but can be used to promote such behavior.

A typical procedural language, such as Pascal or C, has limited forms of type extensibility and encapsulation. Both languages have pointer and record types that provide these features. Additionally, C has an ad hoc scheme of file-oriented privacy, namely static file scope declarations. Languages such as Modula-2 and Ada have more complete forms of encapsulation, namely module and package, respectively. These languages readily allow users to build ADTs and provide significant library support for many application areas. A language such as pure LISP supports dynamic binding. The elements in OOP have been available in different languages for at least 25 years.

LISP, Simula, and Smalltalk have been in widespread use within both the academic and research communities. These languages are in many ways more elegant than C and C++. However, not until OOP elements were added to C was there any significant movement to using OOP in industry. In the face of the notorious software crisis, this is quite mystifying. Indeed, we have in the U.S. a *bandwagon effect* that cuts across companies, product lines, and application areas. Even Ada, a government-mandated language, has not been as well received. Our thesis is that industry needed to couple OOP with the ability to program effectively at a low level.

Also crucial is the ease of migration from C to C++. Unlike PL/1, whose heritage was FORTRAN and COBOL, and Ada, which is rooted in Pascal, C++ had C as a nearly proper subset. The installed base of C code did not need to be abandoned. These other languages required a nontrivial conversion process to modify existing code from their ancestor language.

The conventional academic wisdom is that excessive concern with efficiency is detrimental to good coding practices. This concern misses the obvious: Product competition is based on performance. Consequently, industry values low-level technology. In this environment C is a very effective tool.

9.2 ADTs IN NON-OOP LANGUAGES

Existing languages and methodology supported much of the OOP methodology by combining language features with programmer discipline. Programmer discipline and community conventions do work. It is possible in a non-OOP language to create and use ADTs. Three examples in the C community are the use of the pseudotypes string, Boolean, and file. They are pseudotypes in that they do not enjoy the same privileges as true types. What is gained by looking at these examples is a better understanding of the limits of extensibility in the non-OOP context.

A Boolean type is implicit in C. Namely, logical expressions treat 0 as *false* and nonzero as *true*. Since 0 is a universal value available for all native types, it is by convention used as a sentinel value. An idiom in pointer-based processing is zero used to represent an end-of-list condition.

```
while(p) {          //p == 0  NULL pointer
    . . .           //process list
    p = p -> next;  //traverse
}
```

Frequently an enumerated type is used explicitly to provide better documentation.

```
enum boolean {FALSE, TRUE};

boolean search(int table[], int x, int& where)
{
   where = -1;
   for (int i = 0; i < N; ++i)
      if (x == table[i]){
         where = i;
         break;
      }
   return boolean(where != -1);
}
```

The string type is a combination of programmer discipline and community convention in using the library *string.h*. This library is applicable to the type pointer to character. The end-of-string character is again the zero value. Concatenation, copying, length, and other operations are given by functions in *string.h*. A measure of this success is the extent to which C is used for string processing applications.

The file type is based on the use of *stdio.h*. A system-dependent structure type is defined with the name FILE. Functions such as file opening, closing, and seeking are given in *stdio.h*. These routines expect file pointers as parameters. Specific structure members are not directly manipulated when the programmer stays with these conventions. Again, C has been successfully used in writing operating systems and code that manipulates file systems.

These successes do not argue for the status quo. Instead, they argue for OOP as implemented in a language that ensures that library conventions are not circumvented.

9.3 CLIENTS AND MANUFACTURERS

To fully appreciate the OOP paradigm, one must view the overall coding process as an exercise in shared and distributed responsibilities. We have used the term *client* to mean a user of a class. We have used the term *manufacturer* to mean the provider of the class.

A client of a class expects an approximation to an abstraction. A stack, to be useful, has to be of reasonable size. A complex number must be of reasonable precision. A deck of cards must be shufflable with random outcome in dealing hands. The internals of how these behaviors are computed is not a direct concern of the client. The client is concerned with cost, effectiveness, and ease of operation, but not with implementation. This is the black box principle.

A *black box* for the *client* should be

- Simple to use, easy to understand, and familiar
- Cheap, efficient, and powerful
- In a component relationship within the system

A *black box* for the *manufacturer* should be

- Easy to reuse and modify, and hard to misuse and reproduce
- Cheap, efficient, and powerful
- Profitable to produce with a large client base

The manufacturer competes for clients by implementing an ADT product that is reasonably priced and efficient. It is in the manufacturer's interest to hide details of an implementation. This simplifies what the manufacturer needs to explain to the client. It frees the manufacturer to allow internal repairs or improvements that do not affect the client's use. It restrains the client from dangerous and inadvertent tampering with the product.

Structures and ordinary functions in C allow one to build useful ADTs but do not support a client/manufacturer distinction. The client has ready access to internal details and may modify them in unsuitable ways. Consider a stack in C represented as an array with an integer variable top. A client of such a stack in C can extract an internal member of the array used to represent the stack. This violates the LIFO abstraction that the stack is implementing.

Encapsulation of objects prevents these violations. A data-hiding scheme that restricts access of implementation detail to manufacturers guarantees client conformance to the ADT abstraction. The private parts are hidden from client code, and the public parts are available. It is possible to change the hidden representation but not to change the public access or functionality. If done properly, client code need not change when the hidden representation is modified.

The two keys to fulfilling these conditions are inheritance and polymorphism.

9.4 REUSE AND INHERITANCE

Library creation and reuse are crucial indicators of successful language strategies. Inheritance is used for code sharing and reuse and for developing type hierarchies. Inheritance is the mechanism of deriving a new class from an old one. That is, the existing class can be added to or altered to create the derived class. Through inheritance, a hierarchy of related ADTs can be created that share code and a common interface, a feature critical to the ability to reuse code.

Inheritance influences overall software design by providing a framework that captures conceptual elements that become the focus for system building and reuse. For example, InterViews [1] is a C++ library that supports building graphical user interfaces. Major categories of objects include interactive objects, text objects, and graphics objects. These categories are readily composed to produce different applications, such as a CAD system, browser, or WYSIWYG editor.

The OOP design methodology becomes

1. Decide on an appropriate set of ADTs.

2. Design in their relatedness, and use inheritance to share code and interface.

3. Use virtual functions to process related objects dynamically.

Inheritance also facilitates the black box principle. It is an important mechanism for suppressing detail. Because it is hierarchical, each level provides functionality to the next level that is built on it. In retrospect, structured programming methodology with its process-centered view relied on stepwise refinement to nest routines but did not adequately appreciate the need for a corresponding view of data.

9.5 POLYMORPHISM

Polymorphism is the genie in OOP, taking instruction from a client and properly interpreting its wishes. A polymorphic function has many forms. Following Cardelli and Wegner [2], we make these distinctions:

- *Ad hoc polymorphism—coercion.* A function or operator works on several different types by converting their values to the expected type. An example in ANSI C is assignment conversions of arithmetic types upon function call.

- *Ad hoc polymorphism—overloading.* A function is called based on its *signature*, which is defined as the list of argument types in its parameter list. The C integer division operator and floating-point division operator are distinguished based on their argument lists.

- *Pure polymorphism—inclusion.* A type is a subtype of another type. Functions available for the base type work on the subtype. Such a function can have different implementations that are invoked by a runtime determination of the subtype.

- *Pure polymorphism—parametric.* The type is left unspecified and is later instantiated. Manipulation of generic pointers and templates provide this in C++.

```
//polymorphism - various contexts


a / b        //divide behavior determined by native coercions

cout << a    //ad-hoc polymorphism through function overloading

p -> draw()  //pure polymorphism through virtual function call

stack <window*> win[40]   //parametric polymorphism using templates
```

Polymorphism localizes responsibility for behavior. The client code frequently requires no revision when additional functionality is added to the system through manufacturer-provided code additions.

Polymorphism directly contributes to the black box principle. The virtual functions specified for the base class are the interface used by the client throughout. The client knows that an overridden member function takes responsibility for a specific implementation of a given action relevant to the object. The client need not know different routines for each calculation or different forms of specification. These details are suppressed.

9.6 LANGUAGE COMPLEXITY

C++ extracts a major price for all of its advantages. Language complexity is substantial. This leads to additional training costs and to subtle misuse. Also, the rapid evolution of the language while it is in major use is nearly unprecedented. C is a small, elegant language. The syntax of C++ is similar to that of C, but its semantics are complex. To appreciate these difficulties, we compare some characteristics of Pascal, Modula-2, C++, and Ada.

	Keywords	Statements	Operators	Manual Pages
Pascal	35	9	16	28
Modula-2	40	10	19	25
C	29	13	44	40
C++ version 1.0	42	14	47	66
C++ version 3.0	48	14	52	155
Ada	63	17	21	241

These numbers are only suggestive. Modula-2, by these measures, is slightly more complicated than its ancestor Pascal, and both are on a par with C. C++ is intentionally constructed as an extension of C and follows C-style manual explanations. C++ version 3.0 adds 19 keywords to the 29 found in traditional C, a two-thirds increase. The C++ version 3.0 reference manual has 155 pages compared to 40 pages in the C reference manual, a quadrupling. These two measures suggest that C++ is much more complicated than C. Furthermore many C++ constructs are orthogonal, so that their interactions greatly affect complexity.

An example of this occurs on page 306 of the *C++ Annotated Reference Manual* [3], where a 13×5 table is used to outline distinct cases and features of different function types. The five function characteristics are inherited, virtual, return type, member or friend, and default generation. For example, constructors, destructors, and conversion functions cannot have return type declarations, and new() and delete() must have void* and void, respectively. C has effectively one form of function semantics. This 65-fold expansion is awe inspiring; and while regularities exist in this table and many characteristics are derivable from a conceptual understanding of the language design, Stroustrup still felt it advisable to list these distinctions.

C++ overloads key concepts with several meanings. This causes a great deal of conceptual confusion. A candidate for the worst offender is the keyword static. There can be a local static variable, meaning a variable that retains value upon block exit. There can be a static file scope identifier, meaning a name that has visibility restricted to that file. There can be a class variable that is static, meaning a variable whose existence is independent of the class. There can be static member functions, meaning member functions that do not receive the this pointer arguments. There is a relatedness to these meanings, but there are enough distinctions that one cannot successfully understand them all as derived from a single concept.

C++ as a hybrid OOP language can cause the programmer a "dialectical tension headache." The penchant of C programmers to focus on efficiency and implementation conflicts with the penchant for objectivists to focus on elegance, abstraction, and generality. The two demands on the coding process are reconcilable but require bringing a measure of coordination and respect to the process.

9.7 C++ OOP BANDWAGON

OOP using C++ has had dazzling acceptance in industry, in spite of acknowledged flaws. The reason for this is that it brings OOP technology to industry in an acceptable way. Namely, it is based on an existing successful language in widespread use. It allows portable code to be written that is tight and efficient. Type safety is retained and type extensibility is general. C++ coexists with standard languages and does not require special resources from the system.

C was initially designed as a systems-implementation language, and as such allows coding that is readily translated to efficiently use machine resources. Software products gain competitive advantage from such efficiency. Hence, despite complaints that traditional C was not a safe or robust language to code in, C grew in its range of application. The C community by convention and discipline used structured programming and ADT extensions in ad hoc ways. OOP made inroads into this professional community only when it was wedded to C within a conceptual framework that maintained its traditional point of view and advantages. Key to the bandwagon changeover to C++ has been the understanding that inheritance and polymorphism have additional important advantages over traditional coding practice.

Polymorphism in C++ allows a client to use an ADT as a black box. Success in OOP is characterized by the extent to which a user-defined type can be made indistinguishable from a native type. Polymorphism allows coercions to be specified that integrate the ADT with the coercion rules of the kernel language. Polymorphism permits objects from subtype hierarchies to respond dynamically to function invocation, the messaging principle in OOP. Polymorphism simplifies client protocols. Name proliferation is controlled by function and operator overloading. The availability of all four forms of polymorphism in C++ encourages the programmer to design with encapsulation and data hiding in mind.

OOP is many things to many people. Attempts at defining it are reminiscent of the blind sages attempts at describing the elephant. I offer this equation:

$$OOP = type\ extensibility\ + polymorphism$$

In many languages and systems, the cost of detail suppression was run-time inefficiency or undue rigidity in the interface. C++ has a range of choices that allow both efficiency and flexibility. As a consequence of this, industry will increasingly adopt it.

9.8 PLATONISM: TABULA RASA DESIGN

C++ gives the programmer a tool to *implement* an OOP design. But how do you *develop* such a design? You start with an empty slate—a tabula rasa; no simple methodology exists because each design must be strongly tied to the problem domain and reflect its abstractions. Discovering these abstractions is a design philosophy we call *Platonism*.

In the Platonic paradigm, there is an ideal object. For example, imagine an ideal chair in the heavens and attempt to describe its characteristics. These would be characteristics shared by all chairs. Such a chair would be a subcategory of another ideal—furniture. Chair would have subcategories, such as swivel chair, beach chair, reclining chair, rocking chair, and so on. Useful descriptions would require expertise on chairs and agreement on the nature of "chairness" among producers and users of chairs. The Platonic chair should be easily modified to describe most commonly occurring chairs. The Platonic chair should be described in terms that are consistent with existing chair terminology.

FIGURE 9.1 Philosophers contemplating "chairness"

C++ was influenced by Simula 67, a language specifically invented for simulations. The Platonic paradigm is a modeling or simulation of the concrete world. It involves extra effort in determining a design. The design typically provides a public interface that is convenient, general, and efficient. These interface considerations can be in conflict. Again, there are no simple rules for deciding such tradeoffs.

The extra effort should be very beneficial to offset the increased initial design cost. First and foremost, it imposes an additional level of discipline to the programming process. Increasing programmer discipline always pays dividends. Second, it encapsulates into classes meaningful related pieces of code. Encapsulation and decomposition always pay dividends. Third, it enhances code reuse through inheritance and ADTs. Code reuse always pays dividends. Fourth, it improves prototyping by deferring implementation decisions and providing access to large, conveniently used general libraries. Cheap prototyping always pays dividends.

The Platonic paradigm using OOP techniques is quietly revolutionizing the programming process. It does not displace older techniques, such as structured programming, but uses them in the small to effectively manage the composition of large and more robust software.

9.9 DESIGN PRINCIPLES

Most programming should involve the use of existing designs. For example, the mathematical and scientific community have standard definitions of complex and rational numbers, matrices, and polynomials. Each of these can be readily coded as ADTs. The expected public behavior of these types is widely agreed on.

The programming community has widespread experience with standard container classes. Reasonable agreement exists as to the behavior of stacks, associative arrays, binary trees, and queues. Also, the programming community has many examples of specialized programming languages oriented around a particular domain. For example, SNOBOL and its successor language ICON have very powerful string-processing features. These can be captured as ADTs in C++.

Useful design principles include Occam's razor ("Entities should not be multiplied beyond necessity"), completeness, invertibility, orthogonality, consistency, simplicity, efficiency, and expressiveness. These principles can be in conflict and frequently require one to make tradeoffs in arriving at a design.

Invertibility means that one should have member functions that are inverses. In the mathematical types, addition and subtraction are inverses. In a text editor, add and delete are inverses. Some commands are their own inverses, such as negation. The importance of invertibility in a nonmathematical context can be seen by the brilliant success of the undo command in text editing and the recover commands in file maintenance.

Completeness is best seen in Boolean algebra, in which the *nand* operation suffices to generate all possible Boolean expressions. But Boolean algebra is usually taught with negation, conjunction, and disjunction as the basic operations. Completeness by itself is not enough to judge a design. A large set of operators is frequently more expressive.

Orthogonality is a principle that says each element of a design should integrate and work with all other elements. Also, elements of the basic design should not overlap or be redundant. For example, on a system that manipulates shapes, you should have a horizontal move, a vertical move, and a rotate operation. In effect, these would be adequate to position the shape at any point on the screen.

Designs should be hierarchical. Hierarchy is captured through inheritance. It is a reflection of two principles: decomposition and localization. Both principles are methods of suppressing detail, a key idea in coping with complexity. There is a scale problem in a hierarchical design. How much detail is enough to make a concept useful as its own class? It is important to avoid a proliferation of specialized concepts. How much detail is too much and will render the program hard to master?

9.10 LAST WORDS

C++ is to an extent the 1990s version of PL/1 (1965) or Ada (1980). It is an attempt within the professional programming community to provide a nearly universal programming language. The problem with PL/1 is it mixes too many styles—namely, it combined COBOL, FORTRAN, and elements of ALGOL into the same language. Ada is large, complex, and inefficient. C++ has problems with size and complexity but very importantly builds on existing resources and practice. It also emphasizes efficiency, sometimes to a fault.

Some of its complexity problems can be avoided by keeping a conceptual point of view regarding its features. An example is the fact that a pure virtual function can be defined with executable code.

```
class ABC {
public:
   virtual void f() = 0;
};

void ABC::f() { cout << "pure virtual foo " << endl }

//must be called with qualified name,e.g.  x.ABC::f();
```

It is an eccentricity that this is possible. Conceptually, a pure virtual function is used to defer a definition.

Other complexity issues are fundamental to the C++ language design, such as lack of garbage collection (GC). Several proposals exist [4][5][6], and their implementations support the contention that they can be done without degrading performance in most applications. Most other major OOP languages, such as Smalltalk, CLOS, and Eiffel, support GC. The argument for GC is that it makes the programmer's task distinctly easier. Memory leaks and pointer errors are common when each class provides for its own storage management. These are very hard errors to find and debug. GC is a well-understood technology, so why not?

The argument against GC is that it extracts a hidden cost from all users when employed universally. Also, GC manages memory but not other resources. This would still require destructors for *finalization*. Finalization is the return of resources and other behavior when an object's lifetime is over. For example, the object might be a file, and finalization might require closing the file. Finally, it is not in the tradition of the C community to have free store managed automatically.

OOP attempts to emphasize reuse. Reuse is possible on different scales. On the grandest scale, libraries have been developed that are effective for an entire problem domain. The up side to reuse is that it contributes in the long run to more easily maintained code. The down side is that a particular application does not need costly library development.

OOP requires more programmer sophistication. More sophisticated programmers are better programmers. The down side is training cost and potential misuse of sophisticated tools.

OOP lets client code be simpler and more readily extensible. Polymorphism can be used to incorporate local changes into a large-scale system without the need for global modification. The down side can be run-time overhead.

C++ provides programming encapsulations through classes, inheritance, and templates. Encapsulations hide and localize. As systems get bigger and more complex, there is an increasing need for such encapsulations. Simple block structure and functional encapsulation of languages such as FORTRAN and ALGOL are not enough. The 1970s taught us the need for the module as a programming unit. The 1980s taught us that a module needs to have a logical coherence supported in the language, and that modules need to be derivable from each other. When supported by a programming language, these encapsulations and relationships lead to increased programmer discipline. The art of programming is to blend rigor and discipline with creativity.

9.11 Summary

1. Object-oriented programming (OOP) and C++ have been embraced by industry within a very short time frame. C++ is a hybrid OOP language. As such it allows a multiparadigmatic approach to coding. The traditional advantages of the C language as an efficient, powerful programming language are not lost. The new key ingredient is polymorphism—the ability to assume many forms.

2. Existing languages and methodology supported much of the OOP methodology by combining language features with programmer discipline. It is possible in a non-OOP language to create and use ADTs. Three examples in the C community are the use of the pseudotypes string, Boolean, and file. They are pseudotypes in that they do not enjoy the same privileges as true types. What is gained by looking at these examples is a better understanding of the limits of extensibility in the non-OOP context.

3. A black box for the client should be simple to use, easy to understand and familiar; cheap, efficient, and powerful; and in a component relationship within the system. A black box for the manufacturer should be easy to reuse and modify, and hard to misuse and reproduce; cheap, efficient, and powerful; and profitable to produce with a large client base.

4. The OOP design methodology is

    1. Decide on an appropriate set of ADTs.
    2. Design in their relatedness, and use inheritance to share code and interface.
    3. Use virtual functions to process related objects dynamically.

5. Polymorphism directly contributes to the black box principle. The virtual functions specified for the base class are the interface used by the client throughout. The client knows that an overridden member function takes responsibility for a specific implementation of a given action relevant to the object.

6. C++ as a hybrid OOP language can cause the programmer a "dialectical tension headache." The penchant of C programmers to focus on efficiency and implementation conflicts with the penchant for objectivists to focus on elegance, abstraction, and generality. The two demands on the coding process are reconcilable but require a measure of coordination and respect that must be brought to the process.

7. OOP is many things to many people. I offer this equation:

$$OOP = type\ extensibility + polymorphism$$

In many languages and systems, the cost of detail suppression was run-time inefficiency or undue rigidity in the interface. C++ has a range of choices that allow both efficiency and flexibility.

8. In developing an OOP design, you start with an empty slate—a tabula rasa; no simple methodology exists because each design must be strongly tied to the problem domain and reflect its abstractions. Discovering these abstractions is a design philosophy we call Platonism. In the Platonic paradigm, there is an ideal object. For example, imagine an ideal chair in the heavens and attempt to describe its characteristics. These would be characteristics shared by all chairs.

9. Useful design principles include Occam's razor ("Entities should not be multiplied beyond necessity"), completeness, invertibility, orthogonality, consistency, simplicity, efficiency, and expressiveness. These principles can be in conflict and frequently require one to make trade-offs in arriving at a design.

9.12 Exercises

1. Consider the following three ways to provide a Boolean type:

   ```
   //Traditional C using the preprocessor
   #define TRUE  1
   #define FALSE 0
   #define Boolean int

   //ANSI C and C++ using enumerated types
   enum Boolean {false, true};

   //C++ as a class
   class Boolean {
     . . .
   public:
     //various member functions
     //including overloading  !  &&  ||  ==  !=
   };
   ```

   Discuss the advantages and disadvantages of each style. Keep in mind scope, naming, and conversion problems.

2. C++ originally allowed the this pointer to be modifiable. User-controlled storage management was possible by assigning directly to the this pointer. The assignment of zero meant that the associated memory could be returned to free store. Discuss why this is a bad idea.

3. The rules for deciding which definition of an overloaded function to invoke have changed since the first version of the language. One reason for the changes was to reduce the number of ambiguities. Investigate how these rules have changed. One criticism is that the rules allow matching through conversions that possibly are unintended by the programmer. This can cause run-time bugs that are difficult to detect. One strategy is to have the compiler issue a diagnostic warning in such cases. Another is to use casting defensively to inform the compiler of the intended choice. Discuss these alternatives.

4. List three things that you would drop from the C++ language. Argue why it would not be missed. For example, it is possible to have protected inheritance. It was never used in this text. Should it be in the language for completeness' sake?

5. Describe at least two separate concepts for the keyword virtual as used in C++. Does this cause conceptual confusion?

6. The package *string.h* is a pseudotype. It employs traditional C technology and programmer discipline to provide the ADT string. Why is it preferable to provide class string?

7. Write and test a complete implementation for class string.

9.13 REFERENCES

1. Mark Linton, John Vlissides, and Paul Calder. "Composing User Interfaces with InterViews." *IEEE Computer*, vol. 22, no. 2, 1989, pp. 8–22.

2. Luca Cardelli and Peter Wegner. "On Understanding Types, Data Abstraction, and Polymorphism." *Computing Surveys*, vol. 17, 1985, pp. 471–522.

3. Margret Ellis and Bjarne Stroustrup. *The Annotated C++ Reference Manual*. Reading, Mass.: Addison-Wesley, 1990.

4. Hans–J. Boehm and Mark Weiser. "Garbage Collection in an Uncooperative Environment." *Software—Practice and Experience*, September 1988, pp. 807–820.

5. Daniel Edelson and Ira Pohl. "A Copying Collector for C++." In *Usenix C++ Conf. Proc.*, 1991, pp. 85–102.

6. Daniel Edelson. "A Mark and Sweep Collector for C++." In *Proc. Princ. Prog. Lang.*, January 1992.

7. Grady Booch. *Object-Oriented Design with Applications*. Redwood City, Calif.: Benjamin/Cummings, 1991.

8. Timothy Budd. *An Introduction to Object-Oriented Programming*. Reading, Mass.: Addison-Wesley, 1991.

9. Anthony Wasserman, P. A. Pircher, and R. Muller. "The Object-Oriented Structured Design Notation for Software Design Representation." *IEEE Computer*, vol. 23, no. 3, 1990, pp. 50–63–22.

APPENDIX A

ASCII CHARACTER CODES

ASCII American Standard Code for Information Interchange										
Left/Right Digits	**0**	**1**	**2**	**3**	**4**	**5**	**6**	**7**	**8**	**9**
0	nul	soh	stx	etx	eot	enq	ack	bel	bs	ht
1	nl	vt	np	cr	so	si	dle	dc1	dc2	dc3
2	dc4	nak	syn	etb	can	em	sub	esc	fs	gs
3	rs	us	sp	!	"	#	$	%	&	'
4	(	)	*	+	,	-	.	/	0	1
5	2	3	4	5	6	7	8	9	:	;
6	<	=	>	?	@	A	B	C	D	E
7	F	G	H	I	J	K	L	M	N	O
8	P	Q	R	S	T	U	V	W	X	Y
9	Z	[	\	]	^	_	`	a	b	c
10	d	e	f	g	h	i	j	k	l	m
11	n	o	p	q	r	s	t	u	v	w
12	x	y	z	{			}	~	del		

Some Observations

1. Character codes 0–31 and 127 are nonprinting.
2. Character code 32 prints a single space.
3. Character codes for digits 0 through 9 are contiguous.
4. Character codes for letters A through Z are contiguous.
5. Character codes for letters a through z are contiguous.
6. The difference between a capital letter and the corresponding lowercase letter is 32.

The Meaning of Some of the Abbreviations

nul	null	nl	newline
ht	horizontal tab	esc	escape
cr	carriage return	bs	backspace
bel	bell	vt	vertical tab

APPENDIX B

OPERATOR PRECEDENCE AND ASSOCIATIVITY

The following table shows precedence and associativity for all C++ operators. When in doubt, use parentheses to indicate operation precedence.

Operators	Associativity
:: (global scope) :: (class scope)	left to right
() [] -> . *postfix* ++ *postfix* --	left to right
++ -- ! ~ sizeof (*type*) + (unary) - (unary) * (indirection) & (address) new delete	right to left
.* ->*	left to right
* / %	left to right
+ -	left to right
<< >>	left to right
< <= > >=	left to right
== !=	left to right
&	left to right
^	left to right
|	left to right
&&	left to right
||	left to right
?:	right to left
= += -= *= /= *etc*	right to left
, (*comma operator*)	left to right

APPENDIX C

C++ LANGUAGE GUIDE

This appendix is a concise, convenient guide to the C++ language. It summarizes many of the key language elements of C++ that are not found in older procedural languages, such as Pascal and C.

C.1 LEXICAL ELEMENTS

A C++ program is a sequence of characters that are collected into *tokens*, which comprise the basic vocabulary of the language. There are six categories of tokens: keywords, identifiers, constants, string constants, operators, and punctuators.

Among the characters that can be used to construct tokens are

```
a b c d e f g h i j k l m n o p q r s t u v w x y z
A B C D E F G H I J K L M N O P Q R S T U V W X Y Z
0 1 2 3 4 5 6 7 8 9
+ - * / = ( ) { } [ ] < > ´ " ! # ~ % ^ & _ : ; , . ? \ |
```
white-space characters such as blank and tab

In producing tokens the compiler selects the longest string of characters that constitutes a token.

Comments

C++ has a one-line comment symbol, //.

```
//Compile with version 1.2 or later
const float pi = 3.14159;  //pi accurate to six places
```

C-style comments are also available.

```
/*   * * * * * *
   C++
   Demonstrate Multiple-Inheritance
   OOP - Platonic Designs
 *   * * * * * * */
```

Comments do not nest.

Identifiers

An identifier can be one or more characters. The first character must be a letter or underscore. Subsequent characters can be either letters, digits, or an underscore.

```
speed Speed speedy    //are all distinct
_C_                   //reserved for system use
q213                  //opaque
multi_word            //normal style
MultiWord             //pascal style
```

Good programming style is to pick meaningful identifier names that help document a program. All identifiers containing a double underscore are reserved for use by the system. Avoid using underscore as a starting character because many system programs and libraries use these.

Keywords

Keywords are explicitly reserved identifiers that have a strict meaning in C++. They cannot be redefined or used in other contexts.

Keywords

asm	continue	float	new	signed	try
auto	default	for	operator	sizeof	typedef
break	delete	friend	private	static	union
case	do	goto	protected	struct	unsigned
catch	double	if	public	switch	virtual
char	else	inline	register	template	void
class	enum	int	return	this	volatile
const	extern	long	short	throw	while

Other keywords are specific to different implementations, such as near and far, which are in Borland C++, and typeof, which is in GNU C++.

C.2 CONSTANTS

C++ has constants for each basic type. These include integer, character, and floating-point constants. These constants can also be long and unsigned. String constants are character sequences surrounded by double quotes. The one universal pointer constant is 0. Some examples follow:

```
156   0156  0x156        //int constants: decimal, octal, hexadecimal
1561  156ul              //int constants: long, unsigned long
'A' 'a' '7' '\t'         //char constants - last is tab character
3.14f 3.1415 3.14159L    //float constants of different precision
"A string."              //string constant
```

Suffixes such as u, l, and f are used to indicate unsigned, long, and float, respectively. They can be uppercase.

The character literals are usually given as *'symbol'*. Some nonprinting and special characters require an escape sequence.

```
'\a'   //alert
'\\'   //backslash
'\b'   //backspace
'\r'   //carriage return
'\"'   //double quote
'\f'   //formfeed
'\t'   //tab
'\n'   //newline
'\0'   //null character
'\''   //single quote
'\v'   //vertical tab
'\101' //octal 101 in ASCII 'A'
'\x041' //hexadecimal ASCII 'A'
L'oop' //wchar_t or wide character literal
```

The floating-point constants can be specified with or without signed integer exponents.

```
3.14f  1.234F    //float constant - smallest floating point type
0.1234567        //double constant
0.123456789L     //long double - either l or L
3.  3.0  0.3E1   //all express double 3.0
300e-2           //also 3.0
```

String literals are considered static char[] constants. A string literal is a contiguous array of characters with the null character at its end.

```
""            //empty string  is '\0'
"OOP 4ME"     // 'O' 'O' 'P' ' ' '4' 'M' 'E' '\0'
"my \"quote \" is escaped"    // \" used for "
"a multi-line string \
is also \
possible"
```

String literals that are separated only by white space are implicitly concatenated into a single string.

```
"This is a single string, "
"since it is only separated "
"by white space."
```

Enumerations define named constants. The constants are a list of identifiers that are implicitly consecutive integer values starting with zero. They can be anonymous, as in

```
enum {false, true};   //false == 0 true == 1
```

They are distinct types, as in

```
enum color {red, blue, white, green, orange}; //color is a type
```

They can have specifically initialized values, as in

```
enum {BOTTOM = 50, TOP = 100, OVER}; //OVER == 101
enum grades {F = 60, D = 60, C = 70, B = 80, A = 90};
```

Enumeration constants are promoted to type int in expressions.

The keyword const is used to declare that an object's value is constant throughout its scope.

```
const int N = 100;
double w[N];      //N may be used in a constant expression

const  int bus_stops[5] = {23, 44, 57, 59, 83};
//The element values, bus_stops[i], are constant
```

The use of const differs from the use of constant definitions by #define, as in

```
#define N   100
```

In the const case, N is a nonmodifiable *lvalue*. In the define case, N is a literal. Also, the macro replacement of N occurs regardless of scope.

C.3 DECLARATIONS AND SCOPE RULES

Declarations associate meaning with a given identifier. The syntax of C++ declarations is highly complex because they incorporate many disparate elements that are context dependent. A declaration provides an identifier with a type, a storage class, and a scope. A simple declaration is often a definition as well. For a simple variable, this means the object is created and possibly initialized.

```
void foo()       //foo is declared and defined
{
   int  i = 5;   //i is declared and defined and initialized
                 //i is automatic and local to foo

   . . .
}
```

Complex declarations, such as class, function, and template declarations, are described in their own sections.

C++ has file scope, function scope, block scope, class scope, and function prototype scope. File scope extends from the point of declaration in a file to the end of that file. Function prototype scope is the scope of identifiers in the function prototype argument list and extends to the end of the declaration. Blocks nest in a conventional way, but functions cannot be declared inside other functions or blocks.

Declarations can occur almost anywhere in a block. A declaration can also be an initializing statement of a for statement.

```
for (int i = 0; i < N; ++i) {
   . . .
```

Declarations cannot occur as initializing statements within nested loops. A selection statement, such as an if or switch statement, cannot merely control a declaration. In general, jumps and selections cannot bypass an initialization. This is not true of ANSI C.

```
if (flag)
   int j = 6;     //illegal
else
   j = 19;

if (flag) {
   int j = 6;     //legal within block
   cout << j ;
}
```

C++ introduces the operator ::, called the scope resolution operator. When used in the form :: *variable*, it allows access to the externally named variable. Other uses of this notation are important for classes.

Class member identifiers are local to that class. The scope resolution operator :: can be used to resolve ambiguities. When used in the form *class name* :: *variable*, it allows access to the named variable from that class.

```
class A {
public:
   int  i;
   static void foo();
};

class B {
public:
   char i;
   void foo() {  A :: foo(); . . .}
};
```

A hidden external name can be accessed by using the scope resolution operator.

```
int  i;
void foo(int  i)
{
   i = ::i;
   . . .
}
```

A hidden class, struct, union, or enum identifier can be accessed by using its respective keyword.

```
static union u {
   . . .
};

void foo(int u)
{
   union u U;
   . . .
}
```

Classes can be nested. C++ rules make the inner class scoped within the outer class. This is a source of confusion because the rules have changed and are different from ANSI C rules.

Enumerations declared inside a class make the enumerators have class scope, as in

```
class foo_bool {
public:
   enum boolean {false, true} flag;
};

main()
{
   foo_bool c;
   c.flag = foo_bool::false;
   . . .
}
```

C.4 LINKAGE RULES

Modern systems are built around multifile inclusion, compilation, and linkage. To use C++, one must understand how multifile programs are combined. Linking separate modules requires resolving external references. The key rule is that external nonstatic variables must be defined in exactly one place. Use of the keyword extern together with an initializer constitutes defining a variable. Using the keyword extern without an initializer constitutes a declaration but not a definition. If the keyword extern is omitted, the resulting declaration is a definition, with or without an initializer. The following examples illustrate these rules:

```
//file prog1.c
   char  c;          //definition of c
   . . .

//file prog2.c
   extern char c;    //declaration of c
   . . .

//file prog3.c
   extern int n = 5; //definition of n
   . . .

//file prog4.c
   char          c;  //illegal second definition
   extern float n;   //illegal type mismatch
   extern int    k;  //illegal no definition
   . . .
```

Constant definitions and `inline` definitions at file scope are local to that file; in other words they are implicitly static. Constant definitions can be explicitly declared `extern`. Usually such definitions are placed in a header file to be included with any code that needs these definitions.

A `typedef` declaration is local to its file. It is a synonym for the type it defines.

```
typedef int  BOOLEAN;      //one way to produce BOOLEAN
typedef char *c_string;    //c_string is pointer to char
typedef void (*ptr_f)();   //pointer to function
                           //of no arguments returning void
```

An enumerator declaration is local to its file. Enumerators and `typedefs` that are needed in a multifile program should be placed in a header file. Enumerators defined within a class are local to that class. Access to them requires the scope resolution operator.

```
//types.h    header file
typedef char *c_string;   //c_string is pointer to char
typedef void (*ptr_f)();  //pointer to function

void foo(c_string s);     //function prototypes
void title();
void pr_onoff();

enum {OFF, ON};
extern int x;

//fcns.c to be separately compiled
#include <iostream.h>
#include "types.h"

void foo(c_string s)
{
    cout <<"\noutput: " << s;
}

void title()
{
    cout << "\nTEST TYPEDEFS";
}

void pr_onoff()
{
    if (x == OFF)
        cout << "\nOFF";
    else
        cout << "\nON";
}
```

```
//linkage_ex.c   main program file  CC fcns.o linkage_ex.c
#include <iostream.h>
#include "types.h"
int x = 0;

main()
{
    c_string f = "foo on you";
    ptr_f    pf = &pr_onoff;

    foo("ENTER 0 or 1: ");
    cin >> x;
    if ( x == ON)
        pf = &title;
    pr_onoff();
    pf();
    x = !x;
    pf();
    foo(f);
}
```

C.5 TYPES

The fundamental types in C++ are integral types and floating-point types. The char type is the shortest integral type. The long double type is the longest floating-point type. The following table lists these types from shortest to longest (reading first across and then down the columns).

Simple Data Types

char	signed char	unsigned char
short	int	long
unsigned short	unsigned	unsigned long
float	double	long double

Types can be derived from the basic types. A simple derived type is the enumeration type. The derived types allow pointer types, array types, and structure types. A generic pointer type void* is allowed, as is a reference type. Both anonymous unions and anonymous enumerations are allowed. An anonymous union can only have public data members. A file scope anonymous union has to be declared static. The class type is another extension, and the struct is extended to be a variant of the class type. Union, enumeration, and class names are type names.

```
void*   gen_ptr;              //a generic pointer
int     i, &ref_i = i;        //ref_i is an alias for i
enum    boolean {false, true}; //enumeration
boolean flag;                 //boolean is now a type name
boolean set[10];              //array type

class   card {                //user-defined type
public:
   suit s;                    //public data member
   pips p;
   void pr_card();            //member function
private:
   int  cd;                   //private data member
};
suit card::* ptr_s = &card::s;  //pointer to member
```

The five storage class keywords are:

```
auto         //local to blocks and implicit
register     //optimization advice and automatic
extern       //global scope
static       //within blocks - value retained
typedef      //creates synonyms for types
```

The keyword auto can be used within blocks, but such use is redundant and is normally avoided. Automatic variables are created at block entry and destroyed at block exit. The keyword register can be used within blocks and for function parameters. It advises the compiler that, for optimization purposes, the program wants a variable to reside in a high-speed register. Register variables have behavior that is semantically equivalent to automatic variables.

The keyword extern can be used within blocks and at file scope. It indicates a variable is linked in from elsewhere. The keyword static can be used within blocks and at file scope. Inside a block, static indicates that a variable's value is retained after block exit. At file scope it indicates that declarations have internal linkage.

The type qualifer keywords are:

```
const        //nonmodifiable
volatile     //supresses compiler optimization
```

We discuss const in a number of contexts. It is used to indicate that a variable or function parameter has a nonmodifiable value. The volatile keyword implies that an agent external to the program can change the variable's value.

```
volatile const gmt;  //expect external time signal
```

C.6 CONVERSION RULES

C++ has numerous conversion rules. Many of these conversions are implicit, which makes C++ convenient but potentially dangerous for the novice. Implicit conversions can induce run-time bugs that are hard to detect.

The general rules are straightforward.

Automatic conversion in an arithmetic expression x op y

First:
Any char, short, or enum is promoted to int.
Integral types unrepresentable as int are promoted to unsigned.

Second:
If, after the first step, the expression is of mixed type, then, according to the hierarchy of types

int < unsigned < long < unsigned long < float < double < long double

the operand of lower type is promoted to that of the higher type, and the value of the expression has that type.
Note that unsigned is promoted to unsigned long if long cannot contain all the values of unsigned.

Implicit pointer conversions also occur in C++. Any pointer type can be converted to a generic pointer of type void*. Unlike ANSI C, however, C++ does not have generic pointers that are assignment-compatible with arbitrary pointer types. This means that C++ requires a generic pointer to be cast to an explicit type for assignment to a nongeneric pointer variable.

```
char* mem;
void* gen_p;
gen_p = mem;           //C and C++
mem   = (char*)gen_p; //C and C++
mem   = gen_p;         //legal C and illegal C++
```

The name of an array is a pointer to its base element. The null pointer constant can be converted to any pointer type.

```
char* p = 0;  //p is a null pointer
int*  x = p;  //illegal: need (int*)p
int*  y = 0;  //legal
```

A pointer to a class can be converted to a pointer to a publicly derived base class. This also applies to references.

Explicit conversions are forced by *casts*. Traditional C casts are augmented in C++ by a functional notation as a syntactic alternative. The cast notation has the form

(*type*) *expression*

A functional notation of the form

type-name (*expression*)

is equivalent to a cast. The *type-name* in functional notation must be expressible as an identifier. Thus the two expressions

```
x = float(i);   //C++ functional notation
x = (float) i;  //C   cast notation
```

are equivalent. Functional notation is the preferred style.

A constructor of one argument is de facto a type conversion from the argument's type to the constructor's class type. Consider an example of a string constructor.

```
string::string(const char* p)
{
    len = strlen(p);
    s = new char[len + 1];
    strcpy(s, p);
}
```

This is automatically a type transfer from char* to string. These conversions are from an already defined type to a user-defined type. However, it is not possible for the user to add a constructor to a built-in type — for example, to int or double. In the string example, one may also want a conversion from string to char*. This can be done by defining a special conversion function inside the string class as follows:

```
operator char*() { return s; }   //recall char *s; is a member
```

The general form of such a member function is

```
operator type() { . . . }
```

These conversions occur implicitly in assignment expressions and in argument and return conversions from functions.

Temporaries can be created by the compiler to facilitate these operations. This can require constructor invocation and is system and compiler dependent. It may dramatically and unexpectedly affect execution speeds.

C.7 EXPRESSIONS AND OPERATORS

C++ is an operator-rich language that is expression oriented. The operators have 17 precedence levels (see Appendix B). Operators also can have side effects.

A great variety of expressions are allowed in C++. For example, assignment is an expression. The following is legal C++:

```
a = b + (c = d + 3);
```

The equivalent multistatement code is

```
c = d + 3;
a = b + c;
```

sizeof **Expressions**

The sizeof operator can be applied to an expression or a parenthesized type name. It gives the size in bytes of the type that it is applied to.

```
int   a, b[10];

sizeof(a)           //4 on gnu C++ running on a DECSTATION
sizeof(b)           //40 the array storage
sizeof(b[1])        //4
sizeof(5)           //4
sizeof(5.5L)        //8
```

Autoincrement and Autodecrement Expressions

C++ provides autoincrement (++) and autodecrement (--) operators in both prefix and postfix form. In prefix form the autoincrement operator adds 1 to the value stored at the *lvalue* it acts upon. Similarly, the autodecrement operator subtracts 1 from the value stored at the *lvalue* it acts upon.

```
++i;  is equivalent to  i = i + 1;
--x;  is equivalent to  x = x - 1;
```

The postfix form behaves differently than the prefix form by changing the affected *lvalue* after the rest of the expression is evaluated.

```
j = ++i;   is equivalent to  i = i + 1; j = i;
j = i++;   is equivalent to  j = i; i = i + 1;
i = ++i + i++;  // hazardous practice that is system dependent
```

Note that these are not exact equivalencies. Therefore, for complicated expressions with side effects, results of the two forms can be different.

Arithmetic Expressions

Arithmetic expressions are consistent with expected practice. The following examples are grouped by precedence, with highest first:

```
-i    +w                        //unary minus  unary plus
a * b     a / b   i % 5         //multiplication division modulus
a + b     a - b                 //binary addition and subtraction
```

Arithmetic expressions depend on the conversion rules discussed in Section C.6. For example, the results of the division operator / depend on its argument types.

```
a = 3 / 2;    // a is assigned 1
a = 3 / 2.0;  // a is assigned 1.5
```

The modulus operator % is the remainder from the division of the first argument by the second argument. It can be used only with integer types.

Relational, Equality, and Logical Expressions

In C++, the values zero and nonzero are thought of as false and true and are used to affect flow of control in various statement types. The following table contains the C++ operators that are most often used to affect flow of control:

C++ Operators	Meaning
Relational operators:	
<	less than
>	greater than
<=	less than or equal
>=	greater than or equal
Equality operators:	
==	equal
!=	not equal
Logical operators:	
!	(unary) negation
&&	logical and
||	logical or

The negation operator ! is unary. All the other relational, equality, and logical operators are binary. They operate on expressions and yield either the int value 0 or the int value 1. The value for false can be either 0 or 0.0 (or the null pointer), and the value for true can be any nonzero value.

The logical operators !, &&, and || applied to expressions yield either the int value 0 or the int value 1. Logical negation can be applied to an arbitrary expression. If an expression has the value 0 or 0.0, then its negation will yield the int value 1. If the expression has a nonzero value, then its negation will yield the int value 0.

In the evaluation of expressions that are the operands of && and ||, the evaluation process stops as soon as the outcome (true or false) is known.

This is called *short-circuit evaluation.* For example, given the expressions *expr1* and *expr2*, if *expr1* has zero value, then in

    expr1 && expr2

expr2 is not evaluated because the value of the logical expression is already determined to be 0. Similarly, if *expr1* has a nonzero value, then in

    expr1 || expr2

expr2 is not evaluated because the value of the logical expression is already determined to be 1.

Some examples in C++ are

```
a + 5 && b        parenthesized equivalent is    ((a + 5) && b)
!(a < b) && c     parenthesized equivalent is    ((!(a < b)) && c)
1 || ( a != 7)    parenthesized equivalent is    ( 1 || (a != 7))
```

Note that the last expression always short-circuits to value 1.

Assignment Expressions

In C++, assignment occurs as part of an assignment expression.

```
a = b + 1;  //assign (b + 1) to a
```

The effect is to evaluate the right side of the assignment and convert it to a value compatible with the variable on the left. Assignment conversions occur implicitly and include narrowing conversions.

```
int    i, *p = &i;
double w, *q = &w;

    i = w;          //legal w value converted to int
    *q = i;         //legal integer value promoted to double
    *q = *p;        //legal
    q = p;          //illegal conversion between pointer types
    q = (double *)p; //legal
```

Simple variables are *lvalues.*

C++ allows multiple assignment in a single statement.

a = b + (c = 3); *is equivalent to* c = 3; a = b + c;

C++ provides assignment operators that combine assignments and other operators.

a += b;   *is equivalent to* a = a + b;
a *= a + b;   *is equivalent to* a = a * (a + b);
a *op*= b;   *is equivalent to* a = a *op* b

Comma Expressions

The comma operator has the lowest precedence. It is a binary operator with expressions as operands. In a comma expression of the form

expr1 , expr2

expr1 is evaluated first and then *expr2*. The comma expression as a whole has the value and type of its right operand. The comma operator is a control point. Therefore, each expression in the comma-separated list is evaluated completely before the next expression to its right. An example is

sum = 0, i = 1

If i has been declared an int, then this comma expression has value 1 and type int. The comma operator associates from left to right.

Conditional Expressions

The conditional operator ?: is unusual because it is a ternary operator. It takes as operands three expressions. In a construct such as

expr1 ? expr2 : expr3

expr1 is evaluated first. If it is nonzero (true), then *expr2* is evaluated and that is the value of the conditional expression as a whole. If *expr1* is zero (false), then *expr3* is evaluated and that is the value of the conditional expression as a whole. The following example uses a conditional operator to assign the smaller of two values to the variable x:

```
x = (y < z) ? y : z;
```

The parentheses are not necessary because the conditional operator has precedence greater than the assignment operator. However, parentheses are good style because they clarify what is being tested for.

The type of the conditional expression

expr1 ? *expr2* : *expr3*

is determined by *expr2* and *expr3*. If they are different types, then the usual conversion rules apply. The conditional expression's type cannot depend on which of the two expressions *expr2* or *expr3* is evaluated. The conditional operator ?: associates from right to left.

Bit Manipulation Expressions

C++ provides bit manipulation operators. They operate on the machine-dependent bit representation of integral operands.

Bitwise Operators	Meaning
~	unary one's complement
<<	left shift
>>	right shift
&	and
^	exclusive or
|	or

It is customary to overload the shift operators to perform I/O.

Address and Indirection Expressions

The address operator & is a unary operator that yields the address or location where an object is stored. The indirection operator * is a unary operator that is applied to a value of type pointer. It retrieves the value from the location being pointed at. This is also known as dereferencing.

```
int a = 5, *p = &a; //declarations

&a;        //address or location of a
*p;        //reference to object pointed at by p
*p = 7;    //lvalue in effect a is assigned 7
a = *p +1;//rvalue 7 is added to 1 and a is assigned 8
```

new **and** delete **Expressions**

The unary operators new and delete are available to manipulate *free store*. Free store is a system-provided memory pool for objects whose lifetimes are directly managed by the programmer. The programmer can create an object by using new and destroys the object by using delete.

The operator new is used in the following forms:

new *type-name*
new *type-name initializer*
new (*type-name*)

Each statement has at least two effects. First, an appropriate amount of store is allocated from free store to contain the named type. Second, the base address of the object is returned as the value of the new expression. If new fails, the null pointer value 0 is returned. The initializer is a parenthesized list of arguments. For a simple type, such as an int, the initializer is a single expression. It cannot be used to initialize arrays, but it can be an argument list to an appropriate constructor. If the type being allocated has a constructor, the allocated object is initialized.

The operator delete is used in the following forms:

delete *expression*
delete [ ] *expression*

In both forms the expression is typically a pointer variable used in a previous new expression. The second form is used when returning store that was allocated as an array type. The brackets indicate that a destructor should be called for each element of the array. The operator delete returns a value of type void.

The operator delete destroys an object created by new, in effect returning its allocated storage to free store for reuse. If the type being deleted has a destructor, its destructor is called. The following example uses these constructs to dynamically allocate an array:

```
//Use of new operator to dynamically allocate an array.

#include <iostream.h>

main()
{
   int* data;
   int  size;

   cout << "\nEnter array size: ";
   cin >> size;

   data = new int[size];      //return int* expression
   for (int j = 0; j < size; ++j)
      cout << (data[j] = j) << "\t";
   cout << "\n\n";
   delete []data;
   . . .
}
```

The pointer variable data is used as the base address of a dynamically allocated array whose number of elements is the value of size. The new operator is used to allocate from free store sufficient storage for an object of type int[size]. The operator delete returns to free store the storage associated with the pointer variable data. This can be done only with objects allocated by new. There are no guarantees on what values will appear in objects allocated from free store. The programmer is responsible for properly initializing such objects.

Placement Syntax and Overloading

Operator new has the general form

$$::_{opt} \text{ new } placement_{opt} \text{ } type \text{ } initializer_{opt}$$

The global function operator new() is typically used to allocate free store. The system provides a sizeof(*type*) argument to this function implicitly. The function prototype is

```
void* operator new(size_t size);
```

The operator new can be overloaded at the global level by the addition of parameters and the use of placement syntax to call it. It can be overloaded and used to override the global versions at the class level. But

when an array of objects is allocated, only the default global void* operator new(size_t size) is called.

The global delete operator cannot be overloaded. The global version is

```
void operator delete(void* ptr)
```

A class-specific version can be declared as

```
void operator delete(void* ptr)
```

or as

```
void operator delete(void* ptr, size_t size)
```

but only one of these forms can be used by any one class. When an array
of objects is deallocated, the global version is called. This feature provides a simple mechanism for user-defined manipulation of free store.

```
#include <stddef.h>    //size_t type defined
#include <stdlib.h>    //malloc() and free() defined
class X {
    . . .
public:
    void* operator new(size_t size) { return (malloc(size)); }
    void  operator delete(void* ptr) { free(ptr); }
    X(unsigned size) { new(size); }
    ~X() { delete(this); }
private:
    . . .
};
```

The class X has provided overloaded forms of new() and delete(). When a
class overloads operator new(), the global operator is still accessible using
the scope resolution operator ::.

The *placement syntax* provides for a comma-separated argument list
used to select an overloaded operator new() with a matching signature.
These additional arguments are often used to place the constructed object at a particular address. One form of this can be found in *new.h*.

```
//overloaded new as found in <new.h>
 void* operator new(size_t size, void* ptr) { return (ptr); }

char*  buf1 = new char[1000];  //globally allocated memory
char*  buf2 = new char[1000];  //more global memory

class object {
    . . .
};

main()
{
    object *p = new(buf1) object; //place at beginning of buf1[]
    object *q = new(buf2) object; //place at beginning of buf2[]
    object *r = new(buf2 + sizeof(object)) object;
    . . .
}
```

These class new() and delete() member functions are always static.

Error Conditions

In the absence of implemented exception handling, new returns a zero value indicating an allocation failure.

The standard library *new.h* has the function set_new_handler() that installs the function to be called when new fails. Calling this with value zero means a traditional version of new that does not throw exceptions will be used. Otherwise an xalloc exception will be thrown. The implementation of *new.h* can be system dependent.

Other Expressions

Function calls and array subscripting are expressions. They have the same precedence as the member operator and the structure pointer operator.

```
a[j + 6]         // means  *(a + j + 6)
sqrt(z + 15.5);  // returns a double
```

The global scope resolution operator is of highest precedence. The class scope resolution operator is used with a class name to qualify a local to class identifier.

```
::i             // access global i
A::foo()        // invoke member foo() defined in A
```

The pointer to member operators are

.* and ->*

Their precedence is below the unary operators and above the multiplicative operator. Their use is described in Section C.9.

C.8 STATEMENTS

C++ has a large variety of statement types. It uses the semicolon as a statement terminator. Braces are used to enclose multiple statements, so they are treated as a single unit. Statements are control points. Before a new statement is executed, the previous statements actions must be completed. Inside statements the compiler has some liberty in picking which parts of subexpressions are first evaluated.

```
a = f(i) + f(j);  //compiler can evaluate as it wishes
a = f(i);
a += f(j);        //order is determined
```

Expression Statements

In C++, assignment occurs as part of an assignment expression. There is no assignment statement; instead it is a form of expression statement.

```
a = b + 1;  //assign (b + 1) to a
++i;        //an expression statement
a + b;      //also a statement - but seemingly useless
```

C++ allows multiple assignment in a single statement; therefore,

```
a = b + (c = 3);
```

is equivalent to

```
c = 3; a = b + c;
```

The Compound Statement

A compound statement in C++ is a series of statements surrounded by braces {}. The chief use of the compound statement is to group statements into an executable unit. The body of a C++ function is always a compound statement. In C, when declarations come at the beginning of a compound statement, the statement is called a block. This rule is relaxed in C++, and declaration statements may occur throughout the statement list. Wherever it is possible to place a statement, it is also possible to place a compound statement.

The if and if-else Statements

The general form of an if statement is

```
if (expression)
    statement
```

If *expression* is nonzero (true), then *statement* is executed; otherwise *statement* is skipped. After the if statement has been executed, control passes to the next statement. In the example

```
if (temperature >= 32)
    cout << "Above Freezing!\n";
cout << "Fahrenheit is " << temperature << endl;
```

"Above Freezing!" is printed only when temperature is greater than or equal to 32. The second statement is always executed.

The if-else statement has the general form

```
if (expression)
    statement1
else
    statement2
```

If *expression* is nonzero, then *statement1* is executed and *statement2* is skipped; if *expression* is zero, then *statement1* is skipped and *statement2* is executed. After the if-else statement has been executed, control passes to the next statement.

```
if (temperature >= 32)
    cout << "Above Freezing!\n";
else if (temperature >= 212)
    cout << "Above Boiling!\n";
else
    cout << "Boy it's cold " << temperature << endl;
```

Note that an else statement associates with its nearest if. This rule prevents the *dangling else* ambiguity.

The while Statement

The general form of a while statement is

```
while (expression)
    statement
```

First *expression* is evaluated. If it is nonzero (true), then *statement* is executed and control passes back to the beginning of the while loop. The effect of this is that the body of the while loop, namely *statement*, is executed repeatedly until *expression* is zero (false). At that point control passes to the next statement. The effect of this is that *statement* can be executed zero or more times.

An example of a while statement is the following:

```
int  i = 1, sum = 0;

while (i <= 10) {
    sum += i;
    ++i;
}
```

When this while loop is exited, the value of sum is 55.

The for Statement

The general form of a for statement is

```
for (expression1; expression2; expression3)
    statement
next statement
```

First *expression1* is evaluated. Typically *expression1* is used to initialize a variable used in the loop. Then *expression2* is evaluated. If it is nonzero (true), then *statement* is cxecuted, *expression3* is evaluated, and control passes back to the beginning of the for loop again, except that evaluation of *expression1* is skipped. This iteration continues until *expression2* is zero (false), at which point control passes to *next statement*.

```
for (int i = 1, sum = 0 ; i <= 10; ++i )
    sum += i;
```

When this for loop is exited, the value of sum is 55.

Any or all of the expressions in a for statement can be missing, but the two semicolons must remain. If *expression1* is missing, then no initialization step is performed as part of the for loop. If *expression3* is missing, then no incrementation step is performed as part of the for loop. If *expression2* is missing, then no testing step is performed as part of the for loop. The special rule for when *expression2* is missing is that the test is always true. Thus the for loop in the code

```
for (i = 1, sum = 0 ; ; sum += i++ )
    cout << sum << endl;
```

is an infinite loop.

The do **Statement**

The general form of a do statement is

```
do
    statement
while (expression);
next statement
```

First *statement* is executed. Then *expression* is evaluated and if it is nonzero (true), then control passes back to the beginning of the do statement and the process repeats itself. When the value of *expression* is zero (false), then control passes to *next statement*. An example is the following:

```
do {
    sum += i;
    cin >> i;
} while (i > 0);
```

Transfer Statements

C++ has several statements that transfer flow of control. C++ has the invidious goto statement. Of course, we recommend against its use unless it is unavoidable. The break and continue statements are used to interrupt ordinary iterative flow of control in loops. In addition, the break statement is used within a switch statement. A switch statement can select among several different cases. The return statement is a transfer statement that exits a function call.

The break and continue Statements

To interrupt normal flow of control within a loop, the programmer can use the two special statements

    break; *and* continue;

The break statement, in addition to its use in loops, can also be used in a switch statement. It causes an exit from the innermost enclosing loop or switch statement.

    The following example illustrates the use of a break statement. A test for a negative value is made, and if the test is true, the break statement causes the for loop to be exited. Program control jumps to the statement immediately following the loop.

```
for (i = 0; i < 10; ++i) {
    cin >> x;
    if (x < 0.0) {
        cout << "All done\n";
        break;      // exit loop if value is negative
    }
    cout << sqrt(x) << endl;
}
// break jumps to here
    . . .
```

    The continue statement causes the current iteration of a loop to stop and causes the next iteration of the loop to begin immediately. The following code processes all characters except digits.

```
for (i = 0; i < MAX; ++i) {
    cin.get(c);
    if (isdigit(c))
        continue;
    . . .  // process other characters
// continue jumps to here
}
```

When the continue statement is executed, control jumps to just before the closing brace. Notice that the continue statement ends the current iteration, whereas a break statement would end the loop.

A break statement can occur only inside the body of a for, while, do, or switch statement. The continue statement can occur only inside the body of a for, while, or do statement.

The switch **Statement**

The switch statement is a multiway conditional statement generalizing the if-else statement. Its general form is given by

```
switch (expression)
    statement
```

where *statement* is typically a compound statement containing case labels and optionally a default label. Typically a switch is composed of many cases, and the expression in parentheses following the keyword switch determines which, if any, of the cases get executed.

The following switch statement counts the number of test scores by category:

```
switch (score) {
case 9:    //fall through to next label
case 10:
    ++a_grades; break;
case 8:
    ++b_grades; break;
case 7:
    ++c_grades; break;
default:
    ++fails;
}
```

A case label is of the form

case *constant integral expression*:

In a switch statement, all case labels must be unique.

If no case label is selected, then control passes to the default label, if there is one. A default label is not required. If no case label is selected, and there is no default label, then the switch statement is exited. To detect errors, programmers frequently include a default, even when all the expected cases have been accounted for.

The keywords case and default cannot occur outside of a switch.

The Effect of a switch Statement

1. Evaluates the integral expression in the parentheses following switch.
2. Executes the case label having a constant value that matches the value of the expression found in step 1, or, if a match is not found, executes the default label, or, if there is no default label, terminates the switch.
3. Terminates the switch when a break statement is encountered, or terminates the switch by "falling off the end."

A switch cannot bypass initialization of a variable unless the entire scope of the variable is bypassed.

```
switch (k) {
case 1:
    int very_bad = 3; break;
case 2: //illegal: bypasses initialization of very_bad
    . . .
}

switch (k) {
case 1:
    {
        int d = 3; break;
    }
case 2: //legal: bypasses scope of d
    . . .
}
```

The goto **Statement**

The goto statement is an unconditional branch to an arbitrary, labeled statement in the function. The goto statement is considered a harmful construct in most accounts of modern programming methodology.

A label is an identifier. By executing a goto statement of the form

goto *label*;

control is unconditionally transferred to a labeled statement. An example is

```
if (d == 0.0)
   goto error;
else
   ratio = n / d;
   . . .
error:  cerr << "ERROR:  division by zero\n";
```

Both the goto statement and its corresponding labeled statement must be in the body of the same function.

A goto cannot bypass initialization of a variable unless the entire scope of the variable is bypassed.

```
   if (i < j)
      goto max;  //illegal: bypasses initialization
   int crazy = 5;
max:
   . . .
```

The return **Statement**

The return statement has two purposes: First, when executed, program control is passed back to the calling environment. Second, if an expression follows, then the value of the expression is returned to the calling environment.

A return has the following two forms:

```
return;
return expression;
```

The Declaration Statement

The declaration statement can be placed nearly anywhere in a block. This lifts the C restriction that requires variable declarations to be placed at the head of a block before executable statements. A declaration statement has the form

declaration

Normal block structure rules apply to a variable so declared. Some examples are

```
for (int i = 0; i < N; ++i) { //typical case within for
    a[i] = b[i] * c[i];
    int k = a[i];              //k is local -possibly inefficient
    . . .
}
```

C++ imposes natural restrictions on transferring into blocks passed where declarations occur. These are disallowed, as are declarations that occur only in one branch of a conditional statement.

C.9 CLASSES

C++ and C have structures, which are forms of hetcrogeneous aggregate types. C++ redefines structures to allow data hiding, inheritance, and member functions as major new extensions. In C++ the keyword class or the keyword struct are used to declare user-defined types.

```
class vect {
public:
    //constructors and destructor
    vect() { size = 10; p = new int[10]} //create a size 10 array
    vect(int n);                          //create a size n array
    vect(vect& v);                        //initialization by vect
    vect(int a[], int n);                 //initialization by array
    ~vect() { delete []p; }               //destructor
    //other member functions
    int  ub() { return (size - 1); }      //upper bound
    int& operator[](int i);               //obtain range checked element
private:
    int* p;                               //base pointer
    int size;                             //number of elements
};
```

The keywords public, private, and protected indicate the access of members that follow. The default for class is private, and for struct the default is public. In the previous example, the data members p and size are private. This makes them accessible solely to member functions of the same class.

Member Functions

Member functions are functions declared within a class, and, as a consequence, have access to private, protected, and public members of that class. If defined inside the class, they are treated as inline functions and are also treated when necessary as overloaded functions. In the class vect, the member function

```
    int  ub() { return (size - 1); }   //upper bound
```

is defined. In this example, the member function ub is inline and has access to the private member size.

Member functions are invoked normally by use of the . or -> operators, as in

```
    vect  a(20), b;            //invoke appropriate constructor
    vect* ptr_v = &b;
    int   uba = a.ub(), ubb;   //invoke member ub
    ubb = ptr_v -> ub();       //invoke member ub
```

Constructors and Destructors

A constructor is a member function whose name is the same as the class name. It constructs objects of the class type. This involves initialization of data members and frequently free store allocation using new. For a class to have constructors, it must have either a constructor with a void argument list, or one in which all its arguments use defaults, in order for it to be a base type of an array declaration, where initialization is not explicit. Such a constructor is called the *default constructor*.

```
foo::foo() { . . .}   //default constructor

hoo::hoo(int i = 0} { . . .} //default constructor
```

A destructor is a member function whose name is the class name preceded by the character ˜ (tilde). Its usual purpose is to destroy values of the class type. This is typically accomplished by using delete.

A constructor of the form

```
type::type(const type& x)
```

is used to perform copying of one *type* value into another when one of the following occurs:

- A *type* variable is initialized by a *type* value.
- A *type* value is passed as an argument in a function.
- A *type* value is returned from a function.

This is called the *copy constructor* and, if not given explicitly, is compiler generated. The default is member-by-member initialization of value.

Classes with default constructors can have a derived array type. For example,

```
vect a[5];
```

is a declaration that uses the empty argument constructor to create an array a of five objects, each of which is a size 10 vect.

A class having members whose types require constructors may have these specified after the argument list for its own constructor. The constructor has a comma-separated list of constructor calls following a colon. The constructor is invoked by using the member name followed by a parenthesized argument list. Constructors cannot be virtual, but destructors can be virtual. Constructors and destructors are not inherited.

The this Pointer

The keyword this denotes an implicitly declared self-referential pointer. It can be used *only* in a nonstatic member function. A simple illustration of its use is as follows:

```
// Use of the this pointer

class c_pair {
public:
    c_pair(char b) { c1 = 1 + (c2 = b); }
    c_pair increment() { c1++; c2++; return (*this); }
    unsigned where_am_I() { return ((unsigned)this); }
    void print() { cout << c1 << c2 << "\t"; }
private:
    char    c1, c2;
};
```

The member function increment() uses the implicitly provided pointer this to return the newly incremented value of both c1 and c2. The member function where_am_I() returns the address of the given object. The this keyword provides for a built-in self-referential pointer, as if c_pair implicitly declared the private member c_pair* const this.

Early C++ systems allowed memory management for objects to be controlled by assignment to the this pointer. Such code is obsolete because the this pointer is not modifiable.

static and const Member Functions

An ordinary member function invoked as

```
object.mem(i, j, k);
```

has an explicit argument list i, j, k and an implicit argument list that consists of the members of object. The implicit arguments can be thought of as forming a list that is accessible through the this pointer. In contrast, a static member function cannot access any of the members using the this pointer. A const member function cannot modify its implicit arguments. The following example illustrates these differences:

```
//Salary calculation using
//static and constant member functions.

#include <iostream.h>

class salary {
public:
   salary(int b) : b_sal(b) { }
   void calc_bonus(double perc) { your_bonus = b_sal * perc; }
   static void reset_all(int p) { all_bonus = p; }
   int comp_tot() const
      { return (b_sal + your_bonus + all_bonus); }
private:
   int        b_sal;
   int        your_bonus;
   static int all_bonus;  //declaration
};

int salary::all_bonus = 100; //declaration and definition

main()
{
   salary w1(1000), w2(2000);

   w1.calc_bonus(0.2);
   w2.calc_bonus(0.15);
   salary::reset_all(400);   //equivalently w1.reset_all(400);
   cout << " w1 " << w1.comp_tot() << "   w2 " << w2.comp_tot() << "\n";
}
```

The static member all_bonus requires a file scope definition. It exists independently of any specific variables of type salary being declared. The static member can also be referred to as

```
salary::all_bonus
```

The const modifier comes between the end of the argument list and the front of the code body. It indicates that no data members will have their values changed. As such it makes the code more robust. In effect, it means that the self-referential pointer is passed as const salary* const this.

A static member function can be invoked using either the scope resolution operator or a specific object. Therefore,

```
salary::reset_all(400);
w1.reset_all(400);
(&w2) -> reset_all(400);
```

are equivalent.

Inheritance

Inheritance is the mechanism of deriving a new class from an old one. The existing class can be added to or altered to create the derived class. A class can be derived from an existing class using the form

```
class class-name : (public|protected|private)optional base-class-name
{
    member declarations
};
```

As usual, the keyword class can be replaced by the keyword struct, with the usual implication that members are by default public. The keywords public, private, and protected are available as access modifiers for class members. A public member is accessible throughout its scope. A private member is accessible to other member functions within its own class. A protected member is accessible to other member functions within its class and any class immediately derived from it. These access modifiers can be used within a class declaration in any order and with any frequency.

A derived class must have a constructor if its base class lacks a default constructor. When the base class has constructors requiring arguments, the derived class explicitly invokes the base class constructor in its initializing list. The form of such a constructor is

```
class-name(argument list) : base-class-name :(base class argument list)
{
    . . .
};
```

The base class argument list is used when invoking the appropriate base class constructor and is executed before the body of the derived class constructor is executed.

A publicly derived class is a *subtype* of its base class. A variable of the derived class can in many ways be treated as if it were the base class type. A pointer whose type is pointer to base class can point to objects having the publicly derived class type. A reference to the derived class, when meaningful, may be implicitly converted to a reference to the public base class. It is possible to declare a reference to a base class and initialize it to an object of the publicly derived class.

The following is an example of a derived class:

```
class vect_bnd : public vect {
public:
    vect_bnd();
    vect_bnd(int, int);
    int& operator[](int);
    int  ub() { return (u_bnd); }
    int  lb() { return (l_bnd); }
private:
    int l_bnd, u_bnd;
};

vect_bnd::vect_bnd() : vect(10)
{
    l_bnd = 0;
    u_bnd = 9;
}

vect_bnd::vect_bnd(int lb, int ub) : vect(ub - lb + 1)
{
    l_bnd = lb;
    u_bnd = ub;
}
```

In this example the constructors for the derived class invoke a constructor in the base class with the argument list following the colon.

Multiple Inheritance

Multiple inheritance allows a derived class to be derived from more than one base class. The syntax of class headers is extended to allow a list of base classes and their privacy designation.

```
class tools {
  . . .

};

class parts {
  . . .

};

class labor {
  . . .

};

class plans : public tools, public parts, public labor {
  . . .

};
```

In this example the derived class plans publicly inherits the members of all three base classes. This parental relationship is described by the inheritance *directed acyclic graph* (DAG), which is a graph structure whose nodes are classes and whose directed edges point from base to derived class.

In deriving an identically named member from different classes, ambiguities may arise. These derivations are allowed, provided the user does not make an ambiguous reference to such a member.

With multiple inheritance two base classes can be derived from a common ancestor. If both base classes are used in the ordinary way by their derived class, that class will have two subobjects of the common ancestor. This duplication, if not desirable, can be eliminated by using virtual inheritance.

Constructor Invocation

The order of execution for initializing constructors in base and member constructors is

1. Base classes are initialized in declaration order.

2. Members are initialized in declaration order.

Virtual base classes are constructed before any of their derived classes. They are constructed before any nonvirtual base classes. Their construction order depends on their DAG. It is a depth-first, left-to-right order. Destructors are invoked in reverse order of constructors.

Let us illustrate by elaborating on a previous example.

```
class tools {
   . . .
public:
   tools(char*);
   ~tools();
   . . .
};

class parts {
   . . .
public:
   parts(char*);
   ~parts();
   . . .
};

class labor {
   . . .
public:
   labor(int);
   ~labor();
   . . .
};

class plans : public tools, public parts, public labor {
   . . .
public:
   plans(int m) : labor(m), tools("lathe"), a(m), parts("widget")
      { . . . }
   ~plans();
   . . .
private:
   special a;   //member class with constructor
};
```

In this case the order in which constructor invocation occurs is tools, parts, labor, plans::a and then the body of plans. Destructor invocation occurs with the body of ~plans, plans::~a, ~labor, ~parts, and ~tools.

Abstract Base Classes

A pure virtual function is a virtual member function whose body is normally undefined. Notationally it is declared inside the class as follows:

>   virtual *function prototype* = 0;

A class that has at least one pure virtual function is an *abstract class*. Variables of an abstract base class cannot exist, but pointers of such a class can be defined and used polymorphically.

A pure virtual destructor must have a definition.

Pointer to Class Member

In C++, a pointer to class member is distinct from a pointer to class. A pointer to class member has type $T::*$, where T is the class name. C++ has two operators that act to dereference a pointer to class member. The symbols .* and ->* are the pointer to member operators. Think of *obj.*ptr_mem* as first dereferencing the pointer to obtain a member variable and then accessing the member for the designated *obj*.

```
class object { public: int a, b, c;} x, y, *q = &y;
int object::*p = &object::b;

x.*p            //gets x.b
q ->*p          //gets y.b
```

C.10 FUNCTIONS

In C, functions are strictly call-by-value. Changes in how C++ functions work include use of function prototypes, overloading, call-by-reference, default arguments, and the effects of the keywords `inline`, `friend`, and `virtual`.

Prototypes

In C++ the prototype form is

>   *type name(argument-declaration-list)*;

Examples are

```
double sqrt(double x);
void   pr_int(char*, int);        //definition contains names
void   print(const char* s);      //contents s points at are const
int    printf(char* format, ...); //variable number of args.
```

With the sqrt prototype definition, invoking sqrt guarantees that, if fea-
sible, an argument will be converted to type double. Prototypes are also
found in ANSI C and greatly improve type checking.

Overloading

The term *overloading* refers to use of the same name for multiple meanings of an operator or a function. The meaning selected depends on the
types of the arguments used by the operator or function.

Consider a function that averages the values in an array of double versus one that averages the values in an array of int. Both are conveniently
named avg_arr.

```
double   avg_arr(const double a[], int size);
double   avg_arr(const int a[], int size);

double avg_arr(const int a[], int size)
{
   int  sum = 0;

   for (int i = 0; i < size; ++i)
      sum += a[i];              //performs int arithmetic
   return ((double) sum / size);
}

double avg_arr(const double a[], int size)
{
   double  sum = 0.0;

   for (int i = 0; i < size; ++i)
      sum += a[i];              //performs double arithmetic
   return (sum / size);
}
```

The function argument type list is called its *signature*. The return
type is not a part of the signature, but the order of the arguments is
crucial.

```
int  sqr(int i);          //signature is int
double  sqr(int i);       //signature is int
void print(int i = 0);    //signature is int
void print(int i, double x); //signature is int, double
void print(double y, int i); //signature is double, int
```

In this example sqr() is illegally redeclared, but print() has three distinct signatures. When the print() function is invoked, the compiler matches the actual arguments to the different signatures and picks the best match. In general, there are three possibilities: a best match, an ambiguous match, and no match. If there is no best match, the compiler issues the appropriate syntax error.

```
print('A');               //converts and matches int
print(str[]);             //no match wrong type
print(15, 9);             //ambiguous
print(15, 9.0);           //matches int, double
print();                  //match  int by default
```

The signature-matching algorithm has two parts. The first part determines a best match for each argument. The second part sees if there is one function that is a uniquely best match in each argument. This uniquely best match is defined as being a best match on at least one argument and a "tied-for-best" match on all other arguments.

For a given argument, a best match is always an exact match. An exact match also includes *trivial conversions*. For type T these are

From	To
//equally good	
T	T&
T&	T
T	const T
T	volatile T
T[]	T*
T(*args*)	(*T) (*args*)
//not as good	
T*	const T*
T*	volatile T*
T&	const T&
T&	volatile T&

The first six trivial conversions cannot be used to disambiguate exact matches. The last four are considered worse than the first six. Thus

```
void print(int i);
void print(const int& i);
```

can be unambiguously overloaded.

Whichever overloaded function is to be invoked, the invocation argument list must be matched to the declaration parameter list. The matching algorithm is as follows:

Overloaded Function Selection Algorithm

1. Use an exact match, if found.
2. Try standard type promotions.
3. Try standard type conversions.
4. Try user-defined conversions.
5. Use a match to ellipsis, if found.

Standard promotions are better than standard conversions, which include conversion from float to double, conversion from char, short, or enum to int, and pointer conversions.

An exact match is clearly best. Casts can be used to force such a match. The compiler will complain about ambiguous situations. Thus it is poor practice to rely on subtle type distinctions and implicit conversions that obscure the overloaded function that is called. When in doubt use explicit conversions to provide an exact match.

Call-by-reference

Reference declarations allow C++ to have *call-by-reference* arguments. Let us use this mechanism to write a function greater that exchanges two values if the first is greater than the second.

```
int greater(int& a, int& b)
{
   if (a > b) {          //exchange
      int temp = a;
      a = b;
      b = temp;
      return (1);
   }
   else
      return (0);
}
```

If i and j are two int variables, then

```
greater(i, j)
```

uses the reference to i and the reference to j to exchange, if necessary, their two values. In traditional C this must be accomplished using pointers and indirection.

```
/* traditional C greater */
int greater(int* a, int* b)
{
   if (*a > *b) {          //exchange
      int temp = *a;
      *a = *b;
      *b = temp;
      return (1);
   }
   else
      return (0);
}
```

Inline

The keyword inline suggests to the compiler that the function must be converted to inline code. This keyword is used for the sake of efficiency, generally with short functions, and is implicit for member functions defined within their class. A compiler can ignore this directive for a variety of reasons, including the fact that the function is too long. In such cases the inline function is compiled as an ordinary function.

```
inline float circum(float rad) { return (pi * 2 * rad); }
```

Inline functions are of internal linkage.

Default Arguments

A formal parameter can be given a default argument. However, this can be done only with contiguous formal parameters that are rightmost in the parameter list. A default value is usually an appropriate constant that occurs frequently when the function is called. The following function illustrates this point:

```
int mult(int n, int k = 2)          //k = 2 is default
{
    if (k == 2)
        return (n * n);
    else
        return (mult(n, k - 1) * n);
}
```

We assume that most of the time the function is used to return the value of n squared.

Friend Functions

The keyword friend is a function specifier. It allows a nonmember function access to the hidden members of the class of which it is a friend. A friend function must be declared inside the class declaration of which it is a friend. It is prefaced by the keyword friend and can appear anywhere in the class. A member function of one class can be a friend function of another class. In such a case the member function is declared in the friend's class using the scope resolution operator to qualify its function name. If all member functions of one class are friend functions of a second class, this can be specified by writing friend class *class name*.

The following declarations are typical:

```
class tweedledee {
   . . .
   friend void alice();        //friend function
   int         cheshire();     //member function
   . . .
};

class tweedledum {
   . . .
   friend int tweedledee::cheshire();
   . . .
};

class tweedledumber {
   . . .
   friend class tweedledee;    //all member functions
                               //of tweedledee have access
   . . .
};
```

Operator Overloading

A special case of function overloading is operator overloading. The keyword operator is used to overload the built-in C operators. Just as a function name, such as print, can be given a variety of meanings that depend on its arguments, so can an operator, such as +, be given additional meanings. This allows infix expressions of both user types and built-in types to be written. The precedence and associativity remain fixed.

Operator overloading typically uses either member functions or friend functions because they both have privileged access. To overload a unary operator using a member function, an empty argument list is used because the single operator argument is the implicit argument. Member function binary operator overloading uses, as the first argument, the implicitly passed class variable and, as the second argument, the lone argument list parameter. Friend functions or ordinary functions have both arguments specified in the parameter list.

We demonstrate how to overload a unary operator using ++ as an example. We define the class clock that can store time as days, hours, minutes, and seconds.

```
class clock {
public:
    clock(unsigned long int i); //constructor and conversion
    void print();                 //formatted printout
    void tick();                  //add one second
    clock operator++() { this -> tick(); return(*this); }
private:
    unsigned long int  tot_secs, secs, mins, hours, days;
};
```

This class overloads the autoincrement operator. It is a member function and can be invoked on its implicit single argument. The member function tick adds one second to the implicit argument of the overloaded ++ operator.

The ternary conditional operator ?:, the scope resolution operator ::, and the two member operators . and .* cannot be overloaded.

C++ release 2.1 distinguishes between prefix and postfix autoincrement and autodecrement operators. To stay compatible, only the prefix version of this operator should be used. In the future, postfix will be distinguished by defining the postfix overloaded function as having a single unused integer argument, as in

```
class T {
public:
    void operator++(int);   //postfix invoked as t.operator++(0);
    void operator--(int);
};
```

There will be no implied semantical relationship between the postfix and prefix forms.

Virtual Functions

The keyword virtual is a function specifier that provides a mechanism for dynamically selecting at run-time the appropriate member function from among base and derived class functions. It may be used only to modify member function declarations. A virtual function must be executable code, and when invoked its semantics are the same as other functions. In a derived class it can be overridden. The selection of which function to invoke from among a group of overridden virtual functions is dynamic. In the typical case a base class has a virtual function, and derived classes have their versions of this function. A pointer to a base class type can point at either a base class object or a derived class object. The member function to be invoked is selected at run-time. It corresponds to the object's type, not the pointer's type. In the absence of a derived type member, the base class virtual function is used by default.

Consider the following example:

```
//virtual function selection
#include <iostream.h>

class B {
public:
    int  i;
    virtual void print_i() { cout << i << " inside B\n"; }
};

class D : public B {
public:
    void print_i() { cout << i << " inside D\n"; }
};

main()
{
    B   b;
    B*  pb = &b;
    D   f;

    f.i = 1 + (b.i = 1);
    pb -> print_i();
    pb = &f;
    pb -> print_i();
}
```

The output from this program is:

```
1 inside B
2 inside D
```

In each case a different version of print_i is executed. Selection depends dynamically on the object being pointed at.

Type Safe Linkage

Linkage rules for non-C++ functions can be specified using a linkage specification. Some examples are

```
extern "C" atoi(const char* nptr);  //C linkage

extern "C" {
#include <stdio.h>
}                    //C linkage for these prototypes
```

This specification is at file scope with "C" and "C++" always supported. It is system dependent, if type safe linkage for other languages is provided. Of a set of overloaded functions with the same number, at most one can be declared to have other than C++ linkage. Class member functions cannot be declared with a linkage specification.

C.11 TEMPLATES

The keyword template is used to implement parameterized types. Rather than repeatedly recoding for each explicit type, its own class, the template feature allows a general formulation that can be explicitly instantiated for each type.

```
template <class T>       //parameterize T
class stack {
public:
    stack();
    stack(int s);
    T& pop();
    void push(T);
private:
    T*    item;
    int   top;
    int   size;
    . . .
};
typedef stack<string> str_stack;
str_stack s(100);    //an explicit variable used as a string stack
```

A template declaration has the form

template < *template arguments* > *declaration*

and a template argument can be

class *identifier*
argument declaration

The class *identifier* arguments are instantiated with a type. Other argument declarations are instantiated with constant expressions.

```
template<class T, int n>
class array_n {
public:
    T items[n];  //n will be explicitly instantiated
};

array_n<complex, 1000> w;  //w is an array of complex
```

Member function syntax when external to the class definition is as follows:

```
template <class T>
T& stack<T>::pop()
{
    return(item[top--]);
};
```

The class name used by the scope resolution operator includes the template arguments, and the member function declaration requires the template declaration as a preface to the function declaration.

Function Template

Ordinary functions can be parameterized using a restricted form of template syntax. Only class *identifier* instantiation is allowed. It must occur inside the function argument list.

```
//generic swap
template <class T>
void swap(T& x, T& y)
{
    T temp = x;
    x = y;
    y = temp;
}

//illegal
template <class T>
T foo()
{
  T temp;
  . . .
}
```

A function template is used to construct an appropriate function for any invocation that matches its arguments unambiguously.

```
swap(i, j); //i j int -  okay
swap(c1, c2); //c1, c2 complex -okay
swap(i, ch)  //i int ch char - illegal
```

The overloaded function selection algorithm for template functions is as follows:

1. Exact match on a nontemplate function.

2. Exact match using a function template.

3. Ordinary argument resolution on a nontemplate function.

Note that this algorithm is not universally used. ATT C++ release 3.0 relaxes the exact match condition on function templates, allowing both trivial conversions and base/derived pointer conversions.

In the previous example an ordinary function declaration whose prototype was

```
void swap(char, char);
```

would have been invoked on swap(i, ch).

Friends

Template classes can contain friends. A friend function that does not use a template specification is universally a friend of all instantiations of the template class. A friend function that incorporates template arguments is specifically a friend of its instantiated class.

```
template <class T>
class matrix {
private:
    friend void foo_bar();  //universal
    friend vect<T> product(vect<T> v); //instantiated
    . . .
};
```

Static Members

Static members are not universal but are specific to each instantiation.

```
template <class T>
class foo{
public:
    static int count;
    . . .
};

foo<int> a;
foo<double> b;
```

The static variables `foo<int>::count` and `foo<double>::count` are distinct.

C.12 EXCEPTIONS

Classically an exception is an unexpected condition that a program encounters and cannot cope with. An example is floating-point division by zero. Usually the system aborts the running program.

C++ code is allowed to directly raise an exception in a `try` block by using the `throw` expression. The exception is handled by invoking the appropriate handler selected from a list found in the handler's `try` block. A simple example of this is

```
vect::vect(int n)
{ //fault tolerant constructor
    try {
        if (n < 1)
            throw (n);
        p = new int[n];
        if (p == 0)
            throw ("FREE STORE EXHAUSTED");
    }
    catch (int n) { . . .} //catches an incorrect size
    catch (const char* error) { . . .} //catches free store exhaustion
}
```

Note, that new in this example is the traditional new returning zero for an allocation error. C++ systems define new as throwing an xalloc exception upon failure.

Throwing Exceptions

Syntactically, throw expressions come in two forms:

```
throw
```
throw *expression*

The throw expression raises an exception in a try block. The innermost try block is used to select the catch statement that processes the exception. The throw expression with no argument "rethrows" the current exception. It is used when one typically wants a second handler called from the first handler to further process the exception.

The expression thrown is a static temporary object that persists until exception handling is exited. The expression is caught by a handler that may use this value. An uncaught expression terminates the program.

```
void foo()
{
  int i;
  . . .
  throw i;
}

main()
{
  try {
     foo();
  }
  catch(int n) {  . . . }
}
```

The integer value thrown by throw i persists until the handler with integer signature catch(int n) exits. This value is available for use within the handler as its argument.

An example of rethrowing of an exception is as follows:

```
catch(int n)
{
  . . .
  throw;  //rethrown
}
```

Assuming the thrown expression was of integer type, the rethrown exception is the same persistent integer object that is handled by the "nearest" handler suitable for that type.

Try Blocks

Syntactically, a try block has the form

```
try
compound statement
handler list
```

The try block is the context for deciding which handlers are invoked on a raised exception. The order in which handlers are defined is important because that determines the order in which handlers for a raised exception of matching type will be tried.

```
try {
    . . .
    throw ("SOS");
    . . .
    io_condition eof(argv[i]);
    throw (eof);
    . . .
}
catch (const char*) { . . .}
catch (io_condition& x) { . . .}
```

A throw expression matches the catch argument, if it is one of the following:

- An exact match.

- A public base class of a derived type, which is what is thrown.

- A thrown object type, which is a pointer type convertible to a pointer type that is the catch argument.

It is an error to list handlers in an order that prevents them from being called. An example is

```
catch(void*)  //any char* would match
catch(char*)
catch(BaseTypeError&)  //would always be called for DerivedTypeError
catch(DerivedTypeError&)
```

Handlers

Syntactically, a handler has the form

```
catch ( formal argument )
compound statement
```

The catch looks like a function declaration of one argument without a return type.

```
catch (const char* message)
{
    cerr << message << endl;
    exit(1);
}
```

An ellipsis signature that matches any argument is allowed. Also, the formal argument can be an abstract declaration, meaning it can have type information without a variable name.

Exception Specification

Syntactically, an exception specification is part of a function declaration and has the form

> *function header* throw (*type list*)

The type list consists of types that a throw expression within the function can have. If the list is empty, the compiler may assume that no throw will be executed by the function, either directly or indirectly.

```
void foo() throw(int, over_flow);
void noex(int i) throw();
```

If an exception specification is left off, then the assumption is that an arbitrary exception can be thrown by such a function. It is good programming practice to indicate through specifications what exceptions are to be expected. Violations of these specifications are run-time errors.

terminate() **and** unexpected()

The system-provided handler terminate() is called when no other handler has been provided to deal with an exception. By default, the abort() function is called. Otherwise set_terminate() can be used to provide a handler.

The system-provided handler unexpected() is called when a function throws an exception that was not in its exception-specification list. By default, the abort() function is called. Otherwise set_unexpected() can be used to provide a handler.

C.13 CAUTION AND COMPATIBILITY

C++ is not completely upward-compatible with C. In most cases of ordinary use, it is a superset of C. Also, C++ is not a completely stable language design and currently is in the ANSI standards process. Several novel features are being experimented with, most notably exception handling and parameterized types. The following sections mention features of the language that are problematic.

Nested Class Declarations

The original scoping of nested classes was based on C rules. In effect, nesting was cosmetic, with the inner class globally visible. In C++ the inner class is local to the outer class that encloses it. Accessing such an inner class could require multiple use of the scope resolution operator.

```
int outer::inner::foo(double w) //foo is nested
    . . .
```

It will also be possible to have classes nested inside functions.

Type Compatibilities

In general, C++ is more strongly typed than ANSI C. Some differences include

- Enumerations are distinct types, with enumerators not being explicitly int. This means that enumerations must be cast when making assignments from integer types or other enumerations to each other. They are promotable to integer.

- Any pointer type can be converted to a generic pointer of type void*. However, unlike ANSI C, a generic pointer is not assignment-compatible with an arbitrary pointer type. This means that C++ requires that generic pointers be cast to an explicit type for assignment to a nongeneric pointer variable.

- A character constant in C++ is char, but in ANSI C it is an int. The char type is distinct from both signed char and unsigned char. Functions may be overloaded based on the distinctions, and pointers to the three types are not compatible.

Miscellaneous

The old C function syntax, in which the argument list is left blank, is replaced in ANSI C by the explicit argument void. The signature foo() in

C is considered equivalent to the use of the ellipsis, and both are considered equivalent to the empty argument list in C++.

In early C++ systems, the this pointer could be modified. It could be used to allocate memory for class objects. Although this use is obsolete, a compiler can continue to allow it.

C++ allows declarations to be intermixed with executable statements. ANSI C allows declarations to be only at the heads of blocks or in file scope. However in C++, goto, iteration, and selection statements are not allowed to bypass initialization of variables. This rule differs from ANSI C.

In C++ a global data object must have exactly one definition. Other declarations must use the keyword extern. ANSI C allows multiple declarations without the keyword extern.

Currently, overriding virtual functions requires the same return type. It is expected that this restriction will be relaxed where a derived class replaces the base class as the return type.

```
class Base {
public:
    virtual Base& f1(int n);
    virtual Base* f2(int n);
};

class Derived : public Base {
public:
    Derived& f1(int n); //override Base::f1
    Derived* f2(int n); //override Base::f2
};
```

New and Proposed Features

Exception handling using the keywords catch, throw, and try may not yet be implemented. This is rapidly changing, and most compilers are beginning to have complete implementations of templates and exceptions. Using new with exceptions implemented throws an xalloc exception. This replaces new returning zero upon failure to allocate. The older-style error handling can be retained by using set_new_handler(0). (See vendor manuals for a description of any system-dependent details.)

Currently, garbage collection is not directly supported by the language. Various proposals exist to provide or support garbage-collectible classes.

Mechanisms that dynamically determine object type may enter the language. This is called *run-time type information* (RTTI). Proposed syntax adds the operator typeid(), which is applied to either a type name or an expression. Also added are a variety of *cast-conversion operators*, such as dynamic_cast<*Type*>(*pointer*), whose effect is to either return zero if the cast fails or to perform the cast. In general, such casts will be allowed in polymorphic class hierarchies. (See system manuals for a detailed description of what is implemented.)

C.14 STYLE EXAMPLES AND PRAGMATICS

Our coding style follows the original Kernighan and Ritchie C style of indentation and brace matching.

```
// Code exhibiting style characteristics
#include <iostream.h>
#define MAX   16000

int sum(int n)
{
   int i, total = 0;

   for(i = 0; i < n; ++i) {
     total += i;
     if (total > MAX) {
       cout << "too large" << endl;
       exit(1);
     }
   }
   return (total);
}
```

- Each line consists of only one statement.

- Initial declarations are followed by a blank line.

- A compound statement brace comes on the same line as its controlling expression. Its matching terminating brace is lined up under the initial letter of the keyword starting the statement.

- A pure compound statement, such as a function definition, starts on its own line.

- Everything after the opening (left) brace is indented a standard number of spaces (for example, three spaces in this text). The matching closing (right) brace causes subsequent statements to be lined up under it.

- Return expressions are parenthesized.

- With the exception of the semicolon, a space is added after each token for readability.

- Preprocessor identifiers are capitalized. Ordinary identifiers are lowercase.

- Preprocessor commands and file-level declarations and statements start in column one.

Frequently found variations from these practices include

- Braces are aligned Algol-style, with the initial brace always on its own line.

- Return expressions are not parenthesized.

- Very short statements that are conceptually related can be on the same line.

```
//Algol style matching braces
int order(int& y, int& z)
{
   int temp;

   if (z < y)
   {
      temp = z; z = y; y = temp;
   }
   return z;
}
```

Class-Definition Style

Preferred class-definition style rules include the following:

1. Access privileges are in order—public, protected, and private. This conforms to the most-accessible-first rule. Clients of a class need not know about nonpublic members; therefore, it is logical to place public members first.

2. Member functions are declared but not defined. Textbook examples do so for the sake of brevity of exposition.

```
//Preferred Style as found in this text
//C++ Need to know access - widest first
class string {
public:
    string();                           //default
    string(int n);
    string(const char* p);              //useful conversion
    string(const string& str);          //copy
    ~string();
    string& operator=(string&str);   //overload =
    operator char*();                   //inverse conversion
    friend class string_iterator;
    friend ostream& operator<<(ostream& out, const string& str);
protected:
    void assign(const string& str);
    void print() const;
private:
    str_obj* st;                        //implementation
};

//A friend function of class string.
//This is a typical method for overloading << "put to".
ostream& operator<<(ostream& out, const string& str)
{
    out << str.st -> s;
    return (out);
}
```

Traditional C++ class style derives from Stroustrup's writing and defaults that were historically needed

```
//Traditional C++ class style
class vect {
private:
    int *p;                             //base pointer
    int size;                           //number of elements
public:
    //constructors and destructor
    vect();                             //create a size 10 array
    vect(int l);                        //create a size l array
    vect(vect& v);                      //initialization by vect
    vect(int a[], int l);               //initialization by array
    ~vect() { delete [] p; }
    int  ub() { return (size - 1); } } //upper bound
    int& operator[](int i);             //obtain range checked element
    vect& operator=(vect& v);
    vect operator+(vect& v);
};
```

Style rules include

- In traditional style, access privileges are in order—private, protected, and public. This conforms to early practice when by default private members came first in a class declaration.

- Indentation is as follows: class, access keywords, and closing brace all line up and are placed on separate lines. Member declarations are indented and line up.

- One-line member declarations that are inline can be defined inside the class.

- Constructors come first, then a destructor, and then other member functions.

- Data members are to be private or protected. They are to be accessed and modified using member functions.

APPENDIX D

INPUT/OUTPUT

This appendix describes input/output (I/O) practices in C++ using *iostream.h* and its associated libraries. The software for C++ includes a standard library that contains functions commonly used by the C++ community. The standard input/output library for C, described by the header *stdio.h*, is still available in C++. However, C++ introduces *iostream.h*, which implements its own collection of input/output functions. The header *stream.h* was used on systems before release 2.0 and is still available under many C++ systems.

The stream I/O is described as a set of classes in *iostream.h*. These classes overload the *put to* and *get from* operators « and ». Streams can be associated with files, and examples of file processing using streams are given and discussed in this appendix. File processing often requires the character-handling macros found in *ctype.h*. These are also discussed here.

In OOP, objects should know how to print themselves, and in the book we have frequently made print a member function of a class. Notationally, it is also useful to overload << for user-defined ADTs. In this appendix we develop output functions for card and deck that illustrate these techniques.

D.1 THE OUTPUT CLASS *ostream*

Output is returned to an object of type ostream, as described in *iostream.h*. The operator << is overloaded in this class to perform output conversions from standard types. The operator is left associative and returns a value of type ostream&. The standard output ostream corresponding to stdout is cout, and the standard output ostream corresponding to stderr is cerr.

The effect of executing a simple output statement such as

```
cout << "x = " << x << "\n";
```

is to print to the screen first a string of four characters followed by an appropriate representation for the output of x followed by a newline. The representation depends on which overloaded version of << is invoked.

The class ostream contains public members, such as

```
ostream& operator<<(int i);
ostream& operator<<(long i);
ostream& operator<<(double x);
ostream& operator<<(char c);
ostream& operator<<(const char* s);
ostream& put(char c);
ostream& write(const char* p, int n);
ostream& flush();
```

The member function put outputs the character representation of c. The member function write outputs the string of length n pointed to by p. The member function flush forces the stream to be written. Since these are member functions, they can be used as follows:

```
int c = 'A';
cout.put(c);        //output A
cout.put(98);       //output b  ascii value 98
cout.put(c + 2);    //output C
char* str = "ABCDEFGHI";
cout.write(str + 2, 3);  //output CDE
cout.flush();       //write contents of buffered stream
```

D.2 FORMATTED OUTPUT AND *iomanip.h*

The *put to* operator << produces by default the minimum number of characters needed to represent the output. As a consequence, output can be confusing, as seen in the following example.

```
int  i = 8, j = 9;
cout << i << j ;                    //confused: prints 89
cout << i << "   " << j;            //better: prints 8   9
cout << "i= " << i << " j= " << j;  //best:prints i= 8 j= 9
```

Two schemes that we have used to properly space output are to have strings separating output values and to use \n and \t to create newlines and tabbing, respectively. We can also use manipulators in the stream output to control output formatting.

A *manipulator* is a value or function that has a special effect on the stream it operates on. A simple example of a manipulator is endl defined in *iostream.h*. Its effect is to output a newline followed by flushing the ostream.

```
x = 1;
cout << "x = " << x << endl;
```

This immediately prints the line

```
x = 1
```

Another manipulator, flush, flushes the ostream, as in

```
cout << "x = " << x << flush;
```

which has almost the same effect as the previous example but does not advance to a newline.

The manipulators dec, hex, and oct can be used to change integer bases. The default base is base ten. The conversion base remains set until explicitly changed.

```
//Using different bases in integer I/O.
#include <iostream.h>

main()
{
   int i = 10, j = 16, k = 24;
   cout << i << '\t' << j << '\t' << k << endl;
   cout << oct << i << '\t' << j << '\t' << k << endl;
   cout << hex << i << '\t' << j << '\t' << k << endl;
   cout << "Enter 3 integers, e.g. 11 11 12a" << endl;
   cin >> i >> hex >> j >> k;
   cout << dec << i << '\t' << j << '\t' << k << endl;
}
```

The resulting output is

```
10      16      24
12      20      30
a       10      18
Enter 3 integers, e.g. 11 11 12a
11      17      298
```

The reason the final line of output is 11 followed by 17 is that the second 11 in the input is interpreted as hexadecimal, which is $16 + 1$.

The manipulators discussed above are found in *iostream.h*. Other manipulators are found in *iomanip.h*. For example, the setw(int width) manipulator changes the default field width for the next formatted I/O operation to the value of its argument. This value reverts back to the default. We briefly list the standard manipulators, their function, and where they are defined in the following table.

Manipulator	Function	File
endl	output newline and flush	*iostream.h*
ends	output null in string	*iostream.h*
flush	flush the output	*iostream.h*
dec	use decimal	*iostream.h*
hex	use hexadecimal	*iostream.h*
oct	use octal	*iostream.h*
ws	skip white space on input	*iostream.h*
setw(*int*)	set field width	*iomanip.h*
setfill(*int*)	set fill character	*iomanip.h*
setbase(*int*)	set base format	*iomanip.h*
setprecision(*int*)	set floating-point precision	*iomanip.h*
setiosflags(*long*)	set format bits	*iomanip.h*
resetiosflags(*long*)	reset format bits	*iomanip.h*

D.3 USER-DEFINED TYPES: OUTPUT

User-defined types typically have been printed by creating a member function print. Let us use the types card and deck of Section 5.9 as examples of simple user-defined types. We write out a set of output routines for displaying cards.

```
//card output

#include  <iostream.h>

char pips_symbol[14] = { '?', 'A', '2', '3', '4', '5', '6',
                         '7', '8', '9', 'T', 'J', 'Q', 'K'};
char suit_symbol[4] = { 'c', 'd', 'h', 's'};

enum suit {clubs, diamonds, hearts, spades};

class pips {
public:
   void assign(int n) { p = n % 13 + 1; }
   void print() { cout << pips_symbol[p]; }
private:
   int  p;
};

class card {
public:
   suit s;
   pips p;
   void assign(int n) { cd = n; s = suit(n / 13); p.assign(n); }
   void pr_card() { p.print(); cout << suit_symbol[s] << " "; }
private:
   int  cd;        //a cd is from 0 to 51
};

class deck {
public:
   void init_deck();
   void shuffle();
   void deal(int, int, card*);
   void pr_deck();
private:
   card d[52];
};

void deck::pr_deck()
{
   for (int i = 0; i < 52; ++i) {
      if (i % 13 == 0)       //13 cards to a line
        cout << endl;
      d[i].pr_card();
   }
}
```

Each card will be printed out in two characters. If d is a variable of type deck, then d.pr_deck() prints out the entire deck, 13 cards to a line.

In keeping with the spirit of OOP, we can overload << to accomplish the same aims. The operator << has two arguments, an ostream& and the ADT, and it must produce an ostream&. We want to use a reference to a stream and return a reference to a stream whenever overloading << or >>, because we do not want to copy a stream object. Let us write these functions for the types card and deck.

```
ostream& operator<<(ostream& out, pips x)
{
    return (out << pips_symbol[x.p]);
}

ostream& operator<<(ostream& out, card cd)
{
    return (out << cd.p << suit_symbol[cd.s] << "  " );
}

ostream& operator<<(ostream& out, deck x)
{
    for (int i = 0; i < 52; ++i) {
        if (i % 13 == 0)        //13 cards to a line
            out << endl;
        out << x.d[i];
    }
    return (out);
}
```

The functions that operate on pips and deck need to be friends of the corresponding class because they access private members.

D.4 THE INPUT CLASS *istream*

An operator >> is overloaded in istream to perform input conversions to standard types. The standard input istream corresponding to stdin is cin.

The effect of executing a simple input statement such as

```
cin >> x >> i;
```

is to read from standard input, normally the keyboard, a value for x and then a value for i. White space is ignored.

The class istream contains public members such as

```
istream& operator>>(int& i);
istream& operator>>(long& i);
istream& operator>>(double& x);
istream& operator>>(char& c);
istream& operator>>(char* s);
istream& get(char& c);
istream& get(char* s, int n, char c = '\n');
istream& getline(char* s, int n, char c = '\n');
istream& read(char* s, int n);
```

The member function get(char& c) inputs the character representation to c, including a white-space character. The member function get(char* s, int n, int c = '\n') inputs at most n - 1 characters into the string pointed to by s, up to the specified delimiter character c or an end-of-file character. A terminating '\0' is placed in the output string. The optionally specified default character acts as a terminator but is not placed in the output string. If not specified, the input is read up to the next newline character. The member function getline() works like get(char*, int, char = '\n') except it discards rather than keeps the delimiter character in the designated istream. The member function read(char* s, int n) inputs at most n characters into the string pointed to by s. It sets the failbit (see Section D.7) if an end-of-file character is encountered before n characters are read.

```
cin.get(c);          //one character
cin.get(s, 40);      //length 40 or terminated by '\n'
cin.get(s, 10, '*'); //length 10 or terminated by *
cin.getline(s, 40);  //same as get but '\n' is discarded
```

Other useful member functions include

```
int gcount();        //number of recently extracted characters
istream& ignore(int n = 1, int delimeter = EOF); //skips
int peek();          //get next character without extraction
istream& putback(char c);   //puts back character
```

When overloading the operator >> to produce input to a user-defined type, the typical form of such a function prototype is

```
istream& operator>>(istream& p, user-defined type& x)
```

If the function needs access to private members of x, it must be made a friend of its class. A key point is to make x a reference parameter so its value can be modified.

D.5 FILES AND *fstream.h*

C systems have stdin, stdout, and stderr as standard files. In addition, systems may define other standard files, such as stdprn and stdaux. Abstractly, a file may be thought of as a stream of characters that are processed sequentially.

Written in C	Name	Remark
stdin	standard input file	connected to the keyboard
stdout	standard output file	connected to the screen
stderr	standard error file	connected to the screen
stdprn	standard printer file	connected to the printer
stdaux	standard auxiliary file	connected to an auxiliary port

The C++ stream input/output ties the first three of these standard files to cin, cout, and cerr, respectively. Typically C++ ties cprn and caux to their corresponding standard files stdprn and stdaux. There is also clog, which is a buffered version of cerr. Other files can be opened or created by the programmer. We show how to do this in the context of writing a program to double-space an existing file into an existing or new file. The file names are specified on the command line and passed in to argv.

File I/O is handled by including *fstream.h*. This contains classes ofstream and ifstream for output file stream and input file stream creation and manipulation. To properly open and manage an ifstream or ofstream related to a system file, you first declare it with an appropriate constructor. First we study the ifstream behavior:

```
ifstream();
ifstream(const char*, int = ios::in, int prot = filebuf::openprot);
```

The constructor of no arguments creates a variable that will later be associated with an input file. The constructor of three arguments takes as its first argument the named file. The second argument specifies the file mode. The third argument is for file protection.

File mode arguments are defined as enumerators in class ios as follows:

```
ios::in          //input mode
ios::app         //append mode
ios::out         //output mode
ios::ate         //open and seek to end of file
ios::nocreate    //open but do not create mode
ios::trunc       //discard contents and open
ios::noreplace   //if file exists open fails
```

Thus the default for an ifstream is input mode, and for an ofstream is output mode. If file opening fails, the stream is put into a bad state. It can be tested with operator!.

Let us use this scheme to write a simple file-handling program.

```
//dbl_sp: a program to double space a file
//Usage: executable  f1 f2
//f1 must be present and readable
//f2 must be writable if it exists

#include <fstream.h>     //includes iostream.h
#include <stdlib.h>

void double_space(ifstream& f, ofstream& t)
{
   char  c;

   while (f.get(c)) {
      t.put(c);
      if (c == '\n')
         t.put(c);
   }
}
```

```
main(int argc, char** argv)
{
   if (argc != 3) {
      cout << "\nUsage: " << argv[0]
           << "  infile  outfile\n";
      exit(1);
   }

   ifstream  f_in(argv[1]);
   ofstream  f_out(argv[2]);

   if (!f_in) {
      cerr << "cannot open " << argv[1] << endl;
      exit(1);
   }
   if (!f_out) {
      cerr << "cannot open " << argv[2] << endl;
      exit(1);
   }
   double_space(f_in, f_out);
}
```

■ DISSECTION OF THE *dbl_sp* PROGRAM

```
void double_space(ifstream& f, ofstream& t)
{
   char  c;

   while (f.get(c)) {
      t.put(c);
      if (c == '\n')
         t.put(c);
   }
}
```

- The get member function gets a character from an ifstream.
  The put member function puts a character to an ofstream.
  These functions do not ignore white-space characters. The
  newline character is outputted twice, creating the desired
  double-spacing in the output file.

```
ifstream  f_in(argv[1]);
ofstream  f_out(argv[2]);
```

- The variable f_in is used for input, and the variable f_out is used for output. They are used to create corresponding ifstream and ofstream variables. The corresponding constructors are invoked on the names found in argv[] passed through the command line. If opening the input file succeeds, the ifstream f_in is constructed so it is connected to the file named in argv[1]. If opening the output file succeeds, the ofstream f_out is constructed so it is connected to the file named in argv[2].

```
if (!f_in) {
    cerr << "cannot open " << argv[1] << endl;
    exit(1);
}
if (!f_out) {
    cerr << "cannot open " << argv[2] << endl;
    exit(1);
}
```

- If the constructors for either f_in or f_out fail, they return a bad state tested by operator!, and then an error exit is executed. At this point f_in can be used analogously to cin, and f_out can be used analogously to cout.

```
double_space(f_in, f_out);
```

- The actual double-spacing from the input file to the output file occurs here.

Other important member functions that are found in *fstream.h* include

```
//opens ifstream file
void open(const char*, int = ios::in, int prot = filebuf::openprot);

//opens ofstream file
void open(const char*, int = ios::out, int prot = filebuf::openprot);

void close();
```

These functions can be used to open and close appropriate files. If you create a file stream with the default constructor, you would normally use open() to associate it with a file. You could then use close() to close the file and open another file using the same stream. Additional member functions in other I/O classes allow for a full range of file manipulation.

D.6 THE FUNCTIONS AND MACROS IN *ctype.h*

The system provides the standard header file *ctype.h*, which contains a set of functions used to test characters and a set of functions used to convert characters. These functions can be implemented as macros or inline functions. This is mentioned here because of its usefulness in C++ input/output. Those functions that test only a character return an int value that is nonzero (true) or zero (false). The argument is type int.

Function	Nonzero (true) is returned if:
isalpha(c)	c is a letter
isupper(c)	c is an uppercase letter
islower(c)	c is a lowercase letter
isdigit(c)	c is a digit
isxdigit(c)	c is a hexadecimal digit
isspace(c)	c is a white-space character
isalnum(c)	c is a letter or digit
ispunct(c)	c is a punctuation character
isgraph(c)	c is a printing character, except space
isprint(c)	c is a printable character
iscntrl(c)	c is a control character
isascii(c)	c is an ASCII code

Other functions provide for the appropriate conversion of a character value. Note that these functions do not change the value of c stored in memory.

Function	Effect
toupper(c)	changes c from lowercase to uppercase
tolower(c)	changes c from uppercase to lowercase
toascii(c)	changes c to ASCII code

The ASCII code functions are usual on ASCII systems.

D.7 USING STREAM STATES

Each stream has an associated state that can be tested. The states are as follows:

```
enum io_state {goodbit, eofbit, failbit, badbit, hardfail};
```

The values for a particular stream can be tested using the following public member functions:

```
int good();   //nonzero if not eof or other error bit set
int eof();    //nonzero if istream eofbit set
int fail();   //nonzero if failbit, badbit, or hardfail set
int bad();    //nonzero if badbit, or hardfail set
int rdstate();  //returns error state
void clear(int i = 0);  //resets error state
int operator!();  //return true if failbit or badbit set
operator void*    //return false if failbit or badbit set
```

Testing for a stream being in a nongood state can protect a program from hanging up.

A stream state of *good* means the previous input/output operation worked and the next operation should succeed. A stream state of *eof* means the previous input operation returned an end-of-file condition. A stream state of *fail* means the previous input/output operation failed, but the stream is usable once the error bit is cleared. A stream state of *bad* means the previous input/output operation is invalid, but the stream may be usable once the error condition is corrected. And a stream state of *hardfail* means the previous input/output operation failed irreparably. It is also possible to directly test a stream. It is nonzero if it is either in a good or eof state.

```
if (cout << x )  //output succeeded
   . . .
else
   . . .            //output failed
```

The following program counts the number of words coming from the standard input. Normally this would be redirected to use an existing file. It illustrates ideas discussed in this and the previous two sections.

```
//A word count program
//Usage: executable < file
#include    <iostream.h>
#include    <ctype.h>

main()
{
    int    word_cnt = 0;
    int    found_next_word();

    while (found_next_word())
        ++word_cnt;
    cout << "word count is " << word_cnt << endl;
}

int found_next_word()
{
    char    c;
    int     word_sz = 0;

    cin >> c;
    while ( !cin.eof() && !isspace(c)) {
        ++word_sz;
        cin.get(c);
    }
    return (word_sz);
}
```

■ DISSECTION OF THE *word_cnt* PROGRAM

```
while (found_next_word())
    ++word_cnt;
```

- The function found_next_word attempts to read the next word.
  It returns a positive word length for each word it finds. If it
  reads only the end-of-file character, it returns a word length
  of zero.

```
int found_next_word()
{
   char   c;
   int    word_sz = 0;

   cin >> c;
   while ( !cin.eof() && !isspace(c)) {
      ++word_sz;
      cin.get(c);
   }
   return (word_sz);
}
```

- A non-white-space character is retrieved from the input stream and assigned to c. The while loop tests that adjacent characters are not white space. The loop terminates when either an end-of-file character or a white-space character is found. The word size is returned as zero when the only non-white-space character found is the end-of-file. One last point: The loop cannot be rewritten as

```
while ( !cin.eof() && !isspace(c)) {
   ++word_sz;
   cin >> c;
}
```

   because this would skip white space.

D.8 MIXING I/O LIBRARIES

We have used *iostream.h* throughout this text. It is perfectly reasonable to want to continue using *stdio.h* because it is the standard in the C community and is well understood. Its disadvantage is that it is not type safe. Functions like printf use unchecked variable-length argument lists. Stream I/O requires assignment-compatible types as arguments to its functions and overloaded operators. It is also possible that you would want to mix both forms of I/O. When mixed, synchronization problems can occur because the two libraries use different buffering strategies. This can be avoided by calling

```
    ios::sync_with_stdio();
```

This is illustrated in the following:

```
//Mix C and C++ I/O.

#include <stdio.h>
#include <iostream.h>

unsigned long fact(int n)
{
    unsigned long f = 1;
    for (int i = 2; i <= n; ++i)
        f *= i;
    return (f);
}

main()
{
    int n;

    ios::sync_with_stdio();
    do {
        cout << "\nEnter n positive or 0 to halt: ";
        scanf("%d", &n);
        printf("\n fact(%d) = %ld", n, fact(n));
    } while (n > 0);
    cout << "\nend of session" << endl;
}
```

Note that, for integer values greater than 12, the results will overflow. It is safe to mix stdio and iostream provided they are not mixed on the same file.

INDEX